FORTRAN IV
PROGRAMMING

FORTRAN IV PROGRAMMING

Second Edition

V. Thomas Dock, Ph.D

College of Business Administration
Texas Tech University

RESTON PUBLISHING COMPANY, INC., Reston, Virginia
A Prentice-Hall Company

Library of Congress Cataloging in Publication Data

Dock, V   Thomas.
    Fortran IV programming.

    Includes index.
    1. Fortran (Computer program language) I. Title.
QA76.73.F25D63 1975   001.6'424   75-16346
ISBN 0-87909-279-3

To
Mary, Steven and Jordanna
my wife and children

© 1976 by
Reston Publishing Company, Inc.
A Prentice-Hall Company
Reston, Virginia 22090

10 9 8 7 6 5 4 3 2 1

Printed in the United States of America.

CONTENTS

Chapter 1   **INTRODUCTION TO THE COMPUTER AND FORTRAN IV**   1

Definition of a Computer, 1
Analog and Digital Computers, 1
Introduction to FORTRAN IV, 2
An Example of a FORTRAN Program, 2
The FORTRAN Coding Form, 2
FORTRAN Program Statements, 5
The Comment Statement, 6
The FORTRAN Character Set, 7
Data Cards, 7
Job Control Language Cards, 8
The Card Punch, 8
The Conversion of a Source Program into an Object Program, 8
Questions, 9
Exercise, 10

Chapter 2   **THE COMPOSITION OF FORTRAN STATEMENTS**   11

The FORTRAN Character Set, 11
FORTRAN Key Words, 13
Numbers, 13
Symbolic Names, 16
Expressions, 20
The Categories of FORTRAN Statements, 20
Questions, 20
Exercises, 20

Chapter 3   **INPUT AND OUTPUT STATEMENTS**   30

The READ Statement, 22
The WRITE Statement, 24

The FORMAT Statement, 26
Additional Format Options, 29
Carriage Control Characters, 30
The Format Codes, 30
Vignette FORTRAN Exercises, 43
Answers to Vignette Exercises, 45
Questions, 46

Chapter 4   **ASSIGNMENT STATEMENTS**   **48**

The Arithmetic Statement, 48
The Logical Statement, 53
Relational Operators, 54
Logical Operators, 55
Hierarchy of Execution, 55
An Introduction to Control Statements, 56
The Unconditional GO TO Statement, 56
The STOP Statement, 56
The END Statement, 57
Illustrations of FORTRAN Programs, 57
Questions, 61
Exercises, 62

Chapter 5   **CONTROL STATEMENTS**   **63**

System and Program Flowcharting, 63
Branching, 63
Looping, 71
The CONTINUE Statement, 76
The Reading of Two or More Data Decks, 78
Questions, 79
Exercises, 79

Chapter 6   **ARRAYS**   **103**

The Nature of an Array, 81
The Creation of an Array, 82
Array Dimensions, 85
Subscripts and Array Elements, 86
The Normal Order in Which Array Elements are
     Filled With a Number, 86
The Transfer of Data Into and From *All* of the
     Array Elements of an Array, 88
The Transfer of Data Into and From *Specific*
     Array Elements of an Array, 90
The Transfer of Data Into and From *Part* of the
     Array Elements of an Array, 90
Questions, 96
Exercises, 96

Chapter 7   **SUBPROGRAMS**   120

FORTRAN-Supplied Subprograms, 97
FUNCTIØN Subprograms, 99
The RETURN Statement, 101
SUBRØUTINE Subprograms, 103
Multiple Entry Into a Subprogram, 106
The Use of Subprogram Names, With or Without
     Their Arguments, as Arguments, 108
Statement Functions, 110
The Explicit Specification Statement, 111
Associated Program Statements, 112
Questions, 119
Exercises, 120

Chapter 8   **ADDITIONAL FORTRAN STATEMENTS**   121

A Different Style of Input and Output State-
     ments, 121
The NAMELIST Statement, 123
Additional Format Codes, 125
The PAUSE Statement, 127
The DATA Initialization Statement, 127
The BLØCK DATA Statement, 129
The IMPLICIT Statement, 130
The CØMPLEX Statement, 131
The Length of a Symbolic Name, 132
Questions, 137
Exercises, 138

Chapter 9   **TAPE AND DISK STATEMENTS**   139

Magnetic Tape, 139
Magnetic Disk, 144
Questions, 153
Exercises, 153

Appendix A   **AN INTRODUCTION TO THE IBM 29 CARD
                     PUNCH**   155

Appendix B   **A LIST OF THE FORTRAN IV KEY WORDS**   159

Appendix C   **PROGRAM DEBUGGING**   160

Appendix D   **FLOATING-POINT AND INTEGER NUMBERS
                     WITH A DECIMAL EXPONENT**   184

Appendix E   **ADDITIONAL FORMAT OPTIONS**   **190**

Appendix F   **LOGICAL OPERATIONS**   **192**

Appendix G   **THE READING OR TWO OR MORE DATA DECKS**   **194**

Appendix H   **SYSTEM AND PROGRAM FLOWCHARTING**   **197**

Appendix I   **FORTRAN-SUPPLIED SUBPROGRAMS**   **201**

        ANSWERS TO QUESTIONS AND EXERCISES   **209**

        Index   **227**

PREFACE

Most digital computers in wide use today are capable of using several languages through which objectives can be successfully accomplished. FORTRAN is one of these languages. While there are several versions of FORTRAN, this textbook is concerned with the newest, most widely used version—FORTRAN IV.

The objective of this textbook is to provide the reader with a systematic explanation of the FORTRAN IV language. Those essential FORTRAN IV key words that enable the reader to begin writing a program almost immediately are discussed in the first several chapters. The remaining chapters discuss those key words that provide the reader with an in-depth understanding of the potentiality of the FORTRAN IV language and its versatility in writing a program. The IBM System/360 and System/370 FORTRAN IV language discussed in this textbook is compatible with and encompasses American National Standard (ANS) FORTRAN, including its mathematical function provisions. Thus, the IBM FORTRAN IV language can be compiled and executed on an IBM FORTRAN E, G, and H level compiler, a WATFOR and WATFIV compiler, and an ANS FORTRAN compiler.

The author assumes that the reader has no prior knowledge of this language. Thus, the textbook begins—after several statements concerning the computer—with a fundamental discussion of FORTRAN. The potential applications of the language are presented through discussions of the various statements composing the language and examples of various uses of these statements to obtain one or more objectives. In addition, at the end of each chapter there are several questions and exercises which highlight the material discussed in that chapter and to varying degrees reinforce the material discussed in previous chapters. The answers to these questions and exercises are provided at the end of the textbook so that the reader can immediately determine his correctness in answering them.

While the individuals that have contributed to the writing of this textbook are too numerous to mention, the author desires to express his indebtedness to Dr. Steve Teglovic of the University of Northern Colorado for his suggestions concerning the original manuscript. However, the author assumes full responsibility for any inadequacies and/or discrepancies in this textbook.

V. Thomas Dock

Chapter 1

INTRODUCTION TO THE COMPUTER AND FORTRAN IV

A discussion of FORTRAN IV generally assumes that the reader has a basic understanding of the computer and, specifically, the type of computer that he will use to execute his FORTRAN IV program. Thus, the following is a brief discussion of the general implications of the term "computer" and the two main types of computers.

DEFINITION OF A COMPUTER

The term "computer," while validly applicable to any machine capable of arithmetical calculation, generally implies a machine possessing the following four characteristics:

1. *Electronic.* Achieves its results through the movement of electronic impulses rather than the physical movement of internal parts.

2. *Internal Storage.* Has the ability to simultaneously store program statements and data. This ability enables the computer to consecutively execute program statements at a high rate of speed.

3. *Stored program.* Follows a series of *statements* in its internal storage which instruct it in detail as to both the specific operations to perform and the order in which to perform them.

4. *Program-execution modification.* Can change the course of the execution of program statements (*branch*) because of a decision based on data in its internal storage and/or the results of one or more arithmetic or logical operations.

In summary, a computer is an electronic machine possessing internal storage capabilities, a stored program of instructions, and the capability for modification of the set of instructions during the execution of the program.

ANALOG AND DIGITAL COMPUTERS

There are two main types of computers: digital and analog. A *digital computer* operates directly on numerical representations of either discrete data or symbols. It takes input and gives output in the form of

1

numbers, letters, and special characters represented by holes in punched cards, spots on magnetic tapes, printing on paper, and so on. This is the type of computer most commonly thought of and referred to when the word *computer* is used either by itself or in context.

Digital computers are generally used for business and scientific data processing. Depending upon the particular characteristics of the digital computer and the precision of the data it is processing, the digital computer is capable of achieving varying degrees of accuracy in both intermediate and final values of data. Digital computers are the most widely used type of computers in business. Thus, unless stated otherwise, the discussion of computers in this textbook concerns digital computers.

The *analog computer*, in contrast to the digital computer, measures continuous electrical or physical magnitudes; it does not operate on digits. If digits are involved at all, they are obtained indirectly. Such physical quantities as pressure, temperature, shaft rotations, and voltage are directly measured as a continuous function. The output of an analog computer is often an adjustment to the control of a machine. For instance, an analog computer may adjust a valve to control the flow of fluid through a pipe, or it may adjust a temperature setting to control the temperature in an oven. For these reasons, analog computers are often used for controlling processes such as oil refining or baking. Digital computers can also be used for controlling processes. To do so, analog data must be converted to digital form, processed, and then the digital results must be converted to analog form. A digital computer possesses greater accuracy than an analog computer, but the analog computer can process data faster than a digital computer.

INTRODUCTION TO FORTRAN IV

The acronym FORTRAN is derived from the term FORmula TRANslator. FORTRAN is a scientific-mathematic language. Thus, it is especially appropriate for writing computer programs for applications that involve mathematical computations and other manipulation of numerical data. This does not make the FORTRAN language inappropriate for business data processing, however, as a large amount of the data processed by business is numerical; the language is also capable of processing data containing alphabetic and/or special characters. The IV after the acronym FORTRAN reflects the current version of the language.

AN EXAMPLE OF A FORTRAN PROGRAM

Figure 1-1 is an example of a FORTRAN program. The purpose in immediately introducing a program is that it will serve as the basis for discussing fundamental aspects of the FORTRAN language. Basically, what is occurring during the execution of this program is that a number is transferred from the first 5 punch card columns of a data card located on an input device to a storage location in the computer's memory and is stored under the variable name NUMBER, which is its memory address. A duplicate of this number is then retrieved from memory address NUMBER and printed on the first print line of a new page of paper by the printer. The words THE NUMBER READ FRØM THE FIRST 5 PUNCH CARD COLUMNS IS are printed immediately preceding the printing of this number. This series of events is repeated until there are no more data cards. When the computer detects this, it will terminate execution of the stored program.*

THE FORTRAN CODING FORM

A FORTRAN program is composed of FORTRAN statements and possibly one or more comment statements. A FORTRAN Coding Form (see Figure 1-1) can best be thought of as a convenient tool that may be used in the process of writing these statements. After completion of the writing of the program, the statements composing it are generally correspondingly punched by column number on punch cards. Each 80-column line on the FORTRAN Coding Form represents the 80 columns of an 80-column punch card.

---

*The reader should not become alarmed at this time if he does not fully understand the several concepts, procedures, and rules involved in the execution of this program.

FORTRAN Coding Form

GX28-7327-6 U/M 050**
Printed in U.S.A.

PROGRAM

PROGRAMMER

PUNCHING INSTRUCTIONS

GRAPHIC

PUNCH

PAGE ___ OF ___

CARD ELECTRO NUMBER*

DATE

FORTRAN STATEMENT

IDENTIFICATION SEQUENCE

```
C     AN EXAMPLE OF A FORTRAN PROGRAM
99999 READ (5,150,END=99) NUMBER
150   FORMAT (I5)
      WRITE (6,7346) NUMBER
7346  FORMAT (' ','THE NUMBER READ FROM THE FIRST 5 PUNCH CARD COLUMNS
     1IS',1X,I5)
      GO TO 99999
      STOP
      END
99
```

*A standard card form, IBM electro 888157, is available for punching statements from this form.

**Number of forms per pad may vary slightly

Figure 1-1. An Example of a FORTRAN Program.

3

FORTRAN Coding Form

GX28-7327-6 U/M 050**
Printed in U.S.A.

PROGRAM

PROGRAMMER

DATE

PAGE ___ OF ___

PUNCHING INSTRUCTIONS

GRAPHIC

PUNCH

CARD ELECTRO NUMBER*

IDENTIFICATION SEQUENCE

STATEMENT NUMBER	CONT.	FORTRAN STATEMENT
C		AN EXAMPLE ØF A FØRTRAN PRØGRAM
1		READ (5,2,END=99) NUMBER
2		FØRMAT (I5)
		WRITE (6,3) NUMBER
3		FØRMAT ('1', 'THE NUMBER READ FRØM THE FIRST 5 PUNCH CARD CØLUMNS
		1I5,' IX,', I5)
		GØ TØ 1
		STØP
		END
99		

*A standard card form, IBM electro 888157, is available for punching statements from this form.

**Number of forms per pad may vary slightly.

4

Figure 1-2.   The Same FORTRAN Program as is Shown in Figure 1-1, except for Statement Numbers.

FORTRAN PROGRAM STATEMENTS

As previously mentioned, each line of the FORTRAN Coding Form has 80 columns which represent the 80-column punch card. Each line of the FORTRAN Coding Form is correspondingly punched by punch card column in a punch card. When the FORTRAN statements are compiled (this process is discussed in the last topic of this chapter), they are printed verbatim in the same print line sequence as punched card sequence and compose what is called the source program (this term is also discussed in the last topic of this chapter) listing.

The Numbering of Program Statements   As illustrated in Figure 1-1, it is not necessary to number every program statement. The only program statements that *must* have a statement number are FØRMAT statements and statements to which a transfer is made during execution of the program. While the basis for this statement will be more fully discussed in Chapters 3 and 5, a brief explanation of this basis is presented in the next two paragraphs.

The FØRMAT statement is a program statement that is referred to by either one or more READ and/or WRITE statements. Thus, the computer must have some means of identifying FØRMAT statements.

The computer normally executes statements in the order in which they are located in the program rather than by their statement number. That is, the first program statement is the first statement executed by the computer, the second program statement is the second statement executed by the computer, etc. However, as illustrated in Figure 1-1 through the use of a GØ TØ statement, the FORTRAN language provides the means to transfer to either a preceding or a following program statement. The computer must have some means of identifying the particular preceding or following statement. A statement number is used to identify the particular statement.

Punch Card Columns 1 through 5   As indicated on the FORTRAN Coding Form, punch card columns 1 through 5 of the program statements may only contain the number of that specific statement. This number can be from 1 through 5 numeric characters in length (only numeric characters are allowed in these punch card columns of a statement), and successive numbers do not have to be sequentially numbered. That is, the FORTRAN statements illustrated in Figure 1-1 could be written with the statement numbers illustrated in Figure 1-2. The execution of these statements is the same as the execution of the statements in Figure 1-1. However, the author suggests that for ease of punching and reading the reader should, whenever possible, sequentially number his statement numbers as shown in Figure 1-1.

The author makes an exception to this suggestion, however, when it is necessary to assign a statement number to the STØP statement. The reason for this is that in most FORTRAN programs the reader will not use more than 98 statement numbers and he will normally assign a statement number to the STØP statement. Due to this fact and because the number 99 is both a unique number and easy to remember, the author always assigns this number to the STØP statement.

A statement number can begin and end in any of the 1 through 5 punch card columns, and it need not be consecutive as embedded blanks are not recognized by the computer. Thus, either this method of punching a statement number

```
(card column)    cc│12345│6789...
                      25  │ │
```

or this method of punching a statement number

```
            cc│12345│6789...
              2 5  │ │
```

is acceptable. In both instances, the computer will interpret the statement number as the number 25. However, the author again suggests that for ease of punching and reading the reader should begin a statement number in punch card column 1 and if the statement number is two or more characters, punch them consecutively.

Each program statement number must be a unique number. That is, two statements cannot have the same statement number. The reason for this is that if several statements had the same statement number, the computer would not be able to determine which specific statement was being referenced.

Punch Card Column 6   As also indicated on the FORTRAN Coding Form, punch card column 6 is used exclusively for the continuation of a program statement. The first program statement punch card must contain either a blank or a zero in card column 6. As illustrated in Figures 1-1 and 1-2, when a program statement must be continued on one or more punch cards because it exceeds the 66 punch card columns that are available for a program statement, any alphabetic, numeric, or special character other than either a blank (this character cannot be punched) or a zero must be in card column 6. The reason for this is that the computer interprets a blank or zero in card column 6 as indicating that there is no continuation of the program statement (the statement has been completely punched in one punch card). Thus, it interprets any character other than a blank or zero in card column 6 as indicating that this punch card contains a continuation of a program statement. A program statement can be continued, if necessary, through 19 successive punch cards.

Punch Card Columns 7 through 72   As indicated on the FORTRAN Coding Form, punch card columns 7 through 72 are used for FORTRAN statements. The statements do not have to either begin at card column 7 or, as illustrated in Figures 1-1 and 1-2, end on card column 72. The author suggests, though, that for ease of punching and reading the reader always begin each new statement and, whenever applicable, each punch card that contains a continuation of a statement in card column 7.

Except in specific situations, which will be mentioned when these situations are discussed, spacing within program statements is neither required nor has an influence on the execution of the statements. Thus, as many blanks as desired may be employed throughout a statement to improve its readability.

Punch Card Columns 73 through 80   Finally, as indicated on the FORTRAN Coding Form, punch card columns 73 through 80 are not used for FORTRAN statements. The reason for this is that only the first 72 punch card columns are significant to the FORTRAN compiler. (This term is discussed in the last topic of this chapter.) Card columns 73 through 80 may either be left blank or used for program identification, sequencing, or any other purpose by punching the desired code in either one or more of these card columns. If, for example, the output device is the printer, the punched code will appear on the same print line that the program statement located on that punched card appears.

THE COMMENT STATEMENT

The comment statement is a program statement that is used to identify either an overall FORTRAN program as in Figures 1-1 and 1-2 and/or a specific part of a program. Comment statements are identified by the alphabetic character C that *must* be punched in the first card column.

The comment statement, unlike the FORTRAN statement, may be punched in any of the card columns 2 through 80. Also unlike the FORTRAN statement, the continuation of a comment requires that the alphabetic character C be again punched in card column 1 for every punch card that contains a continuation of the comment. No alphabetic, numeric, or special character is required, however, in card column 6 as is required in the FORTRAN statement. Similar to a FORTRAN statement, though, as many blanks as desired may be employed throughout the statement to improve its readability.

The comment statement is a nonexecutable statement; that is, it is neither processed by the FORTRAN compiler (translated into machine language) nor affects the execution of the FORTRAN program. Rather, it is printed verbatim along with the FORTRAN statements on the source program listing in the same print line sequence as punched card sequence.

One or more comment statements are often placed at the beginning of a program as a means of identifying it. In a program that is either lengthy and/or contains one or more distinguishable parts that the programmer desires to identify, as many comment statements as desired can be inserted throughout the program prior to the END statement. However, a comment statement may not immediately precede a continuation of a FORTRAN statement.

THE FORTRAN CHARACTER SET

The FORTRAN Character Set is composed of the following three categories : alphabetic characters, numeric characters, and special characters. Within these three categories are the characters that may compose FORTRAN statements (see Figure 1-3).

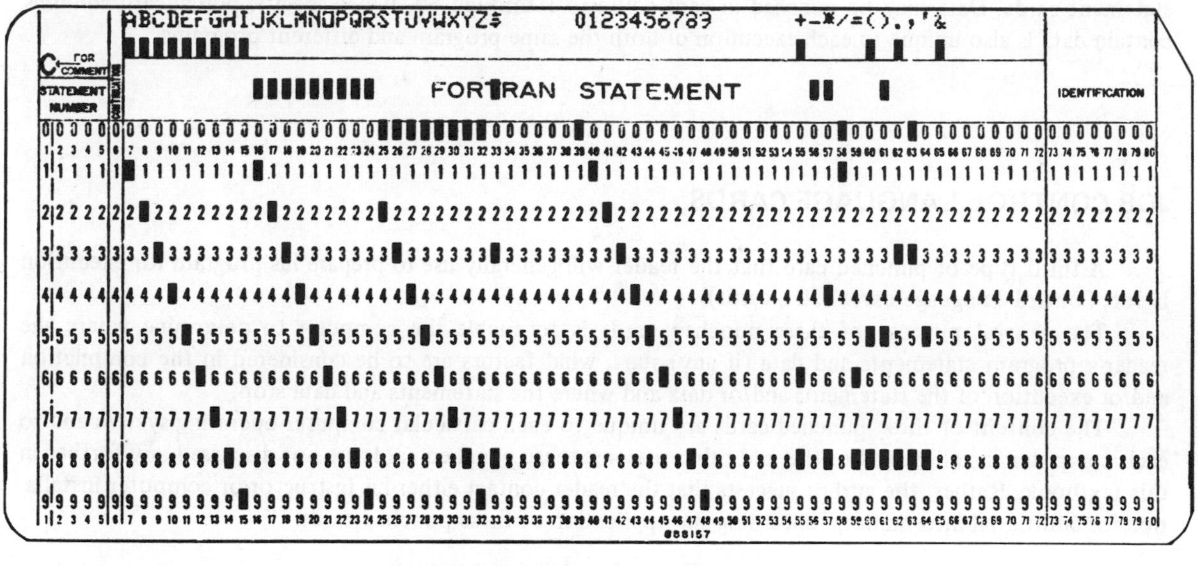

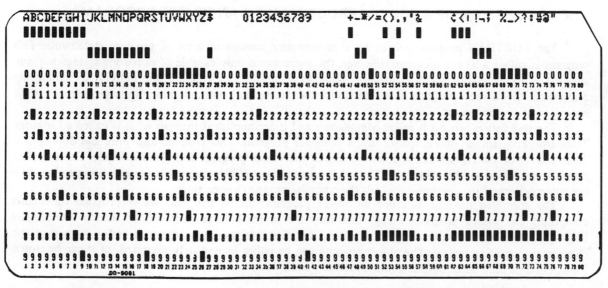

Figure 1-3. FORTRAN Character Set.

DATA CARDS

Data cards are distinct from program statement cards. Although it is possible for a FORTRAN program to generate and process its own data, in most instances this will not successfully accomplish the objective of the program. Thus, there usually is some source of data that is acceptable to the computer. Today, the most common original source of data is the data card.

Data cards, comment statements, and literal data (discussed in Chapter 3) can contain any of the characters of the FORTRAN Character Set, plus any of the additional 15 characters illustrated in Figure 1-4. Since these additional 15 characters are not part of the FORTRAN Character Set, some brand name models of printers are not capable of printing them. Thus, the reader should either ask his instructor or

Figure 1-4. Acceptable Data Card, Comment Statement, and Literal Data Characters.

inquire at his computer installation about whether or not the computer installation's printer is capable of printing these additional characters before using any of them.

Data cards are placed behind the program statement cards when preparing a FORTRAN program for execution by the computer. The number and order of data cards are unique to each execution of both the same program and different programs. Data cards are not subject to the procedures and rules of program statement cards. Data may be punched in card columns 1 through 80. Which specific punch card columns contain data is also unique to each execution of both the same program and different programs.

JOB CONTROL LANGUAGE CARDS

A third type of punched card that the reader will generally use to prepare his program for execution is Job Control Language cards (JCL cards).

The general purpose of these punched cards is to enable the computer to determine where the reader's program statements and data (if any) start, what factors are to be considered in the compilation and/or execution of the statements and/or data and where the statements and data stop.

The content of these punched cards are unique to each particular computer operating system and to each computer installation. For this and other reasons, these punched cards are not discussed any further in this textbook. Rather, the author suggests that the reader contact either his instructor or computer installation for additional information concerning the application of these punched cards.

THE CARD PUNCH

The use of punch cards, whether they be program, data, or JCL requires a basic knowledge of how to use the card punch. With this in mind, the reader may desire to review Appendix A. This appendix contains a brief discussion of the IBM 29 Card Punch for either those readers who have already used it but wish to refresh themselves or those readers who have not had an opportunity to use it.

THE CONVERSION OF A SOURCE PROGRAM INTO AN OBJECT PROGRAM

The FORTRAN program written by a programmer consists of a set of program statements. This program is called a *source* program. However, the computer is only capable of executing statements constructed in its language—machine language. Thus, as illustrated in Figure 1-5, the FORTRAN statements composing the source program must be converted (compiled) into machine language prior to their execution by the computer.

The translation process is called *compilation* and is accomplished through what is called a Language Translator Program or, more specifically, a compiler program. This program also produces appropriate diagnostic error messages when it detects errors in the source program during compilation. The compiler program is located in the computer's Central Processing Unit (CPU) during the compilation process. The operating system of the computer controls the compiler program's operations.

The compiled program is called an *object* program; this is the same set of program statements composing the source program, except that they are in machine language rather than in FORTRAN language form. As with the compiler program, the object program also operates under control of the computer's operating system. The object program can be either immediately executed, or it can be stored for a period of time on an output medium such as a disk, tape, or punched cards.

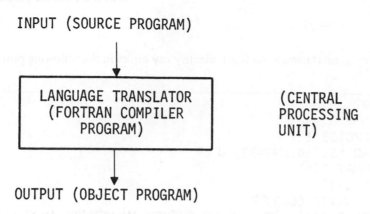

Figure 1-5. The Compilation of a FORTRAN Program.

QUESTIONS

1. Name and briefly discuss the four general implied characteristics of the computer.
2. Name and briefly discuss the two main types of computers.
3. From what term is the acronym FORTRAN derived and for what use is this computer language especially appropriate?
4. Answer the following statements concerning FORTRAN statements with either TRUE of FALSE. If the answer is FALSE, why is the statement false?

   A. The 80 columns of the FORTRAN Coding Form represent the 80 columns of an 80-column punch card.
   B. Every program statement must have a statement number.
   C. FØRMAT program statements are the only program statements that must have a statement number.
   D. Program statement numbers can be any 1 through 5 characters in length.
   E. Program statement numbers do not have to be sequential.
   F. Program statement numbers and the digits composing statement numbers can begin and end in any of the punch card columns 1 through 5, i.e., embedded blanks are not recognized by the computer.
   G. It is acceptable for two or more program statements to have the same statement number.
   H. Punch card column 6 is used for the one or more FORTRAN statement punch cards that are a continuation of a FORTRAN statement.
   I. In a program statement punch card that is a continuation of a FORTRAN statement, column 6 can have any alphabetic, numeric, or special character punched in it.
   J. FORTRAN statements must begin at punch card column 7 and must end at punch card column 72.
   K. As many blanks as desired may be employed throughout a program statement to improve its readability.
   L. Punch card columns 73 through 80 can only be used for program identification, sequencing, etc. of the program statements.

5. What alphabetic character must be punched in what card column of every punch card that either contains a statement or a continuation of a comment statement?
6. What punch columns can a comment statement occupy?
7. Name the three categories of characters composing the FORTRAN Character Set.
8. What is the difference between FORTRAN statements and data cards?
9. What is a source program?
10. What is an object program?
11. What occurs during the process of compilation?

EXERCISE

1. Considering each program statement by itself, identify any errors in the following program statements.

```
cc   123456789...

     C    EXERCISE 1-1
     1    READ (5,150,END=99) J
      150 FØRMAT (I5)
     2A   K = J+100
     150    WRITE (6,3) K
          FØRMAT ('1', 'THE VALUE STØRED IN MEMØRY ADDRESS K IS', I6)
            GØ TØ 1
       9 9 STØP
          END
```

Chapter 2

THE COMPOSITION OF FORTRAN STATEMENTS

In the preceding chapter, the FORTRAN statement was discussed with respect to the basic proce-dures and rules that must be considered when writing it on a line of the FORTRAN Coding Form and, in turn, punching it in a punch card. This chapter discusses the four basic components of the FORTRAN statement—FORTRAN key words, numbers, symbolic names, and expressions. First, however, is a discus-sion of the FORTRAN Character Set, which contains the alphabetic, numeric, and special characters that may compose these four basic components.

THE FORTRAN CHARACTER SET

As shown in Figure 1-3 and again in Figure 2-1, the FORTRAN Character Set is composed of three categories: alphabetic characters, numeric characters, and special characters.

Alphabetic Characters						Numeric Characters				Special Characters		
A	F	K	P	U	Z	0	3	6	9	(Blank)	/	.
B	G	L	Q	V	$	1	4	7		+	=	,
C	H	M	R	W		2	5	8		−	(	' (apostrophe)
D	I	N	S	X						✻	)	& (ampersand)
E	J	O	T	Y								

Figure 2-1. The FORTRAN Character Set.

As illustrated in Figures 1-1 and 1-2, all alphabetic characters are written in capital letter form. When writing characters, care must be taken to be sure they will not be confused with a similarly written character. Eight characters are especially subject to this problem. Thus, in an attempt to avoid this problem, the following characters should be *written* as shown:

Alphabetic Character	Numeric Character
Ø*	0
I	1
Z	2
S	5

*Some computer installations and programmers reverse this convention and slash the numeric char-acter 0 rather than the alphabetic character O. The author suggests the reader follow the above shown convention unless instructed otherwise by either his instructor or computer installation.

Alphabetic Characters   The alphabetic characters are used to form FORTRAN key words and symbolic names and may be used to partially form numbers and expressions.

Numeric Characters   The numeric characters are used to form numbers and may be used to either completely or partially form symbolic names and expressions.

Special Characters   The special characters may be used to partially form numbers and expressions. The following is a discussion of the possible use of each of the special characters:

The special character *blank* is used to space either within or between FORTRAN key words, numbers, symbolic names, and expressions. A blank character results when the card punch Space Bar is struck once. (The same result is obtained by striking a typewriter Space Bar.)

The +, -, *, and / special characters represent addition, subtraction, multiplication, and division, respectively. That is,

$$10 + 5 = 15$$
$$10 - 5 = 5$$
$$10 * 5 = 50$$
$$10 / 5 = 2$$

The special character = normally implies equality between either the datum or data on each side of it. This is *not* the implication in FORTRAN. Rather, it implies either establishment or replacement of the datum stored under the symbolic name on the left side of the equal sign with either the datum or data on the right side. For example, in the equation I = 25, if the variable name I did not have a number stored under it, then the number 25 would be established as the number stored under it. However, if the variable name I already had a number stored under it, say 5, then the number 25 would replace that number. These and other implications of the use of the equal sign are discussed in Chapter 4.

The special character . is used only as a decimal point as there is no sentence period in the FORTRAN language.

The special character & is used in the FORTRAN language.

Delimiters   In the English language, punctuation is used to improve readability and understanding. For basically the same reasons, one of the rules of FORTRAN is that every FORTRAN key word, number, and symbolic name in a FORTRAN statement must be separated by one or more appropriate delimiters. The following characters and punch card column can be used as delimiters:

+ - * / = ( ) . , ' Punch Card Column 73

The following FORTRAN statements are excerpted from the program illustrated in Figure 1-1:

```
cc  123456789...


    |READ (5,2,END=99) NUMBER
 2  |FØRMAT (I5)
```

In the first statement, a parenthesis is used to separate the FORTRAN key word READ from the number 5; a comma is used to separate the numbers 5 and 2; a comma is used to separate the number 2 and the FORTRAN key word END; an equal sign (=) is used to separate the FORTRAN key word END from the number 99; a parenthesis is used to both separate the number 99 from the variable name NUMBER and to comply with the FORTRAN language rule that there must always be an equal number of left and right parentheses in a FORTRAN statement; and punch card column 73 performs the same function as a period at the end of an English sentence. In the second statement, the left parenthesis is used to separate the FORTRAN key word FØRMAT from the integer format code I5, and the right parentheses is used to comply with the FORTRAN language rule that there must always be an equal number of left and right parentheses in a FORTRAN statement. Punch card column 73 again performs the same function as a period at the end of an English sentence.

If a FORTRAN statement is continued on to one or more punch cards, card column 73 is valid as a punctuation character only in the last continued punch card. As a result, if a FORTRAN key word, number, or symbolic name is started in a punch card column close to card column 72 and is too long to be completed, the reader may punch through card column 72, place any alphabetic, numeric, or special character other than either a blank (this character cannot be punched) or zero in card column 6 of the next program statement card, and continue the balance of the FORTRAN key word, number, or symbolic name beginning in card column 7. The computer will interpret the portion on each program statement punch card as one FORTRAN key word, number, or symbolic name.

The author suggests, however, that whenever possible a FORTRAN key word, number, or symbolic name should not be split between two punch cards. Rather, as shown in Figures 1-1 and 1-2, the statement should be continued to another program punch card from a punch card column prior to card column 72.

Blanks   As mentioned in Chapter 1 under the topic "Punch Card Columns 7 Through 72," all FORTRAN key words, numbers, and symbolic names may be separated by as many blanks as desired to improve readability. In addition, embedded blanks within FORTRAN key words, numbers, and symbolic names are not recognized by the computer.

Thus the above two FORTRAN statements may also be written as follows and be identically executed by the computer:

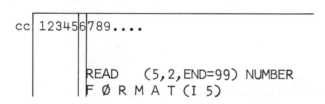

However, the author suggests that for ease of punching the program punch cards, prudent utilization of punch card columns and improvement of readability, the reader not employ either of these allowable practices—especially the second one—unless the situation warrants it.

FORTRAN KEY WORDS

In the English language, words have different meanings; to distinguish between them they are spelled differently; and in many instances they compose either all of or part of an English sentence.

In the FORTRAN language, words have the same implications in FORTRAN statements, i.e., each FORTRAN key word is interpreted differently by the computer with respect to execution, spelled differently, and in many instances, composes either all or part of a FORTRAN statement. Just as the word *read* has a different implication than the word *write* in an English sentence to the reader, the FORTRAN key word READ has a different implication than the FORTRAN key word WRITE in a FORTRAN statement to the computer. In other words, FORTRAN key words are the means by which the computer distinguishes among the FORTRAN statements with respect to the possible types of execution involved in executing a FORTRAN program.

The implications of when, where, and how specific FORTRAN key words are used in FORTRAN statements are discussed in the following chapters of this textbook. Appendix B contains a complete list of the FORTRAN key words.

NUMBERS

All data in a FORTRAN statement that are represented by themselves are called constants in the FORTRAN language. The two most common types of constant data are integer and real numbers. A third type of constant data are floating-point and integer numbers with a decimal exponent.

Integer Numbers   An integer number is composed of one or more numerical characters. Although formally called an integer constant in the FORTRAN language, it is more commonly called a fixed-point or integer number because of the fact that the decimal point is always *assumed* to be located to the right of the last numerical character of the number. In this textbook, the term used is integer number.

An integer number may be either positive, zero, or negative; while a positive integer number can have the special character plus (+) as its leading character, if an integer number is unsigned and nonzero the computer assumes it to be positive. When used in FORTRAN, an integer number must comply with the following five rules:

1. It must be a whole number. That is, it cannot contain a decimal point.

2. If negative, the special character minus (−) must be the leading character.

3. It cannot contain embedded commas.

4. It can be 1 through 10 numerical characters in length.

5. Its maximum magnitude can be either plus or minus 2147483647 or in other words $2^{31}-1$.

The minus or plus sign, if present, is considered by the computer as being an allowable additional character beyond the maximum possible length of 10 numerical characters.

The following are examples of *valid* integer numbers:

```
1
150
2147483647
0
-10
-2147483647
```

The following are examples of *invalid* integer numbers:

15.	(contains a decimal point)
4362−	(minus sign incorrectly located)
8,310	(contains an embedded comma)
15346791264	(exceeds the maximum possible numerical character length)
2371624598	(exceeds the maximum magnitude)

Floating-Point (Real) Numbers   A floating-point number is composed of one or more numerical characters and a decimal point. The decimal point may be followed by one or more numerical characters to form what is called the fraction part of the number. Although formally called a real constant in the FORTRAN language, it is more commonly called a floating-point number to reflect the fact that the decimal point can be moved or *floated* to either the beginning, middle, or end of the numerical characters forming the number. In this textbook, the term used is floating-point.

There are three forms of floating-point numbers:

1. Basic floating-point numbers. (Basic floating-point numbers may be one of two types: single precision or double precision.)

2. Basic floating-point numbers followed by a decimal exponent.

3. Integer numbers followed by a decimal exponent.

All three forms of floating-point numbers may be either positive, zero, or negative. While a positive floating-point number can have the special character plus (+) as its leading character, if a floating-point number is unsigned and nonzero, the computer assumes it to be positive.

Single Precision Floating-Point Numbers   A single precision floating-point number must comply with the following four rules:

1. It can contain 1 through 7 numerical characters.

2. If negative, the special character minus (−) must be the leading character.

3. It must contain a decimal point.

4. It cannot contain embedded commas.

The minus or plus sign, if present, is considered by the computer as being an allowable additional character beyond the maximum possible length of 7 numerical characters.

The following are examples of *valid* single precision floating-point numbers:

.36
2647.198
0.
−.58
−14.78
−93274.65

The following are examples of *invalid* single precision floating-point numbers:

236577.61   (exceeds the maximum possible numerical character length)
73446   (no decimal point)
6742.12−   (minus sign incorrectly located)
19,832.17   (contains an embedded comma)

Double Precision Floating-Point Numbers   A double precision floating-point number must comply with the following four rules:

1. It can contain 1 through 16 numerical characters.

2. If negative, the special character minus (−) must be the leading character.

3. It must contain a decimal point.

4. It cannot contain embedded commas.

The minus or plus sign, if present, is considered by the computer as being an allowable character beyond the maximum possible length of 16 numerical characters.

Double precision floating-point numbers have two basic disadvantages when compared to single precision floating-point numbers:

1. They occupy approximately twice as much computer storage space.

2. They are not processed as quickly by the computer.

Thus, while double precision floating-point numbers do have the advantage of greater numerical character length, they have a negative effect on both the amount of data that may be stored in a specific computer's memory at any one time and the speed with which this data is processed by the computer.

The following are examples of *valid* double precision floating-point numbers:

.64778324
29766239.
00000000.
6379541387.64
−.18875563
−17458645.2

The following are examples of *invalid* double precision floating-point numbers:

34476598823564.192   (exceeds the maximum possible numerical character length)
17845166.5−1   (minus sign incorrectly located)
893447642   (no decimal point)
74,326,598.15   (contains embedded commas)

Floating-Point and Integer Numbers with a Decimal Exponent   Because of the particular use of floating-point and integer numbers with a decimal exponent, the reader is referred to Appendix D for a discussion of this topic. However, unless the reader is specifically interested in this topic, he can omit reading Appendix D without interfering with his learning the FORTRAN language.

SYMBOLIC NAMES

A symbolic name can be a symbolic representation of a number, an alphabetic character, an array of numbers (discussed in Chapter 6), or a subprogram (discussed in Chapter 7). Depending upon which one of these four classes a symbolic name is representing, it has a particular name.

1. When a symbolic name represents an integer, single precision floating-point, or double precision floating-point number or alphabetic character(s) that is either externally supplied to the computer prior to execution of a program or internally calculated by the computer during the execution of the program, it is called a *variable* name. The symbolic name is called a variable name because of the fact that the number or alphabetic character(s) represented by a variable name may change one or more times during the execution of the program. However, a variable name can represent only one number or one group of alphabetic character(s) at a time.

2. When a symbolic name represents a logical constant, it is called a *logical variable* name. The term *variable* is used for the same reason discussed in the previous paragraph.

3. When a symbolic name represents an array, it is called an *array* name.

4. When a symbolic name represents a subprogram, it is called a *subprogram* name.

A symbolic name is composed of 1 through 6 alphabetic and numeric characters. The first character of the symbolic name *must* be an alphabetic character. No special characters can be used in a symbolic name.

The following is an illustration of the use of three variable names:

```
cc | 12345|6|789...
   |
   |
   |      |TAX = TØTPAY ⁛ TXRATE
```

In this example, the quantity represented by the variable name TØTPAY is multiplied by the quantity represented by the variable name TXRATE. The result is stored under the variable name TAX. Thus, the TØTPAY represented the quantity 100.00 and TXRATE represented the quantity .05, the quantity 5.00 would be stored under the variable name TAX.

While it is not a requirement of the FORTRAN language, the author suggests that the reader use, whenever possible, a variable name that is representative of the type of quantity it represents. In other words, while the variable names in the equation of the previous example could have been A = B * C, these variable names would not reflect as well the nature of the quantity each variable name represents as do the variable names used.

Almost all symbolic names are formed by the programmer. A symbolic name that is either composed of or arranged differently by one or more characters is considered by the computer as a different symbolic name from any other symbolic name in the program. The FORTRAN IV key words listed in Appendix B may also be used as symbolic names. The computer distinguishes between a FORTRAN key word used as a FORTRAN key word and as a symbolic name by its location within the program statement.

As previously discussed, integer numbers are distinguished from floating-point numbers by either the presence or absence of a decimal point. Since only alphabetic and numeric characters can compose symbolic names, another technique is used which allows the symbolic name to reflect whether it represents either an integer or a single precision floating-point number. This technique centers around the first character of the symbolic name. If a symbolic name represents an integer number, its first character must be either an I, J, K, L, M, or N. However, if a symbolic name represents a single precision floating-point number, its first character must be represented by one of the alphabetic characters A through H, Ø through Z, or $.

This technique of distinguishing between symbolic names is called *implicit* type specification because the type of number being represented is implied by the first character of the symbolic name.

The following are examples of *valid* symbolic names:

I	(integer)
MØNEY	(integer)
J12345	(integer)
$734	(single precision floating-point)
BASE	(single precision floating-point)
A	(single precision floating-point)

The following are examples of *invalid* symbolic names:

INTEREST	(contains more than 6 characters)
5RUNS	(the first character must be an alphabetic character)
$VALU.	(contains a special character (decimal point))

Specification Statements   A specification statement is a nonexecutable statement that provides the compiler program with certain information concerning the nature of specific data being used in the source program. In addition, it provides the computer with the information it needs to allocate storage space in its memory for this data. While several appropriately indicated specification statements are discussed throughout the remainder of this textbook, it is appropriate to discuss four of these specification statements at this time. These four statements are called "explicit specification statements" because the type of number stored under a symbolic name listed in these statements is determined by the mere presence of the symbolic name in the statement and *not* the symbolic name's initial character. As such, the symbolic name must comply with all of the rules concerning the construction of a symbolic name except one: its first character can be *any* alphabetic character. Also, the specification statement containing the symbolic name must precede the first statement in which the symbolic name is used.

INTEGER Statement   The INTEGER statement is used when it is desirable to store an integer type number under a symbolic name that would normally require a single precision floating-point type number because the first character of the symbolic name is represented by one of the alphabetic characters A through H, Ø through Z, or $. Figure 2-2 illustrates the general form of this statement:

```
cc 123456789...

       INTEGER list
```

where

```
    INTEGER  FORTRAN key word that distinguishes this statement from
             the other kinds of statements in the program.
    list     represents one or more single precision floating-point
             variable names, each of which must be separated by a comma.
```

Figure 2-2.   The General Form of the INTEGER Statement.

The variable names CØUNT, PIECES, and WEIGHT, because of their first alphabetic character, normally imply that a single precision floating-point number will be stored under each of them. However, as shown in the following illustration,

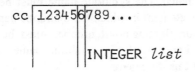

```
cc 123456789...

       INTEGER CØUNT,PIECES,WEIGHT
```

by their presence in the INTEGER statement it is explicitly declared that an integer number will be stored under each of them.

REAL Statement   The REAL statement is used when it is desirable to store a single precision floating-point type number under a symbolic name that would normally require an integer type number because the first character of the symbolic name is represented by one of the alphabetic characters I through N. Figure 2-3 illustrates the general form of this statement:

```
cc 123456789...

        REAL list
```

where

REAL   FORTRAN key word that distinguishes this statement from the other kinds of statements in the program.

list   represents one or more integer variable names, each of which must be separated by a comma.

Figure 2-3.   The General Form of the REAL Statement.

The variable name NUMBER, because of its first alphabetic character, normally implies that an integer number will be stored under it. However, as shown in the following illustration, by its presence in the REAL statement it is explicitly declared that a single precision floating-point number will be stored under it.

```
cc 123456789...

        REAL NUMBER
```

DØUBLE PRECISIØN Statement   A DØUBLE PRECISIØN statement is used when it is desirable to store a double precision floating-point number under a symbolic name. The symbolic name must be used in a DØUBLE PRECISIØN statement that must precede the first statement in which the symbolic name is used. Since each symbolic name that represents a double precision floating-point number must be explicitly declared in a DØUBLE PRECISIØN statement, the first character of the symbolic name can be *any* alphabetic character. Figure 2-4 illustrates the general form of this statement:

```
cc 123456789...

        DØUBLE PRECISIØN list
```

where

DØUBLE PRECISIØN   FORTRAN key word that distinguishes this statement from the other kinds of statements in the program.

list   represents one or more variable names, each of which must be separated by a comma.

Figure 2-4.   The General Form of the DØUBLE PRECISIØN Statement.

The variable names PRICE, CØST, and MARKUP, because of their first alphabetic character, normally imply that a single precision floating-point number will be stored under each of the first two of them and an integer number will be stored under the last of them. However, as shown in the following illustration, by their presence in the DØUBLE PRECISIØN statement it is explicitly declared that a double precision floating-point number will be stored under each of them.

```
cc │123456789...
   │
   │       DØUBLE PRECISIØN PRICE,CØST,MARKUP
```

LØGICAL Statement   There are two basic forms of logical data:

1. *Logical Constants.* A logical constant may specify one of two possible logical values:

.TRUE.

.FALSE.

As indicated above, both logical constants must be immediately preceded and followed by a period. This is the means by which the computer recognizes them as logical constants and not symbolic names.

2. *Logical Variable Names.* A logical variable name is a symbolic name that may have either the logical constant .TRUE. or the logical constant .FALSE. stored under it. A logical variable name must be explicitly declared in a LØGICAL statement. This specification statement must precede the first statement in which the logical variable name is used.

```
cc │123456789...
   │
   │       LØGICAL ln₁, ln₂, ..., lnₙ
```

where

LØGICAL $\qquad$ FORTRAN key word that distinguishes this state-
$\qquad\qquad\qquad$ ment from the other kinds of statements in the
$\qquad\qquad\qquad$ program.

$ln_1, ln_2, ..., ln_n$ $\quad$ represents one or more logical variable names,
$\qquad\qquad\qquad$ each of which must be separated by a comma.

Figure 2-5.   The General Form of the LØGICAL Statement.

Similar to the INTEGER, REAL, and DØUBLE PRECISIØN statements, the LØGICAL statement is an explicit specification statement because the type of datum stored under a symbolic name listed in the statement is determined by the mere presence of the symbolic name in the statement and *not* the symbolic name's initial character. A logical variable name, because it must be explicitly declared in a LØGICAL statement prior to its use in a statement, must comply with all of the rules concerning the construction of a symbolic name except one: its first character can be *any* alphabetic character. For example, the variable names ITEM1, ITEM2, and RESULT, because of their first alphabetic character, normally imply that an integer number will be stored under each of the first two of them and a single precision floating-point number will be stored under the last of them. However, as shown in the following illustration, by their presence in the LØGICAL statement it is explicitly declared that a logical constant will be stored under each of them.

```
cc │123456789...
   │
   │       LØGICAL ITEM1,ITEM2,RESULT
```

EXPRESSIONS

There are two kinds of expressions in FORTRAN: arithmetic and logical. An *arithmetic* expression involves an arithmetical computation. A *logical* expression expresses either a true or false condition. Both of these expressions are discussed in Chapter 4.

THE CATEGORIES OF FORTRAN STATEMENTS

The FORTRAN language is composed of five categories of program statements. These five categories are: specification statements, input and output statements, arithmetic and logical assignment statements, control statements, and subprogram statements. While most FORTRAN programs do not include program statements from all of these categories, many include program statements from the first four categories. The discussion of the remaining chapters of this textbook centers around the different kinds of program statements composing these five categories.

QUESTIONS

1. Name and briefly discuss the four major components of FORTRAN statements.
2. To what extent can each of the three categories of the FORTRAN Character Set be used to form each of the four major components of FORTRAN statements?
3. Name and describe the difference between the four sets of FORTRAN Character Set characters that may be confused because of their similarity in formation.
4. What does the special character = imply in FORTRAN?
5. What is the basic purpose of a FORTRAN key word in a program statement?
6. What is the basic difference between an integer and a floating-point number?
7. What is the basic difference between a single precision floating-point number and a double precision floating-point number?
8. What types of characters can compose a symbolic name?
9. What alphabetic characters can be used as the first character of a symbolic name to implicitly indicate to the computer that the number stored under it is integer mode?
10. What alphabetic characters can be used as the first character of a symbolic name to implicitly indicate to the computer that the number stored under it is single precision floating-point mode?
11. How is it conveyed to the computer that a symbolic name has either a double precision floating-point number or a logical constant stored under it?
12. What type of characters can be used as the first character of either a double precision floating-point name or a logical symbolic name?
13. Name the two possible values of a logical constant.
14. What is a logical variable name?

EXERCISES

1. Which of the following integer numbers are invalid? Why?

(1)	131.	(4)	1540	(7)	2145483647	(10)	3568194176
(2)	-2147483647	(5)	0	(8)	17.2	(11)	+161
(3)	10	(6)	18453621496	(9)	-87	(12)	1,177

2. Which of the following single precision floating-point numbers are invalid? Why?

(1)	347523.5	(4)	185763	(7)	-9861.82	(10)	834.50
(2)	643189.52	(5)	+614.24	(8)	0.	(11)	13,982.10
(3)	-5431.16	(6)	-.1	(9)	835.45-	(12)	27.99

3. Which of the following double precision floating-point numbers are invalid? Why?

    (1) +.71471093   (4) −87243563.8   (7) 91748600.198   (10) 8,291,376.29
    (2) 00000000.   (5) 715839546   (8) 366317.41−1   (11) .615424476
    (3) 214802178963547.37 (6) 4156628.932   (9) +87915248.3   (12) −.411605681

4.* Which of the following single precision floating-point and double precision floating-point numbers are invalid? Why?

    (1) +154563.732D+04   (4) 5447132.5E65   (7) +.92E+1
    (2) 9216.18D   (5) −69750216.323D09   (8) 1031628.23E82
    (3) 671.42E0   (6) 615406.34D8.2   (9) −618.10D−03

5.* Which of the following integer numbers with a decimal exponent are invalid? Why?

    (1) 673142D+08   (4) 495106.5E6   (7) −84751E13
    (2) 278E   (5) +735290678D4   (8) 9178051637D
    (3) −61D−10   (6) 51D83   (9) 2D1

---

*See Appendix D for a discussion of exponents.

Chapter 3

INPUT AND OUTPUT STATEMENTS

While the computer is capable of generating the data to be processed, the source of most data is a data set located on one or more input devices. Although the computer is capable of storing the processed data and the results of this processed data in its memory, in most instances it will be desirable to store the results of this processed data on one or more output devices.

Some of the more common input devices are the card reader, magnetic disk unit, and magnetic tape unit. Some of the more common output devices are the card reader, printer, magnetic disk unit, and magnetic tape unit. While the aspects of the FORTRAN language involved in the input and output of data through all of these input and output devices are discussed in this textbook, only those aspects of FORTRAN that may be involved in input through the card reader and output through the printer are discussed in this chapter.

The FORTRAN statements required to both transfer and control the flow of data between the computer's memory and one or more input and output devices are called input and output statements. The one or more fields of data located on each of the data cards that follow most FORTRAN programs are the original online source of most data read by input statements. Each data card is a *record*; a record is composed of one or more fields of data. Records, in turn, form a *data set* (file), i.e., a data set is composed of one or more related records. Records may be read from and written into several types of input and output media, some of which are: punch cards, print lines, magnetic disk, and magnetic tape.

THE READ STATEMENT

The READ statement causes the reading of data from one or more records located on a specific input device, and the storing of this data in the computer's memory. Figure 3-1 illustrates the general form of this program statement:

```
cc | 123456789...
   |
   | bbbbb | READ (i,n) list
```

where

      bbbbb   represents an unsigned 1 through 5 integer number that is required only if a transfer is made to this statement from another program statement.

READ   FORTRAN key word that distinguishes this statement from the other kinds of statements in the program.

(a special character that is a requirement of the FORTRAN language.

i   represents a data set reference number which is represented by either an unsigned integer number or a variable name which has the integer number stored under it.

,   a special character that is a requirement of the FORTRAN language.

n   represents the statement number of the FØRMAT statement that describes the particular form of the data being transferred into the computer memory.

)   a special character that is a requirement of the FORTRAN language.

list   represents one or more variable, logical variable, and/or array names, each of which must be separated by a comma. The data read from a record of the particular data set designated by *i* is stored in the computer's memory under these one or more variable, logical variable, and/or array names. The array name or names can be subscripted and these subscripts can be indexed (see Chapter 6).

Figure 3-1.   The General Form of the READ Statement.

The READ statement in the following illustration causes the data within one or more records associated with data set reference number 5 to be stored in the computer's memory under the variable names A, B, I, and J. The specific datum of a record to be stored under variable names A, B, I, and J is determined by the FØRMAT statement that has statement number 1 assigned to it. (This program statement is discussed later in this chapter.)

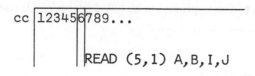

A data set reference number, which can be any number 1 through 99, is associated with a data set that is located on a particular input or output device. The specific data set reference number for a particular input and/or output device is assigned by the computer installation in which the device is located. The same data set reference number is not necessarily assigned to the same particular input and/or output device among computer installations. In this textbook, data set reference number 5 is associated with a data set located on a card reader, data set reference number 6 is associated with a data set located on a printer, and data set reference number 7 is associated with a data set located on a card punch.

Except in two specific situations, which are discussed later in this chapter, a datum cannot be read from a record by a READ statement unless a symbolic name for it is present in the statement. However, a symbolic name should not be present in a READ statement unless a datum is to be stored under it. It is important to remember that a symbolic name must be constructed according to the particular type of datum that is going to be stored under it.

The maximum number of characters of data that can be read from a record located on a particular input device is determined by both the internal storage capacity of the computer's memory and in most instances, more importantly, the maximum possible length of a record in the data set. For a data set stored on punched cards, the maximum number of characters of data that can compose a record is 80 characters. Thus, it is important that no attempt be made to have a READ statement read more than 80 characters of data from a record stored on punched cards.

The READ statement either establishes or replaces the datum stored in the computer's memory under each variable, logical variable, or array name that is present in the statement. For example, if the variable name I in the following illustration did not have a number stored under it, then the number read from a record located on the card reader would establish the number stored under it. However, if the variable name I already had a number stored under it, then the number read would replace that number.

```
cc  123456789...

         READ (5,1) I
```

The END= and ERR= Options FORTRAN offers two options with the READ statement. The general form of the READ statement when these two options are specified is: READ (i,n,END=n,ERR=n) list. The END= option provides the means for the computer to transfer to the program statement indicated by the statement number following the equal sign when the computer attempts to read data from a record and encounters the end of the data set (there are no more data cards to be read). The number following the equal sign must be a statement number assigned to another executable statement in the program. While the statement transferred to is usually the STØP statement, a transfer can be made to *any* executable statement. A transfer to a statement other than the STØP statement is especially appropriate in certain program situations involving branching or looping (Chapter 5) or the reading of array data (Chapter 6) in a program. If the computer attempts to read a record and encounters the end of the data set and the END= option is not specified in the READ statement, execution of the object program is terminated.

The ERR= option provides the means for the computer to transfer to the program statement indicated by the statement number following the equal sign when the computer encounters an error condition during its attempt to read data from a record. When an error condition occurs, no data of the record being read is transferred into the computer's memory and no indication is given by the computer as to which record could not be read. If the computer encounters an error condition during its attempt to read data from a record and the ERR= option is not specified in the READ statement, execution of the object program is terminated.

Either one or both of these options may be specified in a READ statement. If both options are specified, either option may precede the other; also, both options either may or may not transfer to the same statement. In the following illustration, both of these options are included in the READ statement.

```
cc  123456789...

         READ (5,1,END=99,ERR=75) I,J
```

THE WRITE STATEMENT

The WRITE statement causes data to be transferred from the computer's memory and written into one or more records located on a specific output device. Figure 3-2 illustrates the general form of this program statement:

```
cc  123456789...

    bbbbb  WRITE (i,n) list
```

where

> *bbbbb*   represents an unsigned 1 through 5 integer number that is required only if a transfer is made to this statement from another program statement.
>
> WRITE   FORTRAN key word that distinguishes this statement from the other kinds of statements in the program.

(a special character that is a requirement of the FORTRAN language.

i   a data set reference number which is represented by either an unsigned integer number or a variable name which has the integer number stored under it.

,   a special character that is a requirement of the FORTRAN language.

n   represents the statement number of the FØRMAT statement that describes the particular form of the data being transferred from the computer's memory.

)   a special character that is a requirement of the FORTRAN language.

list   represents one or more variable, logical variable, and/or array names, each of which must be separated by a comma. The datum stored under these one or more variable names and/or array names is transferred from the computer's memory and written into one or more records associated with the data set reference number represented by *i*. The array name or names can be subscripted and these subscripts can be indexed (see Chapter 6). The "list" is left blank if the FØRMAT statement designated by *n* contains only literal data.

Figure 3-2.   The General Form of the WRITE Statement.

The WRITE statement in the following illustration causes each number stored in the computer's memory under the variable names A, B, I, and J to be written into one or more records located on a printer. The specific number of characters stored under each variable name to be transferred to the one or more records and the location of the decimal point in each of the numbers stored under variable names A, B, I, and J are determined by the FØRMAT statement that has statement number 1 assigned to it.

```
cc 123456789...

    WRITE (6,1) A,B,I,J
```

Except in three specific situations, which are discussed later in this chapter, a datum cannot be written into a record by a WRITE statement unless either the particular variable, logical variable, or array name under which the datum is stored in the computer's memory is presented in the statement. However, a variable, logical variable, or array name should not be present in a WRITE statement unless a datum has been stored under it by means of a previous program statement.

The maximum number of characters of data that may be written into a record located on a specific output device is determined by both the internal storage capacity of the computer's memory and in most instances, more importantly, the maximum possible length of a record in the data set. For a data set of print lines (each print line is a record), the maximum number of characters of data that may compose each print line on many printers is 132 characters. Thus, the reader should not attempt to have a WRITE statement write more than 132 characters of data on a print line.

The WRITE statement, unlike the READ statement, neither establishes nor replaces the datum stored in the computer's memory under each variable, logical variable, or array name that is present in the statement. Rather, it leaves the datum unchanged and writes a duplicate of it into a record located on a specific output device. For example, a duplicate of the number stored under the variable name I in the following illustration

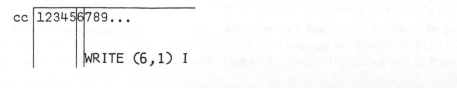

```
cc 123456789...

    WRITE (6,1) I
```

would be written on a print line of a page of printer printout. The number would remain stored in the computer's memory under the variable name I available for duplication as many times as desired in a record located on an output device.

THE FØRMAT STATEMENT

In many instances, the structure of each record located either on an input device or an output device is quite different. Similarly, in many instances the form of data that is either read or written is quite different. For these two reasons, a different FØRMAT statement is usually referred to by each READ statement that reads data from a record located on the card reader and each WRITE statement that writes data into a record located on the printer. Figure 3-3 illustrates the general form of this program statement:

```
cc  123456789...

    ccccc  FØRMAT (ccc₁, fc₁, or '1d₁', ..., cccₙ, fcₙ, or '1dₙ')
```

where

$ccccc$	represents a required 1 through 5 character statement number.
FØRMAT	FORTRAN key word that distinguishes this statement from the other kinds of statements in the program.
(	a special character that is a requirement of the FORTRAN language.
$ccc_1, fc_1, or '1d_1', ..., ccc_n, fc_n, or '1d_n'$	represents the various carriage control characters, format codes, and literal data that can be specified.
)	a special character that is a requirement of the FORTRAN language.

Figure 3-3.   The General Form of the FØRMAT Statement.

The following three factors should be considered when using a FØRMAT statement:

1. The FØRMAT statement is nonexecutable; that is, its only purpose is to provide information for either a READ and/or a WRITE statement.

2. It is permissible for either one or more READ and/or WRITE statements in the program to refer to the same FØRMAT statement.

3. When either reading data from a record or writing data into a record, care must be taken to be sure that no data is attempted to be either read or written beyond the maximum possible length of the record. For example, since the maximum length of a punch card is 80 columns, no attempt should be made to either read data from it or punch data into it beyond this length. Similarly, since the maximum number of print positions on many printers is 132, no attempt should be made to write data on it beyond this length.

The Matching of Symbolic Names and Format Codes   Symbolic names located in the "list" of either a READ or a WRITE statement are matched with a specific format code (this term is discussed later in this chapter) located in the specified FØRMAT statement. The matching process is based on a left to right sequence. That is, the first symbolic name is matched with the first format code, the second symbolic name is matched with the second format code, etc. Thus, in the following illustration the form of the number stored under the variable name I is indicated by the I5 format code, the form of the number stored under the variable name J is indicated by the I3 format code, and the form of the number stored under the variable name K is indicated by the I2 format code.

```
cc  123456789...



          READ (5,1,END=99) I,J,K
1         FØRMAT (I5,I3,I2)
```

Normally, the parentheses of a FØRMAT statement enclose a record. When a FØRMAT statement is referred to by a READ statement, the computer begins at the left parenthesis of the FORMAT statement. The symbolic names in the "list" of the READ statement are matched with the format codes within the parenthesis until it reaches the right parenthesis, at which time it will terminate reading data from that record. As such, each time a READ statement refers to a FORMAT statement, data within a new record are read and the reading of data from this record is terminated at the right parenthesis. In the following illustration, data from the next record will be read and stored in the computer's memory under the variable names I and J when the left parenthesis is encountered and the reading of the data within this record will be terminated when the right parenthesis is encountered.

```
cc  123456789...



          READ (5,1,END=99) I,J
1         FØRMAT (I1,I4)
```

When a FØRMAT statement is referred to by a WRITE statement, the computer begins writing data into a specific record when it encounters the carriage control character (this term is discussed shortly in this chapter) and terminates writing data into that record when it encounters the right parenthesis. In the following illustration, the computer will begin writing a duplicate of each number stored under the variable names I and J into the next record when it encounters the carriage control character and terminates writing data into that record when it encounters the right parenthesis.

```
cc  123456789...



          WRITE (6,1) I,J
1         FØRMAT (' ',I1,I4)
```

In summary, each time a READ statement refers to a FØRMAT statement, it reads data from the next record every time the left parenthesis is encountered. However, each time a WRITE statement refers to a FØRMAT statement, it writes data into a specific record every time a carriage control character is encountered. The reason for this difference is that the computer would reread the data from the previously read record if the computer did not progress to the next record until it encountered the right parenthesis. Conversely, the computer would skip the first record if, during writing, it progressed to a new record each time it encountered the left parenthesis.

If the number of symbolic names in the "list" of the READ statement is greater than the number of format codes within the parentheses of the referred to FØRMAT statement, the computer will match from left to right a symbolic name with a format code until it reaches the right parenthesis. It will then transfer back to the left parenthesis, progress to the next record, and continue matching the remaining symbolic names with the format codes following the left parenthesis. The computer will continue repeating this process until each symbolic name in the "list" has a datum stored under it. Conversely, if the number of symbolic names is less than the number of format codes within the parentheses of the referred to statement, the computer matches from left to right a symbolic name with a format code; any remaining format codes are ignored by the computer.

In the following illustration, the computer will prepare to read and store data in its memory from a new record when it encounters the left parenthesis, then store a number under the variable names I and J using the format codes I3 and I1 respectively. Upon encountering the right parenthesis, the computer will transfer back to the left parenthesis since the variable names K and L have not had a number stored under them. After returning to the left parenthesis, the computer will progress to the next record and begin storing a number under the variable names K and L from that record again using the format codes I3 and I1, respectively.

```
cc  123456789...

         READ (5,1,END=99) I,J,K,L
  1      FØRMAT (I3,I1)
```

Similarly, if the number of symbolic names in the "list" of a WRITE statement is greater than the number of format codes within the parentheses of the referred to FØRMAT statement, the computer will write each datum stored under the symbolic names into a record, matching from left to right a symbolic name with a format code, until it reaches the right parenthesis. It will then terminate the writing of data into that record, transfer back to the left parenthesis, and begin writing the datum stored under the remaining symbolic names in a new record (the specific record being determined by the carriage control character), again matching each symbolic name with a format code from left to right. The computer will continue repeating this process until each symbolic name in the "list" has had a duplicate of its datum written into a record.

In the following illustration, the computer will write a duplicate of each number stored under the variable names I and J into a record using the format codes I3 and I1, respectively. Upon encountering the right parenthesis, it will terminate writing data into that record, and transfer back to the left parenthesis. Upon returning to the left parenthesis, it will begin to write a duplicate of each number stored under the variable names K and L into the next record, again using the format codes I3 and I1, respectively.

```
cc  123456789...

         WRITE (6,1) I,J,K,L
  1      FØRMAT (' ',I3,I1)
```

The Reading, Writing, and Skipping of More Than One Record   In certain situations, it is desirable to either read, write, and/or skip more than one record located on either a card reader or printer during the execution of either a READ or WRITE statement. This is accomplished through the use of one or more consecutive slashes within the FØRMAT statement.

When it is desirable to either read data from more than one record and/or skip one or more records, one slash (/) is appropriately placed within the FØRMAT statement referred to by the READ statement each time it is desired to either select a new record or skip a record. Each slash causes the termination of the reading of data from the record being read and the progression to the next record of the data set. For example, the READ statement in the following illustration will cause a number from the first record, which was selected when the computer encountered the left parenthesis of the FØRMAT statement, to be read

```
cc  123456789...

         READ (5,1,END=99) I,J,K,L,M,N
  1      FØRMAT (I7,I2,/,I1,//,I5,I3,/,I6)
```

and stored in the computer's memory under the variable names I and J using the format codes I7 and I2, respectively. Upon encountering the slash, the computer will terminate reading data from that record and progress to the next record. It will then read and store in its memory a number from that record under the variable name K. Next the computer will, upon encountering a slash, terminate reading data from that record and progress to the next record. However, upon encountering another slash it will immediately progress to the next record without reading any data. The computer will then read and store in its memory a number under the variable names L and M using format codes I5 and I3 respectively. Upon encountering a slash, it will terminate reading data from that record and progress to the next record. The computer will then read and store in its memory a number from the newly selected record under the variable name N using format code I6.

The slash is similarly used in a FØRMAT statement that is referred to by a WRITE statement that is either writing data into more than one record (print line) and/or skipping one or more records located on a printer. Each time the computer encounters a slash within the statement, it terminates writing data into that record and advances to the next record. For example, the WRITE statement in the following illustration causes a duplicate of each number stored under the variable names I and J to be written into a record

```
cc  12345|6789...


         |WRITE (6,1) I,J,K,L,M,N
    1    |FØRMAT ('1',I7,I2,/, 1X ,I1,//, 1X ,I5,I3,/, 1X ,I6)
```

located on the printer. Upon encountering a slash, the computer will terminate writing data into that record and advance to the next record. It will then write a duplicate of the number stored under the variable name K using the format code I1 into this record. The computer will then, upon encountering a slash, terminate writing data into that record and advance to the next record. Upon encountering the second slash, the computer will immediately advance to the next record without writing any data. The computer will then write a duplicate of the number stored under the variable names L and M into this record. Upon encountering a slash, it will terminate writing data into this record and advance to the next record. The computer will then write into the this record a duplicate of the number stored under the variable name N using format code I6. Upon encountering the right parenthesis, it will terminate writing data into this record and advance to the next record. (The 1X's are used so that the first character of the first format code following each of them will be printed. The reason for the use of the 1X's requires the reading of the topics "Carriage Control Characters" and "The Blank (X) Format Code" in this chapter.)

In certain instances of either reading or writing data, the number of records that will be desired to be skipped would cause an abnormal consecutive number of required individual slashes in a FØRMAT statement. To avoid this and still achieve the desired results, and individual slash can be placed within a set of parentheses with the number of records to be skipped preceding it. The statements will cause the computer to skip the first 9 records, read the number located in the first 5 card columns of the 10th record, and store it in its memory under the variable name I.

```
cc  12345|6789...


         |READ (5,1,END=99) I
    1    |FØRMAT (9(/),I5)
```

ADDITIONAL FORMAT OPTIONS

There are several additional options with respect to the last two topics. For a discussion of these options, the reader is referred to Appendix E. However, unless the reader is specifically interested in these options, he can omit reading Appendix E without interfering with his learning the FORTRAN language.

CARRIAGE CONTROL CHARACTERS

Just as the typist uses the carriage return handle to vertically advance the desired number of lines on a page of typing paper before typing, the computer uses a carriage control character as a means of determining the desired number of print lines to vertically advance on a page of printer paper before printing.

Figure 3-4 illustrates the acceptable carriage control characters and the number of print lines caused to advance on a page of printer paper by each character *before* printing.

Carriage Control Character (X)	Number of Lines Vertically Advanced
blank	one line
0	two lines
1	first print line of next page
+	no advance

Figure 3-4.   Carriage Control Characters.

Every FØRMAT statement referred to by a WRITE statement that causes data to be written into one or more records located on a printer must have one of the above carriage control characters as its first character. If a carriage control character is not specified as the first character of a record, the computer will use the first character that is to be printed as the carriage control character. If this first character happens to be one of the carriage control characters, the printer will advance the number of print lines it normally would if that character was specified in one of its two possible forms. However, if the first character is not a carriage control character, the number of print lines the printer will advance is unpredictable.

A carriage control character can be specified in one of either two forms: 'X' or 1HX. The carriage control character and either its enclosed apostrophes or the 1H preceding it are never printed by the printer. If a WRITE statement is writing data into one or more records located on any output device other than a printer, a carriage control character is not necessary.

The following are illustrations of the use of each form of one of the carriage control characters in a FØRMAT statement:

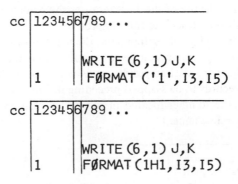

THE FØRMAT CODES

A format code indicates the location, type, field size, and location of the decimal point (if applicable) of a datum that is either read from or written into a record. All of the format codes in a FØRMAT statement must be enclosed in a set of parentheses and must be separated by either a comma and/or one or more slashes. Most of the various types of format codes that can be used in a FØRMAT statement are discussed in the remainder of this chapter.

The Integer (I) Format Code   The I format code is used whenever it is desirable to either read an integer number from a record or write an integer number into a record. A minus sign, when appropriate, or optional plus sign can be read from a record; however, only a minus sign can be written into a record. In both instances, the sign must precede the most significant numerical character. Figure 3-5 illustrates the general form of this format code.

```
cc 123456789...


  ccccc FØRMAT (aIw)
```

where

    a   represents an optional unsigned integer number that specifies the number of times that particular format code is used each time the computer scans from the left to the right parenthesis of the FØRMAT statement. It may be omitted if the format code is to be used only once each time the computer scans from the left to the right parenthesis.

    I   specifies that integer data composes the field of data.

    w   represents an unsigned integer number that specifies the number of characters in the field of data that are to be either read from or written into a record.

Figure 3-5.   The General Form of the I Format Code.

The maximum integer number that can be either read from or written into a record is a 10 numerical character number with a maximum magnitude of either plus or minus 2147483647. Thus, assuming no plus or minus sign, the I format code I10 reflects the maximum number of record positions that can either be read from or written into a record at one time. If either a plus or minus sign precedes the integer number that is to be read from a record or a minus sign precedes the integer number that is to be written into a record, the magnitude of w should be one greater than the number of characters composing the integer number.

Input Considerations   When reading from a record, any leading, embedded, or trailing blanks in the field of data of the record being read are interpreted and stored in the computer as zeros. If the integer number to be read is less than w specified characters, any leading, embedded, or trailing blanks will be replaced with zeros. However, if the integer number to be read is greater than w specified characters, only the leftmost w specified positions are read and stored in the computer's memory.

If an attempt is made to read more than 10 numerical characters from a record at one time, only the 10 most significant characters will be read and stored in the computer's memory.

Output Considerations   When writing into a record, any leading zeros stored in the computer's memory are not written and one blank position is present in the leftmost portion of the field of the record for each leading zero. If the integer number to be written is less than w specified characters, blanks will be inserted in the unused positions to the left of either the most significant numerical character or minus sign, if present. However, if the integer number to be written is greater than w specified characters, asterisks will be written into the record positions specified by the I format code.

If an attempt is made to write more than 10 numerical characters into a record at one time, the characters stored in the computer's memory under either the variable or array name are written into the rightmost positions of the specified field and the unused positions to the left of either the most significant numerical character or minus sign, if present, in the field are left blank.

An Illustration of the I Format Code   In the following illustration, the first five characters of the data card (94632) are read and stored in the computer's memory under the variable name I using the I5 format code; the next three characters of the data card (916) are read and stored in the computer's memory under the variable name J using the I3 format code; the next three characters of the data card (547) are read and stored in the computer's memory under the variable name K again using the I3 format code; and finally, the next character of the data card (9) is read and stored in the computer's memory under the variable name L using the I1 format code. In summary, the first 12 positions of the data card were read and the first 5, next 3, next 3, and next 1 integer characters were stored in the computer's memory under the variable names, I J, K, and L, respectively.

```
cc | 12345|6789...
   |
   |      |READ (5,1) I,J,K,L
 1 |      |FØRMAT (I5,2I3,I1)
   |
```

```
   |            1
cc | 1234567890123...
   | 946329165479
   |
```

The Floating-Point (F) Format Code   The F format code is used whenever it is desirable to either read a floating-point number from a record or write a floating-point number into a record. A minus sign, when appropriate, or optional plus sign can be read from a record; however, only a minus sign can be written into a record. In both instances, the sign must precede the most significant numerical character. Figure 3-6 illustrates the general form of this format code.

```
cc | 12345|6789...
   |
   |ccccc|FØRMAT (aFw.d)
   |
```

where

a represents an optional unsigned integer number that specifies the number of times that particular format code is used each time the computer scans from the left to the right parenthesis of the FØRMAT statement. It may be omitted if the format code is to be used only once each time the computer scans from the left to the right parenthesis.

F   specifies that floating-point data compose the field of data.

w represents an unsigned integer number that specifies the number of characters in the field of data that are to be either read from or written into a record.

is a necessary delimiter between w and d.

d represents an unsigned integer number that specifies the location of the decimal point within the floating-point number.

Figure 3-6.   The General Form of the F Format Code.

Input Considerations   If a decimal point is not located in a floating-point number being read from a record, the computer will place a decimal point to the left of d positions beginning with the least significant numerical character in the number. The decimal point must not be considered in this situation when computing w. However, if a decimal point is located in a floating-point number being read from a record, but d does not indicate the correct location of the decimal point in the number, the computer will ignore d's indication of the location of the decimal point and consider the location of the decimal point in the number as being correct. If present, the decimal point must be considered when computing for w. For example, the F format code illustration in Figure 3-7 will read the number illustrated in Figure 3-8 and store this number in the computer as 654.32. However, if the number illustrated in Figure 3-9 were to be read, the number would be stored in the computer's memory as 654.1 even though the d in the format code specifies that the decimal point should be placed to the left of the two least significant characters in the number. This is due to the fact that when a decimal point is present in the floating-point number, the location of it in the number specified by d is overridden by the location of the decimal point in the number. Also, because the decimal point is present in the number, it is considered as one character when computing w.

```
cc |123456|789...

    |ccccc| FØRMAT (F5.2)
```

Figure 3-7. An Illustration of the F Format Code.

```
cc |123456789...

    |6 5432
```

Figure 3-8. A Data Card.

```
cc |123456789...

    |6 54.1
```

Figure 3-9. A Data Card.

If an attempt is made to read more than 7 numerical characters of a single precision floating-point number from a record, only the 7 most significant numerical characters will be read and stored in the computer's memory. Thus, the F format code illustrated in Figure 3-10 will result in the number illustrated in Figure 3-11 to be read and stored in the computer's memory as -892653.1. The computer places the decimal point to the left of d positions beginning at the least significant w numerical character. If the F format code in Figure 3-10 had been F11.1, and the computer was attempting to read and store in its memory the number illustrated in Figure 3-11, -8926531 would be the number read and stored. Again, the computer will place the decimal point to the left of d positions beginning at the least significant w numerical position. However, because the period is not located among or at the end of the 7 most significant numerical characters, it is not stored in the computer's memory.

```
cc |123456|789...

    |ccccc| FØRMAT (F11.4)
```

Figure 3-10. An Illustration of the F Format Code.

```
cc |123456789...

    |-8926 531754
```

Figure 3-11. A Data Card.

Output Considerations   When writing a floating-point number stored in the computer's memory, w of the F format code is determined by summing the number of numerical characters to the left and right of the decimal point plus 1 for the decimal point and 1 for the minus sign, if present.

If the w of the F format code is greater than the sum of the number of numerical characters, decimal point, and minus sign, if present, composing the stored number being written, the number is written into the sum value rightmost positions and the one or more remaining leftmost positions are left blank. If the d of the F format code is greater than the number of numerical characters to the right of the decimal point in the stored number, the one or more remaining rightmost blank positions of the fractional part of the number are replaced with zeros. However, if the w of the F format code is less than the number of numerical characters to the left of the decimal point in the stored number, asterisks will be written in the w positions of the record specified by the format code. If the d of the F format code is less than the number of numerical characters to the right of the decimal point in the stored number, the one or more additional numerical characters of the fractional part of the number are truncated.

For example, if the single precision floating-point number 1763.17 stored in the computer's memory was to be written using the format code F9.3, the number b1763.170 (where b stands for a blank) would be written. However, if the format code F6.1 was used, the number 1763.1 would be written.

If a fraction is to be written, the computer will write a zero immediately to the left of the decimal point only if a position has been allocated in the F format code. Otherwise, just the decimal point and fraction will be written.

For example, if the single precision floating-point number .8327 stored in the computer's memory was to be written using the format code F6.4, the number 0.8327 would be written. However, if the format code was F5.4, the number .8327 would be written. Only one zero will be written immediately to the left of the decimal point. Any additional positions provided by the F format code are allocated by the computer when writing the number but are left blank. Thus, if the format code was F7.4, the number b0.8327 would be written.

The Logical (L) Format Code   The L format code is used when it is desirable to either read from or write into a record logical information. Figure 3-12 illustrates the general form of this format code.

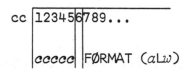

where

a represents an optional unsigned integer number that specifies the number of times that particular format code is used each time the computer scans from the left to the right parenthesis of the FØRMAT statement. It may be omitted if the format code is to be used only once each time the computer scans from the left to the right parenthesis.

L   specifies that logical data compose the field of data.

w represents an unsigned integer number that specifies the number of characters in the field of data that are to be either read from or written into a record.

Figure 3-12.   The General Form of the L Format Code.

Input Considerations   When reading from a field of data within a record, only the leftmost nonblank character is read by the computer. This character must be either a T or an F (if it is any other character, a diagnostic error message will occur). If it is a T, the logical constant .TRUE. will be stored under the logical variable name. However, if it is an F, the logical constant .FALSE. will be stored under the logical variable name. If there are any characters to the right of the leftmost nonblank character in the field, they are ignored by the computer. If the field is blank, the logical constant .FALSE. will be stored under the logical variable name.

Figure 3-13 illustrates the L format code reading data from a logical record of a data set illustrated in Figure 3-14.

```
cc |123456789...
   |
   |    LØGICAL A,B,I,J,K
   |    READ (5,1,END=99) A,B,I,J,K
   |1   FØRMAT (L4,L1,L1,L3,L4)
```

Figure 3-13.   An Illustration of the L Format Code in Reading Data.

```
   |             1
cc |1234567890123...
   |
   |TRUETFT12TIME
```

Figure 3-14.   A Data Card.

The computer will read the first punched card position and store in its memory the logical constant .TRUE. under the logical variable name A. It will then read the fifth position and store the logical constant .TRUE. under the logical variable name B. Next, it will read the sixth position and store the logical constant .FALSE. under the logical variable name I. The computer will then read the seventh position and store the logical constant .TRUE. under the logical variable name J. Finally, it will read the tenth position and store the logical constant .TRUE. under the logical variable name K.

Output Considerations   If a logical variable name has the logical constant .TRUE. stored under it, the alphabetical character T will be written into the rightmost position of the field within a record. However, if a logical variable name has the logical constant .FALSE. stored under it, the alphabetical character F will be written into the rightmost position of the field within a record. Any w – 1 positions in the field to the left of this position will be blank. The following is an illustration of using the L format code to write the data stored in the computer's memory through the illustration in Figure 3-13 into a record:

```
cc |123456789..
   |
   |    LØGICAL A,B,I,J,K
   |    WRITE (6,1) A,B,I,J,K
   |1   FØRMAT ('1',L4,L1,L1,L3,L4)
```

As illustrated below, the computer will advance to the first record of a new page of printer paper and print the alphabetical character T in the 4th print position. The first 3 print positions will be blank. The computer will then print the alphabetical character T in the 5th print position, the alphabetical character F in the 6th print position, and the alphabetical character T in the 9th print position. Print positions 7 and 8 will be blank. Finally, the computer will print the alphabetical character T in the 13th print position and print positions 10, 11, and 12 will be blank.

```
                      |           1
(print position) pp |1234567890123...
                      |
                      |   TTF  T   T
```

Literal Data and Apostrophes   Literal data is used when it is desirable to either read from or write into a record headings, labels, and general information. Any of the FORTRAN Character Set characters, except a single apostrophe, may be "literally" read from or written into a record. If a printer is the output device and it is capable of printing the 15 additional characters, which are not part of the FORTRAN Character Set, these 15 additional characters can be also "literally" written into a record located on that printer.

Input Considerations   Literal data is read from a record through the placement of a number of either identical or different consecutive dummy characters which are equal to the largest number of literal characters that are to be read from a record between apostrophes within the parentheses of a FØRMAT statement. The use of a single apostrophe at the beginning and the end of the dummy characters is the means by which the computer identifies the characters as being dummy characters. The computer replaces verbatim the dummy characters with the data being read from the record. If there are more dummy characters than characters composing the data being read, they are replaced with blanks. Thus, no dummy characters are stored in the computer. Figure 3-15 illustrates the use of dummy characters to read data from a record.

```
cc  123456789...


    READ (5,1,END=99)
1   FØRMAT ('AAAAA',T15,'AAAAA')
```

Figure 3-15.   The Use of Dummy Characters to Read Data from a Record.

In the preceding illustration, the computer will read the first 5 positions of a record and the characters and any blanks located in these positions will replace verbatim the 5 dummy characters located between the first set of apostrophes. The computer will then advance to position 15 of the record, read positions 15 through 19, and the characters and any blanks located in these positions will replace the 5 dummy characters located between the second set of apostrophes. The reader will notice that no symbolic names are located in the "list" of the READ statement. A symbolic name is not required when data is read from a record and stored in the computer's memory through this technique. The reason for this is explained below.

Output Considerations   If literal data has been stored in the computer's memory through the input means just discussed, this literal data is written into a record by referring to the *same* FØRMAT statement that contains the dummy characters through which the literal data was stored in the computer's memory. This is the reason why no symbolic names were required to originally store the data. Figure 3-16 illustrates the use of dummy characters to write the data stored in the computer's memory through the dummy characters within the two sets of apostrophes of the FØRMAT statement illustrated in Figure 3-15.

```
cc  123456789...


    WRITE (6,1)
```

Figure 3-16.   The Use of Dummy Characters to Write Data into a Record.

In the preceding illustration, the computer will refer to the FØRMAT statement assigned statement number 1, advance to the record indicated by the carriage control character, which is the first character of data that replaced the first dummy character immediately following the first parenthesis. The computer will then write verbatim in print positions 1 through 4 the characters and any blanks that replaced the dummy characters and are stored in its memory. Next, the computer will advance to print position 4 and write verbatim in print positions 4 through 8 the characters and any blanks that replaced the second set of dummy characters and are stored in its memory.

Literal data may also be located between a set of apostrophes within the parentheses of a FØRMAT statement. This technique *cannot* be used to originally create and store data in the computer's memory. Rather, literal data located between parentheses can only be used in a FØRMAT statement that is referred to by a WRITE statement. The use of a single apostrophe at the beginning and the end of the literal data is the means by which the computer identifies it as being data that is to be literally written into a record. As previously mentioned, a single apostrophe cannot be used as the computer would interpret this apostrophe as being the end of the literal data when, in fact, it probably is not in most instances. Thus, if it is desirable to make a word of the literal data possessive, two successive apostrophes are written in the literal data. The computer will store only the first apostrophe and thus only one apostrophe will be written into the record.

Literal data can be preceded and followed by any type of format code in the FØRMAT statement. Also, literal data can be located anywhere within the parentheses of the FØRMAT statement. The computer ignores literal data during the process of matching from left to right symbolic names in either the referring READ or WRITE statement and the format codes within the parentheses of the FØRMAT statement. The following is an illustration of the use of literal data within a FØRMAT statement:

```
cc 123456789...


        WRITE (6,1) A,I
   1    FØRMAT ('1','BILL''S ANSWER IS ',F4.1,
        1'  TØM''S ANSWER IS ',I5)
```

In the preceding illustration, the WRITE statement will result in the following being printed within the first record of a new page of printer paper. (It is assumed that the illustrated single precision floating-point number and integer number are stored in the computer's memory under the variable names A and I.)

```
pp 123456789...

   BILL'S ANSWER IS 23.4   TØM'S ANSWER IS 34625
```

It should be noted that while two successive apostrophes are written in two different places in the literal data, only one is written into these places of the record. Also, the blank space between the alphabetical character S of the literal datum IS and the ending apostrophe and the two blank spaces between the beginning apostrophe and the alphabetical character T of the datum TØM"S are correspondingly reflected in the writing into the record. In these three instances, this is a convenient means of spacing for reading purposes. Remember, the computer writes literally what is between the apostrophes and the blank is a special character.

In certain instances, it will be desired to continuously write a specific character several times. While this may be accomplished by continuously literally writing the character the desired number of times in a FØRMAT statement, it may be more easily accomplished by enclosing the character first in a set of apostrophes and then in a set of parentheses with the number of times the character is to be continuously written immediately preceding the set of parentheses. In the following illustration, the computer will continuously print an asterisk 25 times beginning with the first print position of the record.

```
cc 123456789...


        WRITE (6,1)
   1    FØRMAT (' ',25('*'))
```

Literal Data and the Hollerith (H) Format Code   Literal data can also be read from and written into a record through the use of the H format code. However, unlike the just discussed technique no apostrophes are utilized. This code, named for Herman Hollerith, is not as convenient a means of literally transferring headings, labels, and general information either from a record into the computer's memory or from the computer's memory into a record. Figure 3-17 illustrates the general form of this format code.

```
cc│123456789...
  │
  │
  │ccccc│FØRMAT (wHc₁c₂c₃...cₙ)
```

where

> w represents an unsigned integer number that specifies the number of record characters, including blanks, immediately following H that are to be either read from or written into a record.
>
>   H   specifies that literal data compose the field of data.
>
> $c_1c_2c_3...c_n$ represent w characters.

Figure 3-17.   The General Form of the H Format Code.

If the H format code is immediately preceded by either an I, F, L, or T format code, a comma must precede the w of the H format code so that the unsigned integer number represented by w is not interpreted by the computer as being a part of one of these format codes. w positions begins with the first position after H, including blanks. Figure 3-18 illustrates the use of the H format code to read literal data from a record of a data set.

```
cc│12345│6789...
  │
  │     │READ (5,1,END=99)
 │1    │FØRMAT (5HAAAAA,T15,5HAAAAA)
```

Figure 3-18.   The Use of the H Format Code in Reading Data.

In the preceding illustration, the computer will read the first 5 positions of a record and the characters and any blanks located in these positions will replace verbatim the 5 dummy characters immediately following the H. The computer will then advance to position 15 of the record, read positions 15 through 19, and the characters and any blanks located in these positions will replace the 5 dummy characters immediately following the H. The reader will again notice that no symbolic names are located in the "list" of the READ statement. The reason for this is identical to the reason why symbolic names are not used when the literal data is enclosed in apostrophes.

The following is an illustration of the use of the H format code to write the data stored in the computer's memory through the two H format codes of the FØRMAT statement illustrated in Figure 3-18 into a record:

```
cc│12345│6789...
  │
  │     │WRITE (6,1)
```

In the preceding illustration, the computer will refer to the FØRMAT statement assigned statement number 1 and advance to a record indicated by the carriage control character, which is the first character of data that replaced the first dummy character immediately following the H of the format code. The computer will then write verbatim in print positions 1 through 4 the characters and any blanks that replaced the dummy characters and are stored in its memory. The computer will then advance to print position 14 and write verbatim in print positions 14 through 18 the characters and any blanks that replaced the second H format code that are stored in its memory.

Literal data may also be literally located immediately following the H of the H format code in a FØRMAT statement. This technique cannot be used to originally store data in the computer's memory. Rather, literal data that is literally located in a FØRMAT statement can only be referred to by a WRITE statement. When writing literal data into a record, w characters following H, including blanks, are written verbatim into that record. The following is an illustration of the use of the H format code to write literal data into a record:

```
cc  123456789...
         |
         |
         |WRITE (6,1) A
1        |FØRMAT ('1',23HTHE ARITHMETIC MEAN IS ,F5.2)
```

In the preceding illustration, the computer will advance to the first record on a new page of printer paper and begin writing in print position 1 THE ARITHMETIC MEAN IS followed by the single precision floating-point number stored in the computer's memory under the variable name A. There will be a space between the S of the word IS and the first digit of this number because w is one position greater than the total number of positions up to and including the S of the word IS. Since the literal character in the 23rd position following H is a blank, a blank will be left in the 23rd position of the record and the single precision floating-point number will start in print position 24 and continue through print position 28.

If the carriage control character provided in the preceding illustration was not present, the computer would utilize the character in the first position beyond H as the carriage control character. Although this character would not be printed in this instance, the computer will still count the position as part of w.

The Alphanumeric (A) Format Code   The A format code is used within a FØRMAT statement when it is desirable to either read from or write into a record either one or more of the FORTRAN Character Set characters and/or the 15 additional characters in their literal form. (The relevancy of this format code is clarified during the discussion of the topic "The Transfer Of Data Into and From All of The Array Elements Of An Array" in Chapter 6.) Figure 3-19 illustrates the general form of this format code.

```
cc  123456789...
         |
         |
  ccccc  |FØRMAT (aAw)
```

where

  a represents an optional unsigned integer number that specifies the number of times that particular format code is used each time the computer scans from the left to the right parenthesis of the FØRMAT statement. It may be omitted if the format code is to be used only once each time the computer scans from the left to the right parenthesis.

  A   specifies that one or more characters compose the field of data.

  w represents an unsigned integer number that specifies the number of record characters to be either read from or written into a record.

Figure 3-19.   The General Form of the A Format Code.

Input Considerations   When reading data from a record, 4 record positions can be read and their contents stored in the computer's memory if the variable name under which the datum located in these 4 record positions is stored is either integer, single precision floating-point, or logical. If the value of w is greater than 4, w positions will be read from the record but only the characters in the 4 rightmost positions will be stored in the computer's memory under a variable name. However, if the value of w is less than 4, w record positions will be read from the record, blanks are inserted in the 4-w rightmost positions, and these 4 characters are then stored under a variable name.

If the variable name is double precision floating-point, 8 record positions can be read and the datum in these positions stored in the computer's memory under it. If the value of w is greater than 8, w record positions will be read from the record but only the characters in the 8 rightmost positions will be stored in the computer's memory under a variable name. However, if the value of w is less than 8, w record positions will be read from the record, blanks are inserted in the 8-w rightmost positions, and these 8 characters are then stored under a variable name.

Unlike the I and F format codes, any leading, embedded, or trailing blanks are not converted to zeros when read from a record and stored in the computer's memory, but rather remain as blanks in the computer's memory. Also, there is no first-character restriction on the variable names as 4 record positions are read if the variable name has not been explicitly declared as being double precision, and explicitly declared double precision floating-point variable names are automatically considered by the computer as being floating-point names.

The following is an illustration of the use of the A format code in reading data from a record:

```
cc | 123456789...
   |
   |    DØUBLE PRECISIØN C
   |    READ (5,1,END=99) A,B,C,D
 1 |    FØRMAT (2A4,A8,A4)
```

In the preceding illustration, the computer will read and store in its memory the characters located in the first 4 positions of a record under the variable name A and the characters located in the next 4 positions of the record under the variable name B. The computer will then read and store in its memory the characters located in the next 8 positions of the record under the variable name C. It will then read and store in its memory the characters located in the next 4 positions of the record under the variable name D.

Output Considerations   When writing data into a record, 4 record positions can be written if the variable name under which the datum is stored is either integer, single precision floating-point, or logical. If the value of w is greater than 4, w positions will be reserved and 4 characters will be written into the 4 rightmost positions and blanks will be inserted in the w − 4 positions. However, if the value of w is less than 4, only the w leftmost characters will be written into w positions.

If the variable name is double precision floating-point, 8 record positions can be written. If the value of w is greater than 8, w positions will be reserved and 8 characters will be written into the 8 rightmost positions and blanks will be inserted in the w − 8 positions. However, if the value of w is less than 8, only the w leftmost characters will be written into w positions.

The following is an illustration of the use of the A format code in writing data into a record:

```
cc | 123456789...
   |
   |    DØUBLE PRECISIØN C
   |    WRITE (6,1) A,B,C,D
 1 |    FØRMAT ('1',2A4,T21,A8,T46,A4)
```

In the preceding illustration, the computer will advance the first record of a new page of printer paper and write into the first 4 positions of the record the datum stored in the computer's memory under the variable name A and write into the next 4 positions the datum stored in the computer's memory under the variable name B. It will then advance to print position 20 of the record and write the characters stored in the computer under the variable name C into print positions 20 through 27. The computer will then advance to print position 45 of the record and write the characters stored in the computer under the variable name D into print positions 45 through 48.

The Tab (T) Format Code   The T format code specifies the specific record position the computer is to begin either reading from by means of the format code following it or writing into by means of either the format code or literal data following it. It is a means by which the computer can advance either forward or backward to a specific record position. Figure 3-20 illustrates the general form of this format code:

```
cc 123456 789...


   ccccc  FØRMAT (Tw)
```

where

   T   identifies the tab format code.
   w   represents an unsigned integer number that specifies the specific record position the computer is to begin either reading from by means of the format code following it or writing into by means of either the format code or literal data following it.

Figure 3-20.   The General Form of the T Format Code.

A T format code may be either preceded or followed by either any other type of format code or literal data. If more than one T format code is located within a FØRMAT statement, they do not have to be in ascending order.

The following is an illustration of the T format code in reading data from a record:

```
cc 123456 789...

       READ (5,1,END=99) A,I,J
   1   FØRMAT (F4.1,T10,I5,T22,I3)
```

In the preceding illustration, a four character single position floating-point number is read by means of the F format code from the first four positions of the record and is stored in the computer's memory under the variable name A. Upon encountering the T format code, the computer advances to the 10th position of the record. It then reads the integer number in positions 10 through 14 by means of the I format code and stores this number in the computer's memory under the variable name I. Upon encountering the T format code, the computer advances to the 22nd position of the record. It then begins to read the integer number in positions 22 through 24 by means of the I format code and stores this number in the computer's memory under the variable name J.

When using the T format code to specify the specific record position the printer is to begin printing in, remember that the printer always begins counting from the first print position, which is occupied by a carriage control character that is not printed. Thus, each character composing the number stored under the format code or literal data immediately following the T format code is printed one *actual* print position to the left of what is specified.

The following is an illustration of the T format code in writing data into a record:

```
cc 123456 789...


       WRITE (6,1) A,I,J
   1   FØRMAT ('1','THE NUMBERS STØRED UNDER A,I,AND J ARE',
      1T51,F5.1,T76,I5,T101,I3)
```

In the preceding illustration, the printer will advance to the first record of a new page of paper and write THE NUMBERS STØRED UNDER A, I, AND J ARE beginning in print position 1. Upon encountering the T format code, the printer will advance to print position 50 and write in print positions 50 through 54 the single precision floating-point number stored under the variable name A using the F format code. Upon encountering the T format code, the printer will advance to print position 75 and write in print positions 75 through 79 the integer number stored under the variable name I using the I format code. Upon encountering the T format code, the printer will advance to print position 100 and write in print positions 100 through 102 the integer number stored under the variable name J using the I format code.

The Blank (X) Format Code   The X format code is used when it is desirable to either skip one or more positions within a record being read or insert blanks in one or more positions within a record being written into. Figure 3-21 illustrates the general form of the X format code:

```
cc  123456789...


    ccccc  FØRMAT (wX)
```

where

- w represents an unsigned integer number that specifies either the number of positions within a record being read to be skipped or the number of positions within a record being written into to leave blank.
- X   identifies the blank format code.

Figure 3-21.   The General Form of the Blank Format Code.

The X format code may be located anywhere within the parentheses of a FØRMAT statement. The T format code is best used when it is known exactly what position within a record either reading or writing is to begin and the number of blank positions preceding this exact position is not of major concern. The X format code is best used when it is not known exactly at what position within a record either reading or writing is to begin but the exact number of positions to be either skipped or inserted is known. If the X format code is immediately preceded by either an I, F, L, or T format code, a comma must precede the w of the X format code so that the unsigned integer number represented by w is not interpreted by the computer as being a part of one of these format codes.

The following is an illustration of the use of the X format code to skip positions within a record being read:

```
cc  123456789...



    READ (5,1,END=99) I,A,B
1   FØRMAT (I7,3X,F4.1,6X,F5.2)
```

In the preceding illustration, the computer will read and store in its memory under the variable name I the integer number in positions 1 through 7 of a record. The computer will then skip the next 3 positions and read and store in its memory under the variable name A the single precision floating-point number in positions 11 through 14. The computer will then skip the next 6 positions and read and store in its memory under the variable name B the single precision floating-point number in positions 21 through 25.

The following is an illustration of the use of the X format code to insert positions within a record being written into:

```
cc | 12345|6789...
   |
   |
   |      WRITE (6,1) I,A,B
   |    1 FØRMAT ('1',5X,I7,3X,F5.1,5X,F5.2)
```

In the preceding illustration, the computer will advance to the first record of a new page of printer paper, insert 5 blank positions, and write in print positions 6 through 12 the integer number stored in the computer's memory under the variable name I (unlike the T format code, the X format code causes the printer to initially begin counting from the second print position). It will then insert 3 blank positions and write the single precision floating-point number stored in the computer's memory under the variable name A in print positions 16 through 20. The computer will then insert 5 blank positions and write the single precision floating-point number stored in the computer's memory under the variable name B in print positions 26 through 30.

VIGNETTE FORTRAN EXERCISES

The following ten exercises illustrate a possible use of the statements discussed in this chapter. The answers to the exercises immediately follow the exercises. (Before examining the answer to an exercise, attempt to write the appropriate statements yourself.)

1. Which of the following READ statements are invalid? Why?

```
cc | 12345|6789...
   |
   |
   |      READ (5,1,END=99) A,I,B,J
   |      READ (5,99999END=99) RATE,TAX
   |      READ (5,2,000,END=99) $AMT,QUAN
```

2. Which of the following WRITE statements are invalid? Why?

```
cc | 12345|6789...
   |
   |
   |      WRITE (6,100792) PAYRØLL
   |      WRITE (6,1) A,B,C,I
   |      WRITE (6,7852)
```

3. Write a READ and FØRMAT statement to read the data from the data card illustrated in Figure 3-22. Store the data in the computer's memory under the variable names I, A, B, and J respectively and use the I, F, and T format codes in the FØRMAT statement.

```
        1         2         3
cc | 123456789012345678901234567890...
   |
   |
   | 734   19.61 5.6   7543
```

Figure 3-22.   A Data Card.

4. Write a WRITE and FØRMAT statement to write the data illustrated in Figure 3-22, which is stored in the computer's memory under the variable names I, A, B, and J respectively, into the first record of a data set located on a new page of printer paper. Use the I, F, and X format codes. Space 5 positions between the first and second numbers and the second and third numbers and 10 positions between the third and fourth numbers to be written into the record.

5. Write a READ and FØRMAT statement to read the data from the data cards illustrated in Figure 3-23. Store the data in the computer's memory under the variable names ITIME, HRWAG, SALARY, and AINCØM. Use the I, F, and X format codes and the slash.

```
            1         2         3
cc  1234567890123456789012345678901234567890...

    40  4.35 174. 00
```

```
            1         2         3
cc  1234567890123456789012345678901234567890...

    7800. 00
```

Figure 3-23.   Two Data Cards.

6. Write a WRITE and FØRMAT statement to write the data illustrated in Figure 3-23, which is stored in the computer's memory under the variable names ITIME, HRWAG, and SALARY respectively, into the next record and the datum stored in the computer's memory under the variable name AINCØM into the following record of a data set. Space 10 positions between each of the three numbers to be written into the first record and start the number to be written into the second record in the first print position. Use the I, F, and X format codes.

7.* Write a READ and FØRMAT statement to read the data from the data card illustrated in Figure 3-24. Store the data in the computer's memory under the variable names A, B, and C. Use an E exponent format code for the first two numbers and a D exponent format code for the last number. Also use the T format code.

```
            1         2         3         4
cc  12345678901234567890123456789012345678901234567890...

    -596.3E+04          1983.45E2 +9806
```

Figure 3-24.   A Data Card.

8. Write a READ and FØRMAT statement to read the data from the data card illustrated in Figure 3-25. Store the data in the computer's memory under the logical variable names QUES1, QUES2, QUES3, QUES4, and QUES5. Use the L and T format codes.

```
            1         2         3
cc  1234567890123456789012345678901234567890...

    TRUE T  F      TABLE      FEMALE
```

Figure 3-25.   A Data Card.

---

*See Appendix D for a discussion of the E and D exponent FØRMAT codes.

9. Write a READ and FØRMAT statement to read and store in the computer's memory the data from the data card illustrated in Figure 3-26. Use dummy characters enclosed within apostrophes to read the first datum and dummy characters following the H format code to read the second and third datum from the data card. Also use the T format code.

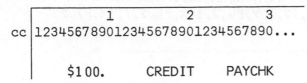

Figure 3-26. A Data Card.

10. Write a READ and FØRMAT statement to read the data from the data card illustrated in Figure 3-27. Store the data in the computer's memory under the variable names WIN, LØSE, and TIE. Use the A and T format codes.

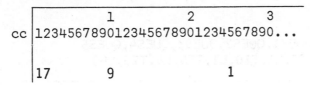

Figure 3-27. A Data Card.

ANSWERS TO VIGNETTE EXERCISES

1. (1) Correct
    (2) The required comma between the FØRMAT statement number 99999 and the key word END is missing.
    (3) The embedded comma in the FØRMAT statement number 2,000 is invalid or three numbers cannot be located prior to the END= option.
2. (1) The program statement number exceeds the maximum number of allowable numerical characters; the variable name (PAYROLL) is too long.
    (2) Correct
    (3) Correct (FØRMAT statement 7852 contains literal data)

3.
```
cc  123456789...



        READ (5,1) I,A,B,J
    1   FØRMAT (I3,T6,F5.2,T12,F3.1,T17,I4)
```

4.
```
cc  123456789...



        WRITE (6,1) I,A,B,J
    1   FØRMAT ('1',I3,5X,F5.2,5X,F3.1,10X,I4)
```

5.
```
cc  123456789...



        READ (5,1) ITIME,HRWAG,SALARY,AINCØM
    1   FØRMAT (I2,2X,F4.2,1X,F6.2,/,F7.2)
```

6.   cc| 123456789...

```
        WRITE (6,1) ITIME,HRWAG,SALARY,AINCØM
    1   FØRMAT (' ',I2,10X,F4.2,10X,F6.2,/,1X,F7.2)
```

7.   cc| 123456789...

```
        READ (5,1)A,B,C
    1   FØRMAT (E10.1,T20,E9.2,T30,D5.0)
```

8.   cc| 123456789...

```
        READ (5,1)QUES1,QUES2,QUES3,QUES4,QUES5
    1   FØRMAT (L4,T7,L1,T10,L1,T15,L5,T25,L6)
```

9.   cc| 123456789...

```
        READ (5,1)
    1   FØRMAT (T5,'AAAAA',T15,6HAAAAAA,T25,6HAAAAAA)
```

10. cc| 123456789...

```
        READ (5,1)WIN,LØSE,TIE
        FØRMAT (A2,T10,A1,T25,A1)
```

QUESTIONS

1.   What is a record?
2.   What is a data set?
3.   What function does the READ statement perform in a computer program?
4.   What is the purpose of the END= and/or ERR= options being placed within the READ statement?
5.   What function does the WRITE statement perform in a computer program?
6.   Why must a FØRMAT statement always be referred to when either reading data from a record located on a punch card reader or writing data into a record located on a printer?
7.   How are symbolic names located in the "list" of either a READ or a WRITE statement matched with a specific format code located in the specified FØRMAT statement?
8.   How may more than one record of a data set be either read or written during the execution of either a READ or WRITE statement?
9.   What function does a carriage control character perform when writing a record of a data set located on a printer?
10. What function does a format code perform in a FØRMAT statement?
11. When is it desirable to use the I format code within a FØRMAT statement?
12. When is it desirable to use the F format code within a FØRMAT statement?

13. When is it desirable to use the E or D exponent format code within a FØRMAT statement?
14. When is it desirable to use literal data either enclosed within apostrophes or following the H format code within a FØRMAT statement?
15. When is it desirable to use the A format code within a FØRMAT statement?
16. When is it desirable to use the T format code within a FØRMAT statement?
17. When is it desirable to use the X format code within a FØRMAT statement?

Chapter 4

ASSIGNMENT STATEMENTS

There are two types of assignment statements in FORTRAN—arithmetic and logical. The arithmetic statement, which is more frequently used in a program, is concerned with computation. The logical statement is concerned with the expression of either a true or false condition.

This chapter examines both of these assignment statements. Following the discussion of these two statements is a discussion of three program control statements.

THE ARITHMETIC STATEMENT

The arithmetic statement is the means through which computations involving exponentiation, multiplication, division, addition, and subtraction are performed. It also provides the means through which both a number can be stored under either a variable name or array element and a number that either is or is not stored under an array element can be utilized in a program. Figure 4-1 illustrates the general form of this statement.

```
cc  123456789...

    bbbbb sn = ae
```

where

- *bbbb* represents an unsigned 1 through 5 integer number that is required only if a transfer is made to this statement from another program statement.
- *sn* represents either a variable name or array element.
- = a special character that is a requirement of the FORTRAN language.
- *ae* represents an arithmetic expression that can be composed of one or more numbers, variable names, array elements, parentheses and arithmetic operators.

Figure 4-1. The General Form of the Arithmetic Statement.

48

General Considerations of the Arithmetic Statement   With respect to both the general appearance and the functioning of the arithmetic operators, the arithmetic statement is similar to an algebraic equation. However, there are four distinct factors that must be considered by the reader in using an arithmetic statement in a FORTRAN program.

1. *Only a single variable name or array element can be located on the left side of the equal sign.* Thus, the following arithmetic statements are incorrect:

```
cc |123456789...
   |
   |A+B = X**2+Y
   |I+6 = A-C+10.
   |5 = J+1
```

2. *The variable name or array element on the left side of the equal sign is "defined" by the result of the evaluation of the expression on the right side of the equal sign.* In FORTRAN, the equal sign means that the result of the expression on the right side of the equal sign either *establishes* or *replaces* the number stored under either the variable name or array element on the left side of the equal sign. Thus, in the following illustration the number stored under the variable name PRICE and the sum of each number stored under the variable names C and D and I and J will be stored under the variable names A, B, and K respectively.

```
cc |123456789...
   |
   |A = PRICE
   |B = C+D
   |K = I+J
```

3. *The variable name or array element on the left side of the equal sign need not be the same type as the operand(s) (numbers and/or symbolic names) composing the arithmetic expression on the right side of the equal sign.* That is, it is acceptable for the operand(s) composing an arithmetic expression to be either the same type (integer, single precision floating-point, double precision floating-point) or a different type than the type of the variable name or array element on the left side of the equal sign. Thus, the four arithmetic statements in the following illustration are correct:

```
cc |123456789...
   |
   |A = X
   |B = 5
   |I = 10
   |J = C
```

4. *The result of an arithmetic expression on the right side of the equal sign is stored under the type of the variable name or array element on the left side of the equal sign.* If the type of the result of the arithmetic expression is the same as the type of the variable name or array element on the left side of the equal sign, a specific problem need not be considered by the reader. However, if the types are not the same then the reader must consider the implications of what occurs in this instance. Specifically, the result of an arithmetic expression on the right side of the equal sign will be changed when it is stored under the variable name or

array element on the left side of the equal sign. For example, in the following illustration the integer number stored under the variable name I and the sum of each integer number stored under the variable names M and N will be changed to single precision floating-point when they are stored under the variable names A and B respectively. Similarly, the single precision floating-point number stored under the variable name Y and the sum of each single precision floating-point number stored under the variable names P and R will be changed to integer when they are stored under the variable names I and K respectively.

```
cc 123456789...


    A = I
    B = M+N
    I = Y
    K = P+R
```

The Arithmetic Expression   An arithmetic expression can be composed of one or more *operands*, generally one or more *arithmetic operators*, and whenever applicable one or more sets of *parentheses*. An operand may be either a number or a symbolic name. Each operand must be separated by one or more arithmetic operators. An arithmetic operator is an arithmetic operational symbol that represents the computer's arithmetic capabilities of either

**	(exponentiation)
*	(multiplication)
/	(division)
+	(addition)
–	(subtraction)

The appropriate arithmetic operational symbol must be used and not the English word that describes it. The result of an arithmetic expression must always be a number. An arithmetic expression is constructed according to the following seven rules:

1. *An arithmetic expression can be composed of either a single number or symbolic name.* Thus, the arithmetic expressions in the following arithmetic statements are correct:

```
cc 123456789...



   NUMBER = NUM
   TØTAL = RENT
   I = 10
   X = 2.5
```

2. *An arithmetic expression can be composed of several numbers and/or symbolic names.* Thus, the arithmetic expressions in the following arithmetic statements are correct:

```
cc 123456789...



   MARK = I+N
   KIT = I/2+N
   F = T+Y
```

3. *A symbolic name cannot be used in an arithmetic expression until it has been "defined" in the program.* That is, a number must be stored under a symbolic name prior to its use in an

arithmetic expression. Thus, the symbolic names composing the arithmetic expressions in the following arithmetic statements must have a number stored under each of them:

```
cc │ 123456789...


       │TAX = PRICE*.05
       │I = K+MN
       │SALARY = HØURS*HRWAGE
```

If a number were not stored under the variable name PRICE, then the computer would not know what number it was to multiply times the number .05. Similarly, if a number were not stored under the variable names K and MN, the computer would not know what two numbers to add, and if a number were not stored under the variables names HØURS and HRWAGE, the computer would not know what two numbers to multiply.

4. *Two or more arithmetic operators cannot appear in sequence in an arithmetic expression.* One or more sets of parentheses must be used to separate sequential arithmetic operators. Thus, in the following illustration

```
cc   123456789...

       │J = K/-5
```

the division sign and the minus sign in the first arithmetic expression cannot be sequential. Rather, the statement should be written as

```
cc 123456789...

       │J = K/(-5)
```

Also, implied multiplication, such as PT to represent multiplying the number stored under the variable name P times the number stored under the variable name T is incorrect. The reason for this is that the computer would interpret PT as a symbolic name. Thus, in the following illustration a multiplication sign must be located between the variable names P and T and the number 5 and variable name X. The computer will not even consider 5X as a symbolic name as the first character of a symbolic name must be alphabetic.

```
cc   123456789...

       │A = PT
       │B = 5X
```

5. *One or more sets of parentheses can be used in an arithmetic expression.* The reader has the option of enclosing in parentheses any combination of operands composing the arithmetic expression. When a set of parentheses is used, the operands of the arithmetic expression enclosed in the parentheses are evaluated prior to evaluating those operands of the arithmetic expression not enclosed in parentheses. If more than one set of parentheses is used in an arithmetic expression, the computer will evaluate from left to right the operands of the arithmetic expression within each set of parentheses.

If one or more sets of parentheses are enclosed within another set of parentheses, the computer will evaluate the operands of the arithmetic expression within each set of parentheses from the innermost set of parentheses to the outermost set of parentheses. Thus, in the first arithmetic statement in the following illustration

```
cc│123456789...
  │
  │    │
  │    │A = B**2.-(YM-T)+1.5
  │    │TIM = 5.+(CA**2.3)/(TØT+X)**(E**2)
  │    │KØUNT = (((7+M**MN)-(KAR**2))**3)
```

the operands of the arithmetic expression within the set of parentheses (YM-T) will be evaluated prior to the evaluation of the operands of the arithmetic expression preceding and following the set of parentheses. In the second arithmetic statement, the operands of the arithmetic expression within the leftmost set of parentheses (CA*2.3) will be evaluated first; the operands within the middle set of parentheses (TØT+X) will be evaluated next; and the operands within the rightmost set of parentheses (E**2) will be evaluated last. In the third arithmetic statement, the operands within the inner leftmost set of parentheses (7+M**MN) will be evaluated first, then the operands within the inner rightmost set of parentheses (KAR*2) will be evaluated next; the result from the inner rightmost set of parentheses will then be subtracted from the result of the inner leftmost set of parentheses (7+M**MN) - (KAR*2). Finally, this result will be exponentiated to the third power.

6. *The evaluation of the various operands comprising an arithmetic expression is based upon a hierarchy of arithmetic operations.* The hierarchy of evaluation, both within and outside a set of parentheses, is in the following order:

    1. All FUNCTIØN subprograms and statement functions are evaluated (Chapter 7).
    2. All exponentiations (**) are performed.
    3. All multiplications (*) and divisions (/) are performed.
    4. All additions (+) and subtractions (–) are performed.

Within this hierarchy of evaluation, another rule of evaluation must be considered by the reader. If the arithmetic operators within the arithmetic expression, excluding exponentiations, are all of the same hierarchy, such as multiplication and division or addition and subtraction, execution of the operands composing the arithmetic expression is from *left to right*. However, if the arithmetic operators are all exponentiations, evaluation of the arithmetic expression is from *right to left*.

Thus, in the arithmetic expression within the first arithmetic statement in the following illustration

```
cc│123456789...
  │
  │    │
  │    │TAB = 5.*C-P/SIG+ET**3
  │    │Y = (4.*A-2.+B)/(A+BZ6-B**2)
  │    │CIR = X**2**D
```

the operand ET**3 will be evaluated first; the operands 5*C will be evaluated next; the operands P/SIG will be evaluated next; then the result from P/SIG will be subtracted from the result of 5*C; and lastly, the result from this subtraction will be added to the result of ET**3. In the second arithmetic expression, the operands within the leftmost set of parentheses will be evaluated prior to the operands within the rightmost set of parentheses. Within the leftmost set of parentheses, the operands 4.*A are evaluated first; the operand –2. will then be subtracted from this result, and the number stored under the operand B will then be added to this result. Within the rightmost set of parentheses, and operand B**2 will be evaluated first, next the operands A+BZ6 will be evaluated; and then the result from B**2 will be subtracted from the result of A+BZ6. Finally, the overall result from the computation of the operands within the leftmost set of parentheses will be divided by the overall result from the computation of the operands within the rightmost set of parentheses. In the third arithmetic statement, the operand 2**D will be evaluated first and then the floating-point number stored under the operand X will be exponentiated to the result of 2**D.

7. *The operands composing an arithmetic expression should be of the same type.* The result of an arithmetic expression is a numerical number that may be one of three types—integer, single precision floating-point, or double precision floating-point. If the operands within an arithmetic expression are all of the same type, then the result of the arithmetic expression is also of that type. However, if one or more operands composing an arithmetic expression are of a different type, the result of the arithmetic expression is the same type as the highest type of operand within the arithmetic expression. The highest type is determined according to the following hierarchy of operand types: Double precision floating-point, single precision floating-point, and integer, with double precision floating-point being the highest type and integer being the lowest type.

While it is possible for an arithmetic expression to be composed of one of more different type operands, the author suggests that the reader avoid this situation for three reasons.

1. A possible problem due to what may occur to the result of the expression when it is stored under the variable or array name on the left side of the equal sign will be curtailed (see general consideration of the arithmetic statement number 4).

2. Since the result of an arithmetic operation involving two operands is the same as the highest type of operand involved in the operation, the result, whether it is then involved in the operation with another operand within the expression or stored under the variable or array name on the left side of the equal sign, may be in a non-desirable type.

3. It is much easier to identify the type of result of an arithmetic expression.

The one exception to the consideration of having operands of the same type composing an arithmetic expression is the exponent involved in the exponentiation of a number. The type of the number involved in the exponentiation and not the type of the exponent determines the type of the result of the exponentiation. Thus, the exponent may be a different type than the number being exponentiated.

THE LØGICAL STATEMENT

The logical statement is the means through which either a true or false condition is stored under either a logical variable name or array element. Figure 4-2 illustrates the general form of this statement:

```
cc │1234 5 6 789...
   │
   │
   │
   │bbbbb│ lv = le
```

where

bbbbb   represents an unsigned 1 through 5 integer number that is required only if a transfer is made to this statement from another program statement.

    lv   represents either a logical variable name or array element.
    =   a special character that is a requirement of the FORTRAN language.
    le   represents a logical expression that can be composed of one or more logical constants, logical variable names, logical array elements, logical FUNCTIØN subprogram and/or statement function references, relational expressions, logical expressions, each of which is enclosed in a set of parentheses, and logical operators.

Figure 4-2.   The General Form of the Logical Statement.

The resultant condition of a logical expression must always be either true or false. This condition, in the form of either the local constant .TRUE. or .FALSE., is stored under either the logical variable name or array element on the left side of the equal sign.

RELATIONAL OPERATORS

Relational operators are symbols by which either a true or false relationship is established between two *arithmetic expressions*.

There are six relational operators, each of which is shown below accompanied by its mathematical meaning and flowchart notation:

Relational Operator Symbol	Mathematical Meaning	Flowchart Notation
.GT.	Greater than	$>$
.GE.	Greater than or equal to	$\geq$
.LT.	Less than	$<$
.LE.	Less than or equal to	$\leq$
.EQ.	Equal to	$=$
.NE.	Not equal to	$\neq$

A relational operator can only compare the resultant values of two arithmetic expressions. As such, a logical expression cannot be used as one of the operands being compared by a relational operator. The basis for this is that a logical expression either is or represents a true or false condition and it would not be logical to compare either two of these conditions or one of these conditions and the resultant value of an arithmetic expression when the desired resultant condition is either true or false.

As indicated above, a period must immediately precede and follow each relational operator for the same reason that a period must immediately precede and follow the two logical constants (see page 19). Like the arithmetic expression, it is possible for a logical expression to be composed of one or more different type operands. However, the author again suggests that the reader avoid this situation.

To illustrate the use of the relational operators, assume the following:

Variable	Type
I, J	Integer
A, B	Single precision floating-point
C, K, R, N	Logical

Considering the preceding information, the first logical expression in the following illustration

```
cc│ 1234567089...
   │
   │C = A .LE. B
   │K = I .NE. J
   │R = A+5. .EQ. 1000.
   │N = I .LT. J-5+K
   │
```

will result in the logical constant .TRUE. being stored under the logical variable name C if the number stored under the variable name A is less than or equal to the number stored under the variable name B. However, if this is not true the logical constant .FALSE. will be stored under the logical variable name C. In the second statement, if the number stored under the variable name I is not equal to the number stored under the variable name J the logical constant .TRUE. will be stored under the logical variable name K. However, if this is not true the logical constant .FALSE. will be stored under the logical variable name K. In the third logical statement, if the result of the arithmetic expression A+5. is equal to the number 1000 the logical constant .TRUE. will be stored under the logical variable name R. However, if this is not true the logical constant .FALSE. will be stored under the logical variable name R. In the last logical statement, if the number stored under the variable name I is less than the result of the arithmetic expression J-5+K the logical constant .TRUE. will be stored under the logical variable name N. However, if this is not true the logical constant .FALSE. will be stored under the logical variable name N.

LOGICAL OPERATORS

Because of the particular use of logical operators, the reader is referred to Appendix F for a discussion of this topic. However, unless the reader is specifically interested in this topic, he may omit reading Appendix F without interfering with his learning the FORTRAN language.

HIERARCHY OF EXECUTION

Like the arithmetic expression, a hierarchy of execution both within and outside a set of parentheses interrupts the normal left to right evaluation of a logical expression. The hierarchy of execution is as follows:

Operation	Hierarchy
All FUNCTIØN subprograms are evaluated (Chapter 7)	1
All arithmetic operations in the following order:	
Exponentiation	2
Multiplication and division	3
Addition and subtraction	4
All relational operators	5
All logical operators in the following order:	
.NØT.	6
.AND.	7
.ØR.	8

Also like the arithmetic expression, the use of one or more than one set of parentheses has an influence on the hierarchical, left to right order of evaluation of a logical expression.

AN INTRODUCTION TO CONTROL STATEMENTS

Control statements are the means by which the process of compilation is terminated, transferring and looping during execution of the program is controlled, and the process of execution is terminated. Except in one instance, the complexity surrounding the use of control statements involved in transferring and looping during execution of a program warrants their not being discussed until Chapter 5. Many FORTRAN programs can be successfully executed without using these control statements. Because of both its simplicity and more common use in FORTRAN programs, however, one control statement involved in transferring during execution of a program is discussed at this point. The two statements that control termination of the process of compilation and the process of execution are both not as difficult to use and must be present in every FORTRAN program. Thus, they too are discussed at this point.

THE UNCONDITIONAL GØ TØ STATEMENT

The unconditional GØ TØ statement causes the computer to unconditionally transfer to another executable program statement. The statement transferred to may either precede or follow the unconditional GØ TØ statement. Figure 4-3 illustrates the general form of this statement.

```
cc 123456789...

   bbbbb GØ TØ sn
```

```
where

    bbbbb   represents an unsigned 1 through 5 integer number that is
            required only if a transfer is made to this statement from
            another program statement.
    GØ TØ   FORTRAN key word that distinguishes this statement from the
            other kinds of statements in the program.
       sn   represents the statement number of the executable program
            statement to which a transfer will be made.
```

Figure 4-3.   The General Form of the GØ TØ Statement.

The unconditional GØ TØ statement in the following illustration

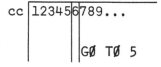

```
cc 123456789...


        GØ TØ 5
```

causes the computer to transfer to the program statement assigned statement number 5.

THE STØP STATEMENT

The STØP statement instructs the computer to terminate execution of an object program. Figure 4-4 illustrates the general form of this statement.

```
cc 123456789...

   bbbbb STØP
          or
   bbbbb STØP n
```

> *bbbbb* represents an unsigned 1 through 5 integer number that is required only if a transfer is made to this statement from another program statement.
> STØP FORTRAN key word that distinguishes this statement from the other kinds of program statements in the program.
> *n* represents an unsigned 1 through 5 integer number.

Figure 4-4. The General Form of the STØP Statement.

A STØP statement may be located anywhere in a program prior to the END statement. The basic consideration in deciding specifically where to place a STØP statement in a program is that it should be located at the *logical* end of the program. If there is more than one logical end to a program, it is appropriate for a STØP statement to be located at each logical end.

If a STØP statement is accompanied by a 1 through 5 integer number, in addition to terminating execution of the object program, that number is printed by the printer.

THE END STATEMENT

The END Statement instructs the computer to terminate compilation of a source program. Figure 4-5 illustrates the general form of the END statement.

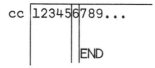

where

> END FORTRAN key word that distinguishes this statement from the other kinds of statements in the program.

Figure 4-5. The General Form of the END Statement.

The END statement, like the comment statement, is a nonexecutable statement; that is, it is neither processed by the FORTRAN Compiler (translated into machine language) nor affects the execution of the FORTRAN program. While the STØP statement can be located anywhere in a program, the END statement must be the last physical statement in the program. As such, there can only be one END statement in a program. Also, the END statement cannot be assigned a statement number.

ILLUSTRATIONS OF FORTRAN PROGRAMS

The statements required to write fundamental FORTRAN programs have now been discussed. Prior to introducing any additional statements, three programs are presented to illustrate a possible use of the statements discussed up to this point in a particular situation. Before examining the author's program to solve each of the problems, attempt to write the program to solve each of them yourself. (Remember, there are several ways to successfully solve almost all problems. Thus, if your program does not contain the same statements in the same order, this does not necessarily mean it is incorrectly written.)

Illustration 1. The Calculation of Employee Weekly Salaries

Problem Write a program that will compute the weekly salary of an unknown number of employees. Each employee has the following data punched in a punch card:
1. Employee ID number   *cc*   1 through 5   (*xxxxx*)
2. Hours worked   *cc* 10 through 11   (*xx*)
3. Hourly wage   *cc* 15 through 17   (*x.xx* (assume decimal point))

After an employee's weekly salary is computed, print his ID number, hours worked, hourly wage, and total salary on a page of printer printout. Begin printing in print position 1 and skip 10 print positions between each unit of information. Double space between the printing of the information concerning each employee. Figure 4-6 is a flowchart of the program. (If desirable, the reader can refer to Appendix H for a discussion of flowcharting.)

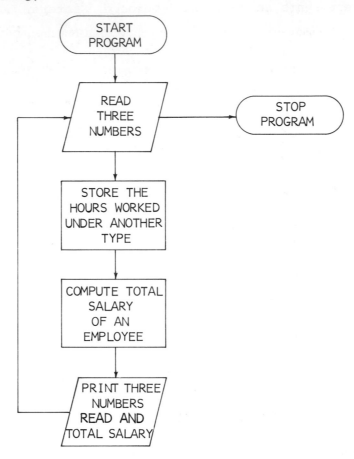

Figure 4-6.   A Flowchart of Illustration 1.

```
cc | 123456789...


   C   | CØMPUTATIØN ØF EMPLØYEE WEEKLY SALARIES
   1   | READ (5,2,END=99) ID,IHR,WAGE
   2   | FØRMAT (I5,T10,I2,T15,F3.2)
       | AHR = IHR
       | TØTWAG = AHR*WAGE
       | WRITE (6,3) ID,IHR,WAGE,TØTWAG
   3   | FØRMAT ('0',I5,10X,I2,10X,F5.2,10X,F6.2)
       | GØ TØ 1
   99  | STØP
       | END
```

Analysis   Although the hours worked are read and stored under the variable name IHR, the number is converted to floating-point prior to using it in the arithmetic statement so as to avoid multiplying a number of one type times a number of another type.

Illustration 2. The Computation of an Arithmetic Mean

Problem Write a program to read an unknown number of records, each of which has a three-digit positive integer number punched in punch card columns 20 through 22, and compute the arithmetic mean of these numbers.

After the arithmetic mean has been calculated, print it at the top of a page of printer printout. Precede the mean by the phrase, THE MEAN IS; allow for one space between the phrase and the number. Since the number of characters that will compose the arithmetic mean is unknown, assume it will be no larger than the maximum possible single precision floating-point number. Allow for a two-digit fraction. Figure 4-7 is a flowchart of the program.

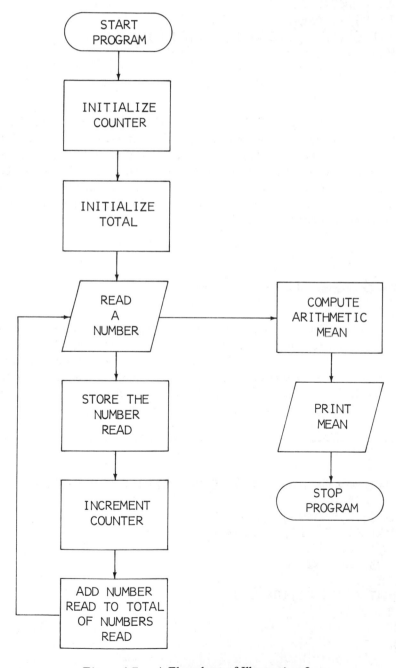

Figure 4-7. A Flowchart of Illustration 2.

```
cc 123456789...

   C     CØMPUTATIØN ØF AN ARITHMETIC MEAN
         CØUNT = 0
         TØTAL = 0
   1     READ (5,2,END=3) NUMBER
         FØRMAT (T20,I3)
   2     BER = NUMBER
         CØUNT = CØUNT+1
         TØTAL = TØTAL+BER
         GØ TØ 1
   3     AMEAN = TØTAL/CØUNT
         WRITE (6,4) AMEAN
   4     FØRMAT ('1','THE MEAN IS',1X,F8.2)
         STØP
         END
```

Analysis   Note that the variable names CØUNT and TØTAL are initialized to zero. The reason for this is that they are both used on the right side of the equal sign in an arithmetic statement and the initial number stored under them would otherwise be unknown. Thus, the first time each arithmetic statement is executed, CØUNT and TØTAL will have the number stored under it. Another point that should be noted is that the computer does not transfer to the STOP statement after the last number is read but rather to the program statement that computes the mean. It is only logical that this arithmetic statement could not be executed until after the last number had been processed.

Illustration 3.   The Comparison of a Final Test Score

Problem   Write a program that will compare a final test score with two previous test scores of an unknown number of students to determine if the final test score is either equal to or greater than the two previous test scores. Each test score is a three-digit integer number. The first test score is punched in punch card columns 1 through 3; the second test score is punched in columns 5 through 7; and the final test score is punched in columns 10 through 12. Print the results of each comparison and double space between the printing of each comparison. Figure 4-8 is a flowchart of the program.

```
cc 123456789...

   C     CØMPARISØN ØF FINAL TEST SCØRE WITH TWØ PREVIØUS TEST SCØRES
         LØGICAL I,J
   1     READ (5,2,END=99) N1,N2,N3
   2     FØRMAT (I3,T5,I3,T10,I3)
         I = N3 .GE. N1
         J = N3 .GE. N2
         WRITE (6,3) I,J
   3     FØRMAT ('0', L1,10X,L1)
         GØ TØ 1
   99    STØP
         END
```

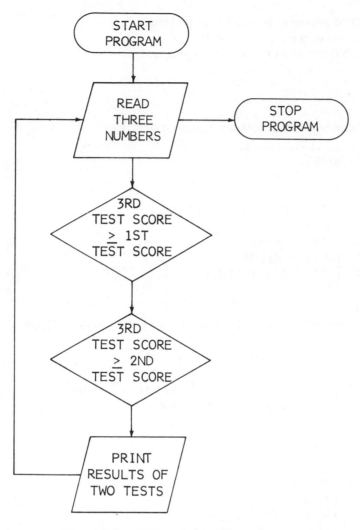

Figure 4-8. A Flowchart of Illustration 3.

Analysis Since the logical variable names I and J were used to store either the logical constant .TRUE. or .FALSE., each had to be explicitly declared in a LØGICAL statement.

QUESTIONS

1. Define the two types of assignment statements.
2. What four factors concerning the use of the arithmetic statement must be considered by an individual?
3. Name the possible components of an arithmetic expression.
4. Briefly discuss the seven rules that must be considered when constructing an arithmetic expression.
5. What are the two possible conditions that may be stored under a logical variable name?
6. Define a relational operator and name the six relational operators and their corresponding arithmetic meaning.
7. The operands being compared by a relational operator may be of what type? What type of operand cannot be compared by a relational operator?
8. What is the function of a logical operator?
9. What is the basic requirement concerning the use of a logical operator?
10. Briefly describe the method of operation of each of the three logical operators.
11. What effect does the hierarchy of execution have on the evaluation of a logical expression?
12. What is the function of the STØP statement?

13. Where may a STØP statement be located in a program?
14. What is the function of the END statement?
15. Where may an END statement be located in a program?

EXERCISES

1. Which of the following arithmetic statements are invalid? Why?

```
cc 123456789...


     XY+5.5 = INCØME*ITAX
     EDUC = YEAR
     DØT = MA+I
     INK = KØLØR
     KK = CØUNT-100.
```

2. Assuming the information provided below, which of the following logical statements are invalid? Why?

Variable	Type
K, L	Integer
C, D	Single precision floating-point
E, M	Logical

```
cc 123456789...


     M = C .LT. D
     D = (K+100) .EQ. 550
     E = K .GT. ((C+D)/10.)
     M = E .NE. D+3.72
     M = K*5/10 LE. 20
     E = .LT. 100
     M = (K*L)/100 .EQ. 5**2+L
```

3. Assuming the information provided below, which of the following logical statements are invalid? Why?

Variable	Type
I, J	Integer
A, B	Single precision floating-point
C, D, K, L	Logical

```
cc 123456789...


     C = (A**I*B .GT. 1000.) .ØR. K
     D = J .AND. L
     K = .ØR. C
     C = A .EQ. B .AND. .NØT. L
     D = K .AND. .ØR. L
     C = D .AND. .NØT. K .ØR. A .LT. B
     K = .NØT. (I .EQ. J) ØR. L
```

Chapter 5

CONTROL STATEMENTS

There are three basic groups of program control statements. One group, composed of the STØP and END statements, was discussed in Chapter 4 and is concerned with the termination of a program. In this chapter, a second and third group of control statements are discussed.

As discussed in Chapter 1, the computer normally executes program statements in the order in which they are located in the program. The second and third groups of control statements are a means of altering the normal sequence of program statement execution. The second group of statements is concerned with branching to a specific program statement. As will be appropriately indicated, one of the statements in this group was discussed in Chapter 4. The third group of statements is concerned with looping one or more program statements a specific number of times.

SYSTEM AND PROGRAM FLOWCHARTING

A simple yet quite helpful aid in preparing to write a program is the preparation of a flowchart. The more complicated a program the greater assistance a flowchart can provide in writing the program. For these reasons, the author suggests that the reader refer to Appendix H for a discussion of system and program flowcharting prior to reading any further in this chapter.

BRANCHING

Program control statements that provide the computer with the capability of branching make it possible for it to choose between two or more sequences of program statement execution during execution of the program. This ability is vital as it provides the computer with the capability of executing specific sequences of program statements based upon a decision it arrives at without human intervention.

The Arithmetic IF Statement   The arithmetic IF statement causes the computer to evaluate an arithmetic expression and, depending upon the result of the evaluation, to transfer to one of three possible program statements. Figure 5-1 illustrates the general form of this statement:

cc $\overline{123456}$789...

$bbbbb$ IF $(ae)\, sn_1, sn_2, sn_3$

where

bbbbb	represents an unsigned 1 through 5 integer number that is required only if a transfer is made to this statement from another program statement.
IF	FORTRAN key word that distinguishes this statement from the other kinds of statements in the program.
(	a special character that is a requirement of the FORTRAN language.
ae	represents an arithmetic expression that is evaluated to determine its current value.
)	a special character that is a requirement of the FORTRAN language.
sn_1	represents a statement number assigned to the executable program statement the computer will transfer to if the current value of the arithmetic expression is less than zero.
,	a special character that is a requirement of the FORTRAN language.
sn_2	represents a statement number assigned to the executable program statement the computer will transfer to if the current value of the arithmetic expression is equal to zero.
,	a special character that is a requirement of the FORTRAN language.
sn_3	represents a statement number assigned to the executable program statement the computer will transfer to if the current value of the arithmetic expression is greater than zero.

Figure 5-1.   The General Form of the Arithmetic IF Statement.

The way the arithmetic statement operates is illustrated in Figure 5-2.

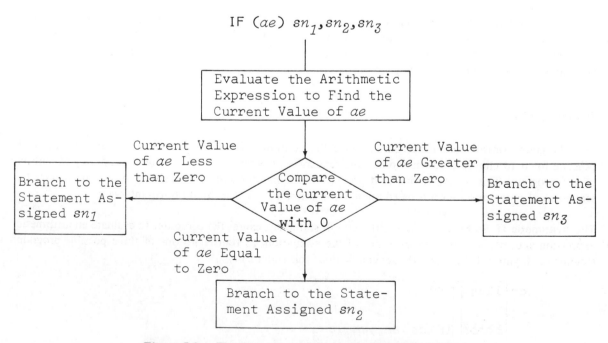

Figure 5-2.   The Operation of the Arithmetic IF Statement.

The following is an illustration of the arithmatic IF statement:

```
cc | 123456789...
   |        |
   |        | IF (I-10) 3,7,10
```

In the preceding illustration, the computer will evaluate the arithmetic expression I-10. If the current value of the arithmetic expression is less than zero, the computer will transfer to the program statement assigned statement number 3; if the current value of the arithmetic expression is equal to zero, the computer will transfer to the program statement assigned statement number 7; and if the current value of the arithmetic expression is greater than zero, the computer will transfer to the program statement assigned statement number 10.

In some instances, it may be desirable to transfer to one of only two possible program statements. This may be accomplished by placing the same program statement number in the two appropriate positions. For example, assume that it is desirable to transfer to the program statement assigned statement number 1 if the current value of the arithmetic expression is either less than zero or greater than zero; and it is desirable to transfer to the program statement assigned statement number 2 if the current value of the arithmetic expression is equal to zero. The arithmetic IF statement would be constructed in the following manner to accomplish this:

```
cc | 123456789...
   |        |
   |        | IF (100/L) 1,2,1
```

While it is possible to place the same statement number in all three positions, the author suggests that this not be done as there is a more appropriate statement, the unconditional GØ TØ statement which is discussed later in this chapter, to use in this situation.

The Logical IF Statement   The logical IF statement causes the computer to evaluate a logical expression and, depending upon the result of the evaluation, to transfer to either the true or false branch. Figure 5-3 illustrates the general form of this statement.

```
cc | 123456789...
   |       |
   | bbbbb | IF (le) t
```

where

bbbbb   represents an unsigned 1 through 5 integer number that is required only if a transfer is made to this statement from another program statement.

   IF   FORTRAN key word that distinguishes this statement from the other kinds of statements in the program.

   (a special character that is a requirement of the FORTRAN language.

le   represents a logical expression that is evaluated to determine whether it is true or false.

)   a special character that is a requirement of the FORTRAN language.

t   represents any executable program statement except a DØ or another logical IF statement that will be executed if the logical expression is evaluated as being true.

Figure 5-3.   The General Form of the Logical IF Statement.

The way the logical statement operates is illustrated in Figure 5-4.

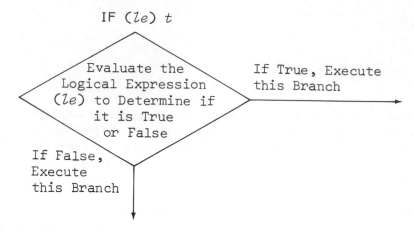

Figure 5-4. The Operation of the Logical IF Statement.

The following is an illustration of the logical IF statement:

```
cc | 123456789...
   |
   |    IF (A .GT. B) GØ TØ 17
```

In the preceding illustration, the computer will evaluate the logical expression A .GT. B. If it is evaluated as being true, the computer will transfer to the true branch and execute that statement. However, if the logical expression is evaluated as being false, the computer will proceed to the next executable statement and execute it.

If a transfer is made to the true branch and that statement does not transfer the computer to another program statement, after the computer has executed that statement it proceeds to the next executable statement and executes it. For example, in the following illustration

```
cc | 123456789...
   |
   |
   |    IF (TØT .LT. X) I = 15
   |    READ (5,1) NUMBER
 1 |    FØRMAT (I5)
```

the computer will store the number 15 under the variable name I and then proceed to and execute the READ statement.

An Illustration of the Arithmetic and Logical IF Statements   The following program reads in an unknown number of punched cards, each of which has punched in it three thermometer readings. The highest of the three temperature readings on each punched card is determined and that temperature reading is printed by the printer. Figure 5-5 is a flowchart of the program. In the following program, two logical IF statements are used to determine the highest temperature. The first logical IF statement determines the highest temperature between the first two temperatures read in and the second logical IF statement determines the highest temperature of the three temperatures by comparing the highest temperature of the first two temperatures with the third temperature. Also note how an arithmetic IF statement is used to determine when to go to the top of a page to print the first highest temperature reading and when to start double spacing between the printing of subsequent highest temperature readings.

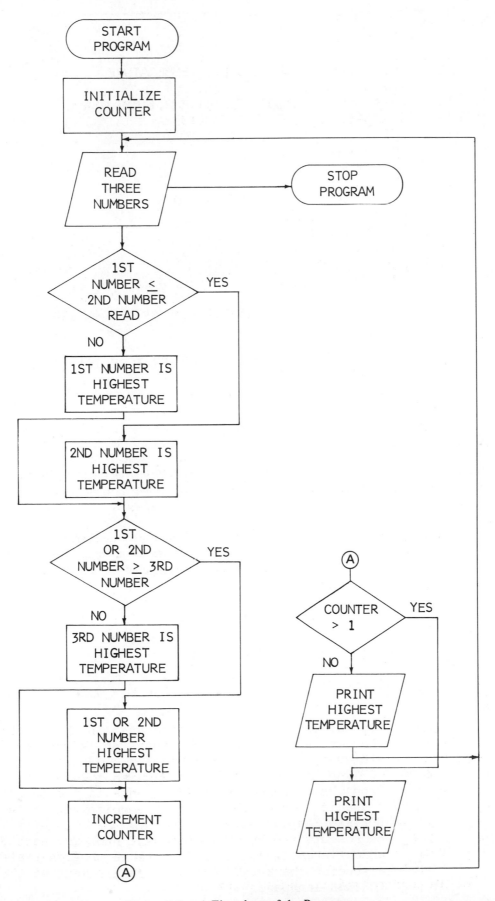

Figure 5-5. A Flowchart of the Program.

```
cc  123456789...


C        SELECTIØN ØF THE HIGHEST TEMPERATURE
         KØUNT = 0
1        READ (5,2,END=99) ITEM1,ITEM2,ITEM3
2        FØRMAT (T5,I3,T15,I3,T30,I3)
         IF (ITEM1 .LE. ITEM2) GØ TØ 3
         IHIGH1 = ITEM1
         GØ TØ 4
3        IHIGH1 = ITEM2
4        IF (IHIGH1 .GE. ITEM3) GØ TØ 5
         IHIGH2 = ITEM3
         GØ TØ 6
5        IHIGH2 = IHIGH1
6        KØUNT = KØUNT+1
         IF (KØUNT-1) 7,7,9
7        WRITE (6,8) IHIGH2
8        FØRMAT ('1','THE HIGHEST TEMPERATURE IS',1X,I3)
         GØ TØ 1
9        WRITE (6,10) IHIGH2
10       FØRMAT ('0','THE HIGHEST TEMPERATURE IS',1X,I3)
         GØ TØ 1
99       STØP
         END
```

The Unconditional GØ TØ Statement   This statement is considered one of the group of program statements capable of branching to another statement. It was discussed in Chapter 4, however, and thus will not be discussed at this point.

The Computed GØ TØ Statement   The Computed GØ TØ statement causes the computer to transfer to an executable statement on the basis of the current value of a number stored under an integer variable name. The statement transferred to may either precede or follow the computed GØ TØ statement. Figure 5-6 illustrates the general form of this statement:

```
cc  123456789...


bbbbb  GØ TØ (sn₁,sn₂,...,snₙ), iv
```

where

bbbbb	represents an unsigned 1 through 5 integer number that is required only if a transfer is made to this statement from another statement.
GØ TØ	FORTRAN key words that distinguish this statement from the other kinds of statements in the program.
(	a special character that is a requirement of the FORTRAN language.
$sn_1, sn_2, \ldots, sn_n$	represents two or more statement numbers, each of which is assigned to an executable program statement.
)	a special character that is a requirement of the FORTRAN language.

, a special character that is a requirement of the
FORTRAN language.

iv represents an integer variable name. The number
stored under it determines which executable statement the computer will transfer to. If the number
is 1, the statement assigned the first statement
number, from left to right, will be transferred to;
if the number is 2, the statement assigned the
second statement number will be transferred to, etc.

Figure 5-6. The General Form of the Computed GØ TØ Statement.

The computed GØ TØ statement is an appropriate statement to use in situations where it is desirable
to transfer to one of several possible statements in a program based upon a number. For example, assume
that it is desired to process certain data of a large number of armed service personnel. The desired data of
each serviceman is punched in a punch card. The particular branch of service of which a serviceman is a
member determines the manner in which the data punched in the serviceman's punch card is to be
processed. The number 1 is punched in the first punch card column if the serviceman is a member of the
Army; the number 2, if he is a member of the Air Force; the number 3, if he is a member of the Marines;
and the number 4, if he is a member of the Navy. The partially completed READ statement in the
following illustration

```
cc│ 123456789...
  │
  │
  │  READ (5,1) I,...
 1│  FØRMAT (I1,...
  │  GØ TØ (2,19,6,3),I
  │  .
  │  .
  │  .
```

causes the computer to read the desired data of each serviceman and if the number stored under the
variable name I is 1, the computer will transfer to the program statement assigned statement number 2; if
the stored number is 2, the computer will transfer to the program statement assigned statement number 19;
if the stored number is 3, the computer will transfer to the program statement assigned statement number
6; and, if the stored number is 4, the computer will transfer to the program statement assigned statement
number 3.

The number stored under the integer variable name must be greater than zero, but cannot be larger
than the number of statement numbers enclosed within parentheses. Like the arithmetic IF statement, one
statement number may be used only once or the same statement number may be used several times.
However, again it is impracticable to use only one statement number; the uncondition GØ TØ statement
should be used instead in this situation.

The ASSIGN and Assigned GØ TØ Statements   The ASSIGN statement, in conjunction with the assigned
GØ TØ statement, also causes the computer to transfer to an executable statement on the basis of the
current value of a number stored under an integer variable name. Figure 5-7 illustrates the general form of
the ASSIGN and accompanying assigned GØ TØ statements:

```
cc│ 123456789...
  │
  │
*bbbbb*│ASSIGN *sn* TØ *iv*
*bbbbb*│GØ TØ *iv*,(*sn*₁,*sn*₂,...,*sn*ₙ)
```

where

bbbbb	represents an unsigned 1 through 5 integer number that is required only if a transfer is made to this statement from another statement.
ASSIGN	FORTRAN key word that distinguishes this statement from the other kinds of statements in the program.
sn	represents a statement number assigned to an executable statement. This statement number must be one of the statement numbers located in an assigned GØ TØ statement.

TØ	FORTRAN key word that distinguishes this statement from the other kinds of statements in the program.
iv	represents an integer variable name.

GØ ·TØ	FORTRAN key word that distinguishes this statement from the other kinds of statements in the program.
iv	represents the same integer variable name as the one located in an ASSIGN statement.
,	a special character that is a requirement of the FORTRAN language.
(	a special character that is a requirement of the FORTRAN language.
$sn_1, sn_2, \ldots, sn_n$	represents two or more statement numbers, each of which is assigned to an executable statement.
)	a special character that is a requirement of the FORTRAN language.

Figure 5-7.   The General Form of the ASSIGN and Assigned GØ TØ Statements.

The following are two illustrations of the ASSIGN and accompanying assigned GØ TØ statements:

```
cc  123456789...



    ASSIGN 20 TØ I
    GØ TØ I,(5,10,15,20,25)
```

In the preceding illustration, the computer will assign the number 20 to the variable name I. It will then execute the assigned GØ TØ statement and transfer to the program statement assigned statement number 20. In the following illustration, after executing several program statements the computer will assign the number 15 to the variable name NUMBER. It will then execute several other program statements located between the ASSIGN and assigned GØ TØ statements. Upon executing the assigned GØ TØ statement, the computer will transfer to the program statement assigned statement number 15. It will execute this statement and the next one, which assigns the number 5 to the variable name NUMBER. The computer will then execute the next statement and transfer to the program statement assigned statement number 1. Upon again executing the assigned GØ TØ statement, the computer will transfer to the program statement assigned statement number 5. After executing this statement, the computer will execute the statements following it.

Any executable program statement that immediately follows any branching statement other than a logical IF statement must be assigned a statement number. Otherwise, there will be no way to refer to them for execution at the appropriate time.

```
cc  123456789...
          .
          .
          .
          ASSIGN 15 TØ NUMBER
          .
          .
          .
     1    GØ TØ NUMBER,(5,10,15,20,25)
          .
          .
          .
          A = B+C
          .
          .
          .
          B = C+D
    15    ASSIGN 5 TØ NUMBER
          GØ TØ 1
          .
          .
          .
     5    I = (10+L)/100
          .
          .
          .
```

LOOPING

The DØ statement provides the computer with the capability of looping, making it possible to execute the same set of program statements a desired number of times. Because of the capability the DØ statement provides the computer, it is considered the most powerful program control statement. Figure 5-8 illustrates the general form of this statement:

```
cc  123456789...

    bbbbb  DØ sn iv = in₁, in₂, in₃
```

$$cc \quad 123456789... $$
$$bbbbb \quad DØ\ sn\ iv = in_1, in_2, in_3$$

where

bbbbb	represents an unsigned 1 through 5 integer number that is required only if a transfer is made to this statement from another program statement.
DØ	FORTRAN key word that distinguishes this statement from the other kinds of statements in the program.
sn	represents the statement number assigned to a program statement located after the DØ statement. This program statement is the last statement included in the range of the DØ statement.

iv represents an integer variable name called the DØ variable. After the last program statement in the range of the DØ statement has been executed, the value of the number stored under this variable name is incremented by in_3.

=   a special character that is a requirement of the FORTRAN language.

in_1 represents either an integer number or integer variable name whose value is the initial value of iv during the first time the statements within the range of the DØ statement are executed. This value must be greater than zero.

,   a special character that is a requirement of the FORTRAN language.

in_2 represents either an integer number or integer variable name whose value is compared with the current value of iv after the last statement in the range of the DØ statement has been executed. If the value of iv exceeds the value of in_2, the computer transfers to the next executable statement after sn. The value of in_2 must be greater than zero but must not exceed $2^{31} - 2$.

,   a special character that is a requirement of the FORTRAN **language.**

in_3 represents either an integer number or integer variable name whose value is added to the current value of iv after the last statement in the range of the DØ statement has been executed, but before the comparison between in_2 and iv is made.

The value must be greater than zero. It is optional if it is the value 1, i.e., iv will be incremented by the value 1 if it is not present. If in_3 is not present, the otherwise immediately preceding comma is also omitted.

Figure 5-8.   The General Form of the DØ Statement.

The way the DØ statement operates is illustrated in Figure 5-9.

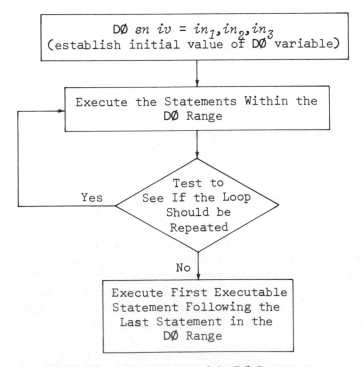

Figure 5-9.   The Operation of the DØ Statement.

The following is an illustration of the DØ statement:

<table>
<tr><td colspan="3">DØ 10 I = 1,25</td></tr>
<tr>
<td>STATEMENT</td>
<td>DØ</td>
<td>The key word DØ indicates that the computer is to execute this statement and all other statements up to and including the statement assigned statement number 10.</td>
</tr>
<tr>
<td>RANGE</td>
<td>10</td>
<td>The range of the DØ includes the statements that are to be executed repeatedly. The last statement must be identified by a statement number following the DØ statement.</td>
</tr>
<tr>
<td>DØ VARIABLE</td>
<td>I</td>
<td>Each DØ statement has associated with it an integer variable name called the DØ variable, which is chosen by the programmer.</td>
</tr>
<tr>
<td>INITIAL VALUE</td>
<td>1</td>
<td>The programmer exercises complete control over the DØ variable by indicating its initial value.</td>
</tr>
<tr>
<td>TEST VALUE</td>
<td>25</td>
<td>Upon each execution of the statements in the DØ range, the value of the DØ variable is compared with the test value, which in this case is twenty-five. When the value of the DØ variable exceeds the test value, the DØ is considered satisfied and control passes outside the range of the DØ. Control passes to the first executable statement following the last statement in the DØ range.</td>
</tr>
<tr>
<td>INDEXING INCREMENT</td>
<td></td>
<td>Another control over the DØ variable is obtained by specifying how much the DØ variable is to increase after each execution of the statement in the range--in this case, 1. (If no value is specified for incrementation, it is understood that the increment is to be 1.) The incrementation occurs <u>before</u> the comparison between the DØ variable and the test value.</td>
</tr>
</table>

In many instances, an arithmetic or logical IF or unconditional, computed, or assigned GØ TØ statement may be used instead of the DØ statement to accomplish the same goal. However, the DØ statement is specifically designed for the purpose of looping and in most instances it is more convenient to use and the process of looping is executed faster. A particular instance when the arithmetic or logical IF statement might be more appropriately used for the purpose of looping is when the decision whether or not to repeat the loop is based upon the result of certain calculations performed by one or more program statements within the loop rather than the counting of the number of repetitions of the loop.

With respect to using the DØ statement, the following seven factors must be considered:

1. The DØ variable, *iv* may be used in appropriate program statements within the range of the DØ statement to either calculate data or as a subscript or an element of a subscript to designate a specific array element of an array.

2. The number stored under the DØ variable name is controlled by the computer during the execution of the program statements within the range of the DØ statement. Thus the number cannot be changed by one of these statements.

3. If variable names are used for in_1, in_2, and/or in_3, the number stored under each of them cannot be changed while the program statements within the range of the DØ statement are being executed.

4. The statement immediately following a DØ statement must be an executable program statement.

5. The program statements within the range of a DØ statement may be located within the range of one or more other DØ statements. In this instance, the statements within the range of the outermost DØ statement are not in the range of any other DØ statement. However, the statements of a DØ statement within the range of another DØ statement are said to be "nested" within that DØ statement.

6. The last program statement within the range of a DØ statement must be an executable statement. However, it cannot be a GØ TØ statement of any form, a PAUSE, a STØP, a RETURN, an arithmetic or logical IF, or another DØ statement.

7. When the computer transfers to the next executable program statement after *sn*, the number stored under the DØ variable name becomes undefined. As such, the number stored under the DØ variable name either may or may not be its last value.

Program statements within the range of an inner DØ statement must be within the range of the next outer DØ statement of the nest. It is permissible, however, for the last program statement within the range of the inner DØ statement to be the same statement as the last program statement within the range of the next DØ statement of the nest.

The computer can transfer out of the range of a DØ statement at any point during the execution of the program statements within its range. However, a return to a program statement within the range of a DØ statement can be made only under the following circumstances:

1. The values of *iv*, in_1, in_2, and in_3 must not have been changed by a program statement outside the range of the DØ statement.

2. If a DØ statement is nested within the range of one or more other DØ statements, both the transfer and return must be made from and to the innermost DØ statement.

Partial Illustrations of the Use of the DØ Statement   The following three partially illustrated programs depict a possible use of the DØ statement. The first program uses a DØ statement to read, process, and write 25 records of a data set:

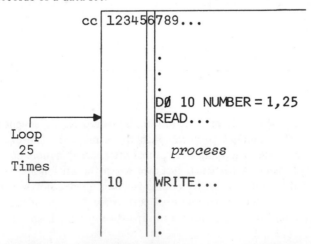

A program may also require the use of multiple DØ statements. Multiple DØ statements may take the form of either two or more independent DØ statements and/or two or more "nested" DØ statements. The next program illustrates the use of two independent DØ statements:

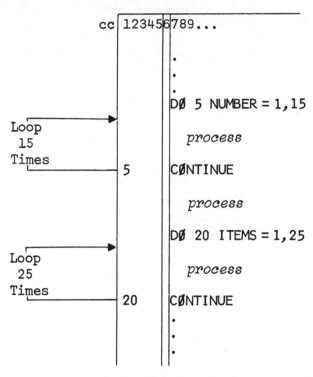

The computer will execute the statements between the first DØ and CØNTINUE statements, repeating this process of execution a total of 15 times. It will then execute the statements between CØNTINUE statement and the second DØ statement. Finally, the computer will execute the statements between the second DØ statement and the second CØNTINUE statement, repeating this process of execution a total of 25 times.

As previously mentioned, the use of multiple DØ statements in a program might take the form of "nested" DØ statements:

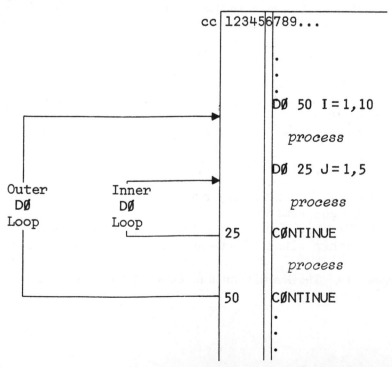

The computer will execute the statements from the first DØ statement down to the second DØ statement. It will then execute the statements from the second DØ statement down to the first CØNTINUE statement, repeating this process of execution a total of 5 times. The computer will then execute the statements between the first and second CØNTINUE statements. Next, the computer will loop back to the statement following the first DØ statement. This entire process will be repeated a total of 10 times.

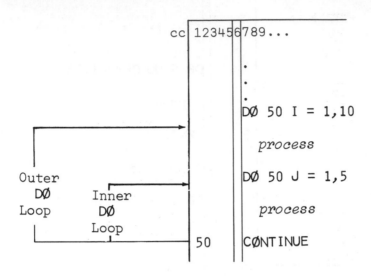

In the preceding illustration, the computer will iterate the inner DØ loop 50 times and the outer DØ loop 10 times. This is due to the fact that the inner loop will iterate 5 times each time the inner DØ statement is encountered by the computer in the process of executing the outer DØ loop.

THE CØNTINUE STATEMENT

The CØNTINUE statement is a non-executable statement that can be used as the last statement within the range of a DØ statement. It is especially appropriate when the last statement might otherwise be one of the forbidden statements. It is also a convenient statement to use when an arithmetic and/or logical IF statement is used within the range of a DØ statement. Figure 5-10 illustrates the general form of this statement:

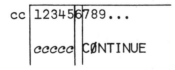

where

        ccccc   represents a normally required 1 through 5 character
                 statement number.
  CØNTINUE   FORTRAN key word that distinguishes this statement from
                 the other kinds of statements in the program.

Figure 5-10.   The General Form of the CØNTINUE Statement.

In the following illustration,

```
cc  123456789...

    C        THE USE ØF THE CØNTINUE STATEMENT
             DØ 4 I = 1,25
             READ (5,1,END=99) NUMBER
    1        FØRMAT (I3)
             IF (NUMBER-100) 4,2,2
    2        WRITE (6,3) NUMBER
    3        FØRMAT (' ',T11,I3)
    4        CØNTINUE
    99       STØP
             END
```

each of the 25 numbers read is compared to the number 100. If the number read is less than 100, the computer will branch to the CØNTINUE statement; if it is either equal to or greater than 100, the computer will branch to the WRITE statement.

A Complete Illustration of the Use of the DØ Statement   The following program reads 100 numbers, one at a time. Each number is compared against the value 500 to determine if it is greater than it. If the number read is greater than 500, the computer branches to the CØNTINUE statement. However, if the number is not greater than 500, the number is squared and the number and its square are printed by the printer. After the one hundredth number has been read and processed, the computer leaves the loop and executes the next executable statement, which is the STØP statement. Figure 5-11 is a flowchart of the program.

```
cc  123456789...

    C        THE USE OF A DØ LØØP TØ READ AND PRØCESS SEVERAL NUMBERS
             WRITE (6,1)
    1        FØRMAT ('1',T26,'NUMBER',T51,'SQUARE ØF THE NUMBER')
             DØ 4 I = 1,100
             READ (5,2,END=99) NUMBER
    2        FØRMAT (I3)
             IF (NUMBER .GT. 500) GØ TØ 4
             ISQR = NUMBER**2
             WRITE (6,3) NUMBER,ISQR
    3        FØRMAT ('0',T28,I3,T60,I7)
    4        CØNTINUE
    99       STØP
             END
```

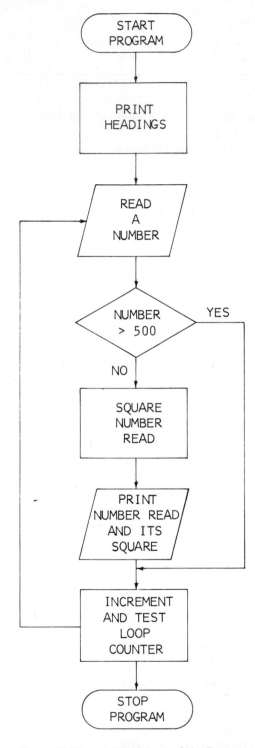

Figure 5-11. A Flowchart of the Program.

THE READING OF TWO OR MORE DATA DECKS

Because of the particular way in which two or more sequential data decks are read, the reader is referred to Appendix G for a discussion of this topic. However, unless the reader is specifically interested in this topic, he may omit reading Appendix G without interfering with his learning the FØRTRAN language.

QUESTIONS

1. What is the general purpose of each of the three groups of control statements and which program statements compose each group?
2. Why is it important for a computer to have the capability of branching?
3. What does the arithmetic IF statement cause the computer to do?
4. What does the logical IF statement cause the computer to do?
5. What does the computed GØ TØ statement cause the computer to do?
6. What does the ASSIGN statement, in conjunction with the assigned GØ TØ statement, cause the computer to do?
7. What does the DØ statement cause the computer to do?
8. What is the "range" of a DØ statement? How is it indicated?
9. What must be the mode of the DØ variable in the DØ statement?
10. What kind of program statement must be the first statement in the range of a DØ statement?
11. What kind of program statement must be used as the last statement in the range of a DØ statement and what specific program statements cannot be used?
12. May the DØ variable be used in program statements located within the range of a DØ statement?
13. When the range of a DØ statement is left normally, what is the next program statement executed?
14. Under what circumstances may the computer transfer out of and back into the range of a DØ statement?
15. What is the function of the CØNTINUE statement?

EXERCISES

1. Which of the following arithmetic IF statements are incorrect? Why?

```
cc│ 123456789...



    │IF (A-C) 5,10,15
 25 │IF (X**2.+Y*Z) 10,10,25
    │IF (I+100 1,2,3
    │IF (A-C) 51,75
    │IF (M) 100,200,300
    │IF (H**T-B*C) 50,50,50
    │IF (M+100N) 5,10,15
    │IF (50-25+5) 31,41,51
    │IF (K+7-J) 17,34,63
```

2. Which of the following logical IF statements are incorrect?

```
cc│ 123456789...



    │IF (A .GT. B) I = 50
    │IF Y .LT. Z GØ TØ 10
    │IF (I .LE M) STØP
    │IF (Z) GØ TØ 75
    │IF (H .GL. T) I = 10*J
    │IF (100-J .EQ. 1000) GØ TØ 100
```

3.   Which of the following computed GØ TØ statements are incorrect? Why?

```
cc 123456789...

        GØ TØ (100,3,10)I
        GØ TØ (15,25),Z
        GØ TØ (25,20,15,20),I      (where I = 50)
        GØ TØ (35,50,10),M
```

4.   Which of the following pairs of ASSIGN and assigned GØ TØ statements are incorrect? Why?

```
cc 123456789...

        ASSIGN 20 TØ A
        GØ TØ A,(5,10,15,20,25)
        .
        .
        .
        ASSIGN 50 TØ I
        GØ TØ I,(15,25,35,45,55)
        .
        .
        .
        ASSIGN 12 TØ N
        GØ TØ N(3,6,9,12,15)
        .
        .
        .
        ASSIGN 30 TØ M
        GØ TØ M,(10,20,30)
```

Chapter 6

ARRAYS

In certain instances, it is necessary to nonsequentially process several related numbers during execution of the program. In such situations, it is desirable to reflect in a program the fact that these numbers are related and retain each number's identity for processing purposes. In FORTRAN, the array is the means through which this can be accomplished.

An array is an ordered set of computer memory storage spaces identified by an array name. The entire array can be referred to through the use of the array name or a specific storage space within the array can be referenced through the use of the array name accompanied by a subscript. The following discussion of an array emphasizes its use in the input and output of data and in one or more calculations on data.

THE NATURE OF AN ARRAY

Figure 6-1 illustrates a partial listing of a weekly payroll of a company:

Employee No.	Amount
1	123.65
2	104.10
3	151.04
4	133.73
5	118.52
.	.
.	.
.	.
50	127.34

Figure 6-1. A Partial Listing of a Company's Weekly Payroll.

81

In Chapter 3, the READ statement was discussed as a means through which the weekly amount earned by each employee could be stored in the computer's memory. Specifically, one of two possible methods could be used:

```
cc  123456789...

        READ (5,1,END=99) EMPL1
        READ (5,1,END=99) EMPL2
        READ (5,1,END=99) EMPL3
        READ (5,1,END=99) EMPL4
        READ (5,1,END=99) EMPL5
        .
        .
        .
        READ (5,1,END=99) EMPL50
    1   FØRMAT (F6.2)
```

or

```
cc  123456789...

        READ (5,1,END=99) EMPL1,EMPL2,EMPL3, ... EMPL50
    1   FØRMAT (F6.2)
```

The use of either method would result in either the writing of 50 READ statements or the writing of a very long READ statement. However, the same 50 amounts could be stored in the computer's memory with much less writing by creating an array named EMPL, specifying that it was composed of 50 storage spaces, and using the following statement:

```
cc  123456789...

        READ (5,1,END=99) EMPL
    1   FØRMAT (F6.2)
```

If the objective was to write the 50 amounts stored in the computer's memory into one or more records of a data set, either one of the more lengthy methods could be used or the shorter method, assuming the amounts had been stored in an array when they were originally read from a record of a data set, could be employed. (A detailed explanation of exactly what is occurring when the shorter method is employed will be presented later in this chapter.)

THE CREATION OF AN ARRAY

An array is created in the computer's memory by means of a specification statement. While there are seven specification statements that can be used to create an array, only the DIMENSIØN, INTEGER, REAL, DØUBLE PRECISIØN, and LØGICAL statements will be discussed in this chapter. The CØMMØN and CØMPLEX statements are discussed in Chapters 7 and 8 respectively.

The DIMENSIØN Statement   The DIMENSIØN statement assigns an array name to one or more arrays and specifies the number of computer memory storage spaces that are allocated to each array. A DIMENSIØN statement must precede any other program statement that refers to an array name located in the specification statement. Figure 6-2 illustrates the general form of the DIMENSIØN statement:

```
cc 123456789...

   bbbbb  DIMENSIØN an_1(in_1,in_2,in_3),...,an_n(in_n,in_n,in_n)
```

where

bbbbb	represents an optional unsigned 1 through 5 integer number.
DIMENSIØN	FORTRAN key word that distinguishes this statement from the other kinds of statements in the program.
$an_1,an_2,...,an_n$	represents an array name.
(	a special character that is a requirement of the FORTRAN language.
$in_1,in_2,in_3,...,$ in_n,in_n,in_n	represents one, two, or three unsigned integer numbers, each of which can be 1 through 7 characters in length, which specify the number of storage spaces to be allocated to the immediately preceding array name. If there is more than one integer number, they must be separated by a comma. One, two, or three numbers are used, depending upon whether it is a one-, two-, or three-dimensional array.
)	a special character that is a requirement of the FORTRAN language.
,	a special character that is optional if more than one array name is present.

Figure 6-2.   The General Form of the DIMENSIØN Statement.

The DIMENSIØN statement in the following illustration causes the computer to allocate the single-dimensional array named EMPL 50 storage spaces in its memory.

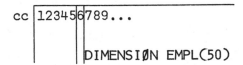

```
cc 123456789...

      DIMENSIØN EMPL(50)
```

As such, the weekly salary of the 50 employees partially listed in Figure 6-1 can be simultaneously stored in the computer's memory under this array name. An important point to remember is that once a number of storage spaces have been allocated to an array name, any of those storage spaces which are not filled with data through the use of that array name cannot be used to store data through the use of any other symbolic name in the program. In other words, those unused storage spaces will remain allocated to the array name they were originally allocated to and in effect are "wasted" storage space. Thus, keep in mind that there is not an unlimited amount of computer memory storage space available and you will waste possible needed storage space if you allocate more storage space to an array name than is actually required. To alleviate this problem, when allocating storage space to an array name attempt to allocate no more storage space than you believe you need for the amount of data you are going to store under that array name. However, be sure you allocate enough storage space.

The Explicit Specification Statements   As previously mentioned, the INTEGER, REAL, DØUBLE PRECISIØN, or LØGICAL statements may also be used to assign a name to one or more arrays and specify the number of computer memory storage spaces that are to be allocated to each array. This ability is in addition to their ability to specify the type of an array name. As such, if it is necessary to specify the type of an array name in addition to allocating storage spaces, it probably would be desirable to use the appropriate explicit specification statement and thus be able to accomplish both in one program statement. However, if it is not necessary to specify the type of an array name, then the author suggests that the DIMENSIØN statement be used. Like the DIMENSIØN statement, the appropriate explicit specification statement must precede any other program statement that refers to an array name located in the explicit specification statement. Figure 6-3 illustrates the general form of this statement.

```
cc 123456789...

     Type an_1(in_1,in_2,in_3),an_2(in_1,in_2,in_3),...,
          an_n(in_n,in_n,in_n)
```

where

$Type$	represents either the key word INTEGER, REAL, DØUBLE PRECISIØN, or LØGICAL.
$an_1, an_2, \ldots, an_n$	represents an array name.
(	a special character that is a requirement of the FORTRAN language.
$in_1, in_2, in_3, \ldots,$ in_n, in_n, in_n	represents one, two, or three unsigned integer numbers, each of which can be 1 through 7 characters in length, which specify the number of storage spaces to be allocated to the immediately preceding array name. If there is more than one integer number, they must be separated by a comma. One, two, or three numbers are used, depending upon whether it is a one-, two-, or three-dimensional array.
)	a special character that is a requirement of the FORTRAN language.
,	a special character that is optional if more than one array name is present.

Figure 6-3.   The General Form of the Explicit Specification Statement.

The following is an illustration of the use of an explicit specification statement:

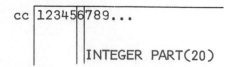

```
cc 123456789...

     INTEGER PART(20)
```

In the preceding illustration the array named PART, which because of its first alphabetic character normally implies that one or more single precision floating-point numbers will be stored under it, instead, because of its presence in this specification statement, explicitly indicates that one or more integer numbers will be stored under it. Also, 20 storage spaces are allocated to this array name.

ARRAY DIMENSIONS

As previously mentioned, an array may be either one-, two-, or three-dimensional. The particular dimension of an array is determined by whether there are one, two, or three unsigned integer numbers enclosed in parentheses immediately following an array name in either a DIMENSIØN or explicit specification statement. The first number specifies the number of allocated rows of storage space; the second number (if present) specifies the number of allocated columns of storage space; and the third number (if present) specifies the number of allocated ranks of storage space composing an array.

In the following illustration, the single-dimension array named PRICE is allocated 10 rows of storage space; the two-dimensional array named TØTAL is allocated 3 rows and 2 columns of storage space; and the three-dimensional array named DISCNT is allocated 2 rows, 3 columns, and 3 ranks of storage space.

```
cc │1234567789...
   │
   │DIMENSIØN PRICE(10),TØTAL(3,2)DISCNT(2,3,3)
```

The following list and tables exemplify the storage space allocation of the arrays named PRICE, TOTAL, and DISCNT:

$PRICE_1$

$PRICE_2$

$PRICE_3$ $DISCNT_{1,1,3}$ $DISCNT_{1,2,3}$ $DISCNT_{1,3,3}$

$PRICE_4$ $TOTAL_{1,1}$ $TOTAL_{1,2}$ $DISCNT_{1,1,2}$ $DISCNT_{1,2,3}$ $DISCNT_{1,3,2}$

$PRICE_5$ $TOTAL_{2,1}$ $TOTAL_{2,2}$ $DISCNT_{1,1,1}$ $DISCNT_{1,2,1}$ $DISCNT_{1,3,1}$

$PRICE_6$ $TOTAL_{3,1}$ $TOTAL_{3,2}$

$PRICE_7$ $DISCNT_{2,1,3}$ $DISCNT_{2,2,3}$ $DISCNT_{2,3,2}$

$PRICE_8$ $DISCNT_{2,1,2}$ $DISCNT_{2,2,2}$ $DISCNT_{2,3,2}$

$PRICE_9$ $DISCNT_{2,1,2}$ $DISCNT_{2,2,2}$ $DISCNT_{2,3,2}$

$PRICE_{10}$

If it is desirable to know the total number of storage spaces allocated to an array, multiply the number of rows times the number of columns (if present) times the number of ranks (if present). Thus, in the preceding illustration, the first array is composed of 10 storage spaces, the second array is composed of 6 storage spaces, and the third array is composed of 18 storage spaces.

SUBSCRIPTS AND ARRAY ELEMENTS

A subscript is composed of either 1 through 7 unsigned integer numbers, variable names with an unsigned integer number stored under each of them, and/or array elements—each of which is separated by a comma—enclosed in a set of parentheses. A subscript always immediately follows an array name. The array name and accompanying subscript are called an array element; an array element is a particular storage space in an array. The construction of a subscript must be based on the following six rules:

1. A subscript may be composed of any elements that an arithmetic expression may be composed of (operands, arithmetic operators, parentheses). The only requirement is that there may be only 1 through 7 operands.

2. A subscript may take any form that an arithmetic expression may take.

3. The hierarchy of evaluation of the operands composing a subscript is identical to the hierarchy of evaluation of an arithmetic expression.

4. An operand composing a subscript and the evaluated result of a subscript must be a number greater than zero.

5. If the evaluated result is not integer, the fractional portion is truncated prior to and the decimal point is ignored in determining the specific array element in an array.

6. Except in a few specific instances that will be clearly identified, an array element can be used in any program statement in which a variable name can be used.

The following is an illustration of creating an array named EMPL through the use of the DIMENSIØN specification statement and then storing a single precision floating-point number in the 10th array element of the array:

```
cc   123456789...


     DIMENSIØN EMPL(50)
     READ (5,1,END=99) EMPL(10)
1    FØRMAT (F6.2)
```

There is a distinct difference in meaning between an array name and accompanying dimension(s) located in either a DIMENSIØN or explicit specification statement and an array name and accompanying subscript in another type of statement, such as a READ, WRITE, or arithmetic or logical assignment statement. If it is located in one of the former statements, the computer is provided information which specifies the type of data that will be stored in the array and the number of storage spaces to be allocated to the array. However, if it is located in one of the latter statements, reference is being made to a specific array element within that array.

THE NORMAL ORDER IN WHICH ARRAY ELEMENTS ARE FILLED WITH A NUMBER

The normal order in which the array elements composing an array are filled with a datum is dependent upon whether the array is one, two, or three dimensional. For example, the normal order in which the array elements composing the single-dimension array in the following illustration would be as follows:

```
cc 123456789...

    DIMENSIØN CUB(10)
```

Order No.	Array Element
1	CUB(1)
2	CUB(2)
3	CUB(3)
4	CUB(4)
5	CUB(5)
6	CUB(6)
7	CUB(7)
8	CUB(8)
9	CUB(9)
10	CUB(10)

If the array was two-dimensional, like the one shown in the following illustration, the normal order in which the array elements composing the array would be filled with data is as follows:

```
cc 123456789...

    DIMENSIØN CUB(3,2)
```

Order No.	Array Element
1	CUB(1,1)
2	CUB(2,1)
3	CUB(3,1)
4	CUB(1,2)
5	CUB(2,2)
6	CUB(3,2)

Finally, if the array was three-dimensional, like the one shown in the following illustration, the normal order in which the array elements composing the array would be filled with data is as follows:

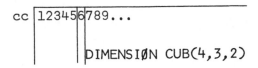

```
cc 123456789...

    DIMENSIØN CUB(4,3,2)
```

Order No.	Array Element
1	CUB(1,1,1)
2	CUB(2,1,1)
3	CUB(3,1,1)
4	CUB(4,1,1)
5	CUB(1,2,1)
6	CUB(2,2,1)
7	CUB(3,2,1)
8	CUB(4,2,1)
9	CUB(1,3,1)
10	CUB(2,3,1)
11	CUB(3,3,1)
12	CUB(4,3,1)
13	CUB(1,1,2)
14	CUB(2,1,2)
15	CUB(3,1,2)
16	CUB(4,1,2)
17	CUB(1,2,2)
18	CUB(2,2,2)
19	CUB(3,2,2)
20	CUB(4,2,2)
21	CUB(1,3,2)
22	CUB(2,3,2)
23	CUB(3,3,2)
24	CUB(4,3,2)

It should be noted that the normal order of filling array elements with data is via rows first, then columns (if present), and finally ranks (if present). That is why the first number increases most rapidly and the last number increases least rapidly.

THE TRANSFER OF DATA INTO AND FROM *ALL* OF THE ARRAY ELEMENTS OF AN ARRAY

There are instances when it will be desirable to transfer a datum either into or from each of the array elements of an array. This may be accomplished by using the array name without subscripts in either a READ or WRITE statement. One datum is either read into or written from each array element in the array. For example, in the following illustration, by placing the unscripted array named MNT in the READ statement, and integer number will be read into each of the 10 array elements composing the array.

```
cc  123456789...


      DIMENSIØN MNT(10)
      READ (5,1,END=99) MNT
  1   FØRMAT (10I3)
```

The same result could have been attained by using the less efficient method illustrated below:

```
cc  123456789...


        DIMENSIØN MNT(10)
        READ (5,1,END=99) MNT(1),MNT(2),MNT(3),MNT(4),MNT(5),
       1MNT(6),MNT(7),MNT(8),MNT(9),MNT(10)
    1   FØRMAT (10I3)
```

In certain instances, it is desirable to read a name composed of 5 or more characters from a record and then, at some later point in the program, write this name into a record of a data set. The following two programs do this by transferring data into all of the array elements of an array by means of the A format code.

In the following illustration,

```
cc  123456789...


        DIMENSIØN TITLE(20)
        READ (5,1,END=99) TITLE
    1   FØRMAT (20A4)
        WRITE (6,2) TITLE
    2   FØRMAT ('1',T51,20A4)
   99   STØP
        END
```

80 columns of a data card are read and stored under the array named TITLE. The characters stored under the name are then printed on the first print line of a page of printer paper.

In the following illustration,

```
cc  123456789...


        DIMENSIØN NAME(3),DATE(4)
        READ (5,1,END=99) NAME,DATE
    1   FØRMAT (3A4,4A4)
        WRITE (6,2) NAME,DATE
    2   FØRMAT ('1',3A4,T26,4A4)
   99   STØP
        END
```

the first 12 columns of a data card are read and stored under the array named NAME and then the next 16 columns of the data card are read and stored under the array named DATE. The characters stored under these two names are then printed on the first print line of a page of printer paper.

THE TRANSFER OF DATA INTO AND
FROM *SPECIFIC* ARRAY ELEMENTS OF AN ARRAY

The use of an array element is the means through which a number is transferred into and from a specific storage space in an array. For example, in the first arithmetic statement of the following illustration the number 25 will be stored under the array element JØB(1); in the second arithmetic statement, the number stored under the array element NUM(8) will be stored under the variable name LØG; and in the last arithmetic statement, the result of the number stored under the array element CAT(2) minus the number 10. will be stored under the variable name PAK.

```
cc | 123456789...


     JØB(1) = 25
     LØG = NUM(8)
     PAK = CAT(2)-10.
```

An array element may also be used in either a READ or WRITE statement to transfer a number either into or from a specific storage space in an array. For example, in the following illustration an integer number will be stored under the array element LINK(5) and the array element LINK(9).

```
cc | 123456789...



     DIMENSIØN LINK(9)
     READ (5,1,END=99) LINK(5),LINK(9)
   1 FØRMAT (2I4)
```

Whether an array be one-, two-, or three-dimensional, it is not necessary that all of the data be either read into or written from an array by means of the same format code. For example, in the following illustration a number will be stored under the array element SAL(5) by means of the format code F3.2; a number will be stored under the array element SAL(10) by means of the format code F5.1; and a number will be stored under the array element SAL(15) by means of the format code F7.3.

However, the type of the array element and format code must be in agreement.

```
cc | 123456789...

     DIMENSIØN SAL(15)
     READ (5,1,END=99) SAL(5),SAL(10),SAL(15)
   1 FØRMAT (F3.2,F5.1,F7.3)
```

THE TRANSFER OF DATA INTO AND FROM *PART* OF THE ARRAY ELEMENTS OF AN ARRAY

In some instances, it will be desirable to transfer more data either into or from certain array elements of an array than is economically feasible by means of listing all of the individual array elements. This may be accomplished through the use of an *indexed subscript* in either a READ or WRITE statement. Because of the identical manner in which an array name with an indexed subscript performs its sequence of actions, it is sometimes referred to as an "implied DØ loop". Figure 6-4 illustrates the general form of an *indexed subscript*:

```
cc 123456789...

   bbbbb  ...(an(iv),iv=in₁,in₂,in₃)
```

where

$bbbbb$　represents an optional unsigned 1 through 5 integer number.

$...$　represents either the key word READ or WRITE.

$($　a special character that is a requirement of the FORTRAN language.

an　represents an array name.

$($　a special character that is a requirement of the FORTRAN language.

iv　represents an integer variable name used as an *indexed subscript*. After each array element datum is either read into or written from the array an, the value of iv is increased by the value of in_3 and thus a new array element is designated.

$)$　a special character that is a requirement of the FORTRAN language.

$,$　a special character that is a requirement of the FORTRAN language.

iv　represents identically the iv described above.

$=$　a special character that is a requirement of the FORTRAN language.

in_1　represents either an integer number or integer variable name whose value is the initial value of iv. This value must be greater than zero.

$,$　a special character that is a requirement of the FORTRAN language.

in_2　represents either an integer number or integer variable name whose value is compared with the current value of iv at the completion of either reading into or writing from the datum stored in each array element. When the current value of iv becomes greater than the value of in_2, the reading or writing operation is terminated. The value of in_2 must be greater than zero.

$,$　a special character that is a requirement of the FORTRAN language.

in_3　represents either an integer number or integer variable name whose value is added to the current value of iv after each array element datum is either read or written but before the comparison between in_2 and it is made. The value of in_3 must be greater than zero. It is optional if it is the number **1**, i.e., iv will be incremented by the number 1 if it is not present. If in_3 is not present, the otherwise immediately preceding comma is also omitted.

$)$　a special character that is a requirement of the FORTRAN language.

Figure 6-4. The General Form of an Indexed Subscript.

The following is an illustration of the use of an indexed subscript to read a number of values into certain array elements of an array:

```
cc  12345 6789...

         DIMENSIØN FIG(15)
         READ (5,1,END=99) (FIG(I),I = 1,15)
1        FØRMAT (F5.1)
```

In the preceding illustration, a single precision floating-point number will be stored under array elements FIG(1) through FIG(15). The sequence of actions involved in this occurrence is as follows: the variable name I has the number 1 stored under it. Then the first value is read and stored in array element FIG(1). Next the number stored under the variable name I is incremented by the number 1. Then the value 15 is compared against the value of I, which is now 2. Since the number stored under the I is not greater than 15, the next number is read and stored under array element FIG(2). This process continues until the number stored under the variable name I is greater than 15.

As previously mentioned, an indexed subscript is sometimes referred to as an "implied DØ loop." The bases for this reference is illustrated in the following example, which shows the use of a DØ loop to accomplish the same task as the previous illustration.

```
cc   12345 6789...

         DIMENSIØN FIG(15)
         DØ 2 I = 1,15
         READ (5,1) FIG(I)
1        FØRMAT (F5.1)
2        CØNTINUE
```

If the incremented value (in $_3$) was changed so that it was 3, as illustrated below, instead of the presently implied 1, a number would be stored only under array elements FIG(1), FIG(4), FIG(7), FIG(10), and FIG(13), because the value stored under the variable name I would be incremented by 3 instead of 1 each time.

```
cc  12345 6789...

         DIMENSIØN FIG(15)
         READ(5,1,END=99) (FIG(I),I = 1,15,3)
1        FØRMAT (F5.1)
```

An indexed subscript in a READ or WRITE statement that references the two-dimensional array named RATE is shown in the following illustration:

```
cc   12345 6789...

         DIMENSIØN RATE(5,5)
         READ (5,1) ((RATE(I,J),J=1,5),I=1,5)
1        FORMAT (5F3.2)
```

The following illustration shows the use of a nested DØ loop to accomplish the same task as the previous illustration:

```
cc 123456789...

        DIMENSIØN RATE(5,5)
        DØ 2 I = 1,5
        DØ 2 J = 1,5
        READ (5,1) RATE(I,J)
1       FØRMAT (5F3.2)
2       CØNTINUE
```

If it is desirable, several subscripted array names can be indexed in the same READ or WRITE statement and the array names can have one, two, or three subscripts depending upon whether the array was one-, two-, or three-dimensional. For example, in the following illustration the arrays named RATE and CØMP have two subscripts reflecting the fact that they are two-dimensional arrays:

```
cc 123456789...

        DIMENSIØN RATE(4,3),CØMP(4,3)
        READ (5,1,END=99 ((RATE(IØ,ID),CØMP(IØ,ID=1,3),
1       IØ=1,4)
1       FØRMAT (3F5.2)
```

In the preceding illustration, the data would be stored in array elements of each array in the following sequence:

```
RATE(1,1)
CØMP(1,1)
RATE(1,2)
CØMP(1,2)
RATE(1,3)
CØMP(1,3)
RATE(2,1)
CØMP(2,1)
RATE(2,2)
CØMP(2,2)
RATE(2,3)
CØMP(2,3)
RATE(3,1)
CØMP(3,1)
RATE(3,2)
CØMP(3,2)
RATE(3,3)
CØMP(3,3)
RATE(4,1)
CØMP(4,1)
RATE(4,2)
CØMP(4,2)
RATE(4,3)
CØMP(4,3)
```

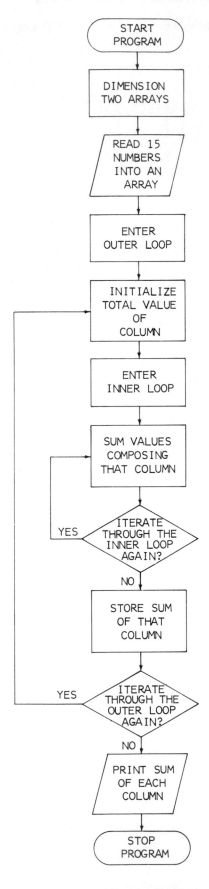

Figure 6-5. A Flowchart of the Program.

Note that the normal order of filling array elements with data is not being followed in the three illustrations on page 93. Rather, starting with the first row all of the column array elements in that row are filled from left to right prior to the filling of any of the array elements in the second row. Next, all of the column array elements in the second row are filled from left to right prior to the filling of any of the array elements in the third row. Finally, all of the array elements in the third row are filled from left to right. If there are not enough data to fill all of the array elements of an array, the unfilled array elements will contain data of some nature. However, as long as these unfilled array elements are not used in the program, there is no problem. However, if they are to be used then some programming action is required to store desired data in these array elements.

If there is more available data than is capable of being stored in the array elements of an array, it will not be read into the computer's memory by the READ statement.

A Complete Illustration of the Implied DØ Loop   The following program reads 15 numbers into a two-dimensional array. The sum of each column of the array is then calculated and printed by the printer.

```
cc  123456789...


C       CALCULATIØN ØF THE SUM ØF EACH CØLUMN ØF AN ARRAY
        DIMENSIØN TØTAL(3),SPACE(5,3)
        READ (5,1,END=99) ((SPACE(I,J),J = 1,3), I = 1,5)
1       FØRMAT (3F5.2)
        DØ 4 J=1,3
        SUM = 0
        DØ 3 I=1,5
        SUM = SUM+SPACE(I,J)
3       CØNTINUE
        TØTAL(J) = SUM
4       CØNTINUE
        WRITE (6,5) TØTAL
5       FØRMAT ('1','THE SUM ØF EACH ØF THREE CØLUMNS
       1ØF THE ARRAY NAMED SPACE IS',1X,F7.2,5X,F7.2,
       25X,F7.2)
99      STØP
        END
```

In the preceding program, an implied DØ loop is used to read the 15 numbers into the two-dimensional array named SPACE, which has 5 rows and 3 columns. A "nested" DØ loop is used to calculate the sum of each column and store it under an array element of the array named TØTAL. After the sum of each of the columns is calculated, the three sums are printed by the printer.

QUESTIONS

1. What is an array?
2. When is it desirable to use an array?
3. What is the function of the DIMENSIØN specification statement?
4. What additional ability do the explicit specification statements have over the DIMENSIØN specification statement?
5. Where must a specification statement creating an array be located in a program?

6. If in a specification statement an array name had three unsigned integer numbers enclosed in parentheses immediately following it, what does each number specify?

7. What is a subscript?

8. What is the distinct difference in meaning between an array name and accompanying one, two, or three unsigned integer numbers enclosed in parentheses located in a specification statement and an array name and accompanying subscript in another type of program statement such as a READ, WRITE, or arithmetic or logical assignment statement?

9. What is the normal order of filling the array elements composing an array with data?

10. What is the function of an array element?

11. What is the function of an indexed subscript?

12. In what kind of program statements may be indexed subscript be located?

EXERCISES

1. Write the program statements necessary to transfer a two-character integer number into array elements NØB(1), NØB(3), and NØB(5) of a single-dimensional array named NØB, which must be created and allocated 5 storage spaces.

2. Write the program statements necessary to transfer a 1 through 5 integer number into the first 25 array elements of a single-dimensional array named M, which must be created and allocated 50 storage spaces.

3. Rewrite the program statements written in response to exercise number 2 to transfer a number into each even-numbered array element of the array.

4. Write the program statements to transfer a one-character integer number into all of the array elements of a single-dimensional array named IN, which must be created and allocated 100 storage spaces.

5. Rewrite the program statements written in response to exercise number 4 to transfer each number stored in the odd array elements of the array into a record located on a printer.

Chapter 7

SUBPROGRAMS

In certain situations, it is desirable to write a program that requires, at various points within the program, identical computation to be performed on different data. While it is possible to rewrite the group of statements at each point within the program, it is more efficient to write what is called a *subprogram* composed of this group of statements and refer to it at each appropriate point in the program. This has the same effect as though the group of statements were written at each appropriate point in the program.

A subprogram is a group of statements that solves part of an overall problem and as such cannot be used by itself, but rather as part of a larger program. The use of a subprogram simplifies the writing of a program that requires the performance of the same computations on different data at various points within the program.

A subprogram is either directly or indirectly connected to a main program by a *calling* program. The calling program may be either the main program itself or another subprogram that is either directly or indirectly connected to the main program. A subprogram can never directly, indirectly, or through any of its entry points refer to itself.

There are two classes of programmer-supplied subprograms in the FORTRAN language: FUNCTIØN subprograms and SUBRØUTINE subprograms. In addition, there is a group of FUNCTIØN subprograms supplied as part of the FORTRAN system, which has been written by either the computer manufacturer or staff programmers at various computer installations. Finally, statement functions, although not subprograms, are similar to FUNCTIØN subprograms and thus are discussed in this chapter.

FORTRAN-SUPPLIED SUBPROGRAMS

A FORTRAN-supplied subprogram is a group of statements that is part of the FORTRAN compiler. As such, the statements need not be written, but rather only called by writing the subprogram name, immediately followed by one or more arguments, is an *arithmetic expression* located in the calling program. The number stored under each of the one or more arguments is transferred to its appropriate location in the sub-program; the program statements composing the subprogram are executed; and the resultant value is transferred back to the calling program where it replaces the subprogram name and its arguments. Figure 7-1 illustrates the general form of the FORTRAN-supplied subprogram statement:

```
cc  123456 789...

    bbbbb  ...sn(arg₁,arg₂,...,argₙ)...
```

where

$bbbbb$ represents an unsigned 1 through 5 integer number that is required only if a transfer is made to this statement from another program statement.

sn represents the subprogram name.

(a special character that is a requirement of the FORTRAN language.

$arg_1, arg_2, \ldots, arg_n$ represent one or more arguments, each of which must be separated by a comma, that are either literally transferred or are the means through which number(s) are transferred to the subprogram from the calling program. An argument can be a specific type of number, variable name, arithmetic expression, array element, FORTRAN-supplied subprogram name, FUNCTIØN subprogram name, or SUBRØUTINE subprogram name. A subprogram name may or may not be accompanied by one or more arguments.

)   a special character that is a requirement of the FORTRAN language.

Figure 7-1. The General Form of the FORTRAN-Supplied Subprogram Statement.

Each FORTRAN-supplied subprogram performs a specific function. While most of these subprograms perform a specific mathematical function, several of them convert one type of number to another type of number. Figure 7-2 is a partial listing of these subprograms and their functions (Appendix I contains a complete list of these subprograms and their functions):

FORTRAN-Supplied Subprogram Name	Function
EXP	Exponential
ALØG1Ø	Common logarithm
SIN	Trigonometric sine
CØS	Trigonometric cosine
SQRT	Square root (single precision floating-point number)
DSQRT	Square root (double precision floating-point number)
IABS	Absolute value (integer number)
ABS	Absolute value (single precision floating-point number)
FLØAT	Convert an integer type number to a single precision floating-point type number
IFIX	Convert a single precision floating-point number to an integer number

Figure 7-2. A Partial Listing of FORTRAN-Supplied Subprograms.

The following is an illustration of the SQRT subprogram with the various types of possible arguments:

```
cc  123456789...

           DIMENSIØN TØTAL(50)
    1      A = SQRT(31.10)
    2      B = SQRT(Z)
    3      C = SQRT(X-Y+100.)
    4      D = SQRT(TØTAL(I))
    5      E = SQRT(ABS(Z))
    6      F = SQRT(PRICE(A))
    7      G = SQRT(SUM(A))
```

In the first arithmetic statement of the preceding illustration, the square root of the number 31.10 will be stored under the variable name A; in the second arithmetic statement, the square root of the single precision floating-point number stored under the variable name Z will be stored under the variable name B; in the third arithmetic statement, the square root of the result of the evaluation of the arithmetic expression X−Y+100. will be stored under the variable name C; in the fourth arithmetic statement, the square root of the single precision floating-point number stored under the array element TØTAL(I) will be stored under the variable name D; in the fifth arithmetic statement, the square root of the absolute value of Z, which is returned from the execution of the FORTRAN-supplied subprogram named ABS, will be stored under the variable name E; in the sixth arithmetic statement, the square root of the number returned from the execution of the FUNCTIØN subprogram named PRICE will be stored under the variable name F; and in the last arithmetic statement, the square root of the number returned from the execution of the SUBRØUTINE subprogram named SUM will be stored under the variable name G.

FUNCTIØN SUBPROGRAMS

A FUNCTIØN subprogram is a group of statements that is written to perform a specific task. The group of statements composing the subprogram should immediately follow the calling program. This makes it possible for the subprogram to be called at the appropriate time during execution of the calling program. Similar to a FORTRAN-supplied subprogram, the FUNCTIØN subprogram name and the immediately following one or more arguments are written in an *arithmetic expression* located in the calling program.

The FUNCTIØN statement must be the first statement in the subprogram. Any kind of statement, except another FUNCTIØN, SUBRØUTINE, or BLØCK DATA statement, can be located in the subprogram. If an IMPLICIT statement (see Chapter 8) is located in the subprogram, it must immediately follow the FUNCTIØN statement. Figure 7-3 illustrates the general form of the FUNCTIØN subprogram statement:

```
cc  123456789...

    bbbbb  Type FUNCTIØN sn(darg₁,darg₂,...,dargₙ)
```

where

> *bbbbb* represents an optional unsigned 1 through 5 integer number.
>
> *Type* represents either the optional key word INTEGER, REAL, DØUBLE PRECISIØN, LØGICAL, or COMPLEX. One of these five key words is

                    to be used only if the type of the number
                    returned to the calling program is to be
                    different from the type implied by the first
                    alphabetic character of the subprogram name.
FUNCTIØN   FORTRAN key word that distinguishes this state-
                    ment from the other kinds of statements in the
                    program.
      sn represents the subprogram name. It must appear
                    at least once in the subprogram either (1) in
                    the list of a READ statement, (2) as the sym-
                    bolic name on the left side of the equal sign
                    of either an arithmetic or logical statement,
                    or (3) as an argument in a CALL statement.
        (a special character that is a requirement of
                    the FORTRAN language.
$darg_1, darg_2, \ldots, darg_n$ represents one or more dummy arguments, each
                    of which can be a variable, logical variable,
                    array element, array name, FORTRAN-supplied
                    subprogram name, another FUNCTIØN subprogram
                    name, or a SUBRØUTINE subprogram name. The
                    dummy arguments must be separated by a comma.
                    There must be at least one dummy argument and
                    each symbolic name can be used only once. A
                    subprogram name may or may not be accompanied
                    by one or more of its arguments. Each var-
                    iable, logical variable, and array name can
                    be enclosed in slashes.
)   a special character that is a requirement of
                    the FORTRAN language.

Figure 7-3. The General Form of the FUNCTIØN Subprogram Statement.

The following is an illustration of this statement:

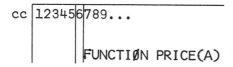

```
cc 123456789...

    FUNCTIØN PRICE(A)
```

In the preceding illustration, a FUNCTIØN subprogram is assigned the name PRICE and the variable name
A is a dummy argument. When the FUNCTIØN subprogram name is written in an arithmetic expression of
an arithmetic statement located in a calling program, it will be immediately followed by an argument
enclosed in a set of parentheses. If there is a number stored under that argument, it will be transferred and
stored under the dummy argument A at the beginning of the execution of the subprogram. The dummy
argument A is then used within the subprogram wherever the number stored under the argument in the
calling program is required. When execution of the subprogram is completed, the number stored under the
subprogram named PRICE is transferred back to and stored under the subprogram named PRICE in the
arithmetic expression of the calling program.

     A FUNCTIØN subprogram name must be assigned a datum in the subprogram. In addition, one or
more of the dummy arguments accompanying the subprogram name can also return a datum to the calling
program. Similar to the subprogram name, each dummy argument that is to return a datum to the calling
program must appear in the subprogram either (1) in the list of a READ statement, (2) as the symbolic
name on the left side of the equal sign of either an arithmetic or logical statement, or (3) as an argument in

a CALL statement. Each of the returned data will be stored under its corresponding argument in the arithmetic expression of the arithmetic statement in the calling program. However, if a datum are returned to both the FUNCTION subprogram name and one or more of its arguments, only the datum stored under the FUNCTIØN subprogram name will be used by the computer in calculating the arithmetic expression's resultant value.

Similar to a FORTRAN-supplied subprogram name and its argument(s), the first character of a FUNCTIØN subprogram name and its argument(s) normally indicates the type of datum that can be stored under it. However, if the FUNCTIØN subprogram name and/or any of its arguments of a called subprogram is specified to be a different type than the type implied by its character, the type of the subprogram name and/or any of its dummy arguments in the calling program must be similarly specified.

The one or more arguments accompanying the FUNCTIØN subprogram name in a calling program and their corresponding dummy argument accompanying the subprogram name in the FUNCTIØN statement in a called subprogram must agree in order, number, and type. That is, the first argument in a calling program replaces the first dummy argument in a called subprogram, etc.; the number of arguments in a calling program must be equal to the number of dummy arguments in a called subprogram; and the type of the arguments in a calling program must be the same as the type of their corresponding dummy arguments in a called subprogram. The symbolic name of an argument in a calling program can be either the same as or different than the symbolic name of its corresponding dummy argument in the called subprogram.

If an array name is used as a dummy argument, it must be specified as an array in either a DIMENSIØN or explicit specification statement in the subprogram prior to any other statement that references it. The number of allocated computer memory storage spaces can be either the same as or less than the number of storage spaces allocated to the array in the calling program. The basis for allocating less than the number of storage spaces allocated to the array in the calling program would be the need to use fewer than the allocated number of storage spaces during this particular calling of the subprogram. To provide for reallocating the number of storage spaces for an array each time the subprogram is called, the argument(s) and variable dummy argument(s) that are to be used as subscript(s) should be variable names instead of integer numbers, so that the unsigned integer numbers specifying the number of storage spaces that are to be allocated each time to the array can be transferred from the calling program to the called program.

If a dummy argument is enclosed in slashes, it is referred to in the subprogram by its location. When a dummy argument is referenced by location, the subprogram in which it is located reserves no storage space for it, which it would otherwise do if the dummy argument were not enclosed in slashes. Instead, the subprogram uses the storage space reserved for the corresponding argument of the dummy argument in the calling program for its arithmetic or logical calculations.

The statement numbers and symbolic names used in a FUNCTIØN subprogram are completely independent of those used in the calling program and those used in any other subprograms called by that calling program. As such, the same statement numbers and symbolic names can be used in a calling program and each of its called subprograms with the same effect as if they were unique.

THE RETURN STATEMENT

After executing the appropriate program statements in a FUNCTIØN subprogram, the computer does not stop execution of the program, but rather returns to the calling program. For this reason, one or more RETURN statements are appropriately used in a subprogram rather than the STØP statement. Figure 7-4 illustrates the general form of this statement:

```
cc │123456│789...
   │      │
   │bbbbb │RETURN
```

where

     bbbbb   represents an unsigned 1 through 5 integer number that is required only if a transfer is made to this statement from another program statement.

RETURN   FORTRAN key word that distinguishes this statement from
the other kinds of statements in the program.

Figure 7-4.   The General Form of the RETURN Statement.

Upon executing the RETURN statement, execution of the statements in the subprogram is terminated and
the computed data and control are returned to the calling program. The normal sequence of program
execution after control is returned to the calling program is for the computer to execute the next executable statement following the statement that referenced the subprogram. For the same reason discussed in
Chapter 4, the last physical statement of a FUNCTIØN subprogram must be an END statement.

Figure 7-5 illustrates two calling statements and Figure 7-6 illustrates the called FUNCTIØN
subprogram.

```
cc│ 12345│6│789...



        .
        .
        .
    │CØST = DEL(A)+STØR
        .
        .
        .
    │IF (Z-DEL(B)) 3,7,12
        .
        .
        .
```

Figure 7-5.   A Calling Program.

```
cc│ 12345│6│789...


    │FUNCTIØN DEL(A)
    │IF (A) 5,10,15
  5 │DEL= A*2.5
    │RETURN
 10 │DEL = A+5.
    │RETURN
 15 │DEL = A/10.
    │RETURN
    │END
```

Figure 7-6.   The Called FUNCTIØN Subprogram.

In executing the arithmetic statement illustrated in Figure 7-5, the computer will first call the
subprogram named DEL (Figure 7-6) and transfer to and store under the dummy argument A the number
stored under the argument A. The subprogram will then execute the IF statement and depending upon
whether the number stored under the argument A is negative, zero, or positive, transfer to the program
statement assigned statement number 5, 10, or 15, respectively. After executing that statement, the number
stored under the subprogram named DEL will be returned to the calling program where it will replace DEL.

That number and the number stored under the variable name STØR will then be added together and the sum stored under the variable name CØST.

In executing the IF statement illustrated in Figure 7-5, the computer will again first call the subprogram named DEL and perform the same sequence of steps that was performed in executing the arithmetic statement. The returned number will replace DEL in the calling program and then be subtracted from the number stored under the variable name Z. Depending upon whether the result is negative, zero, or positive, the computer will transfer to the program statement assigned either statement number 3, 7, or 12, respectively.

SUBRØUTINE SUBPROGRAMS

The general operation of a SUBRØUTINE subprogram is in many respects similar to a FUNCTIØN subprogram. The three principal differences between the two classes of subprograms are (1) whereas a FUNCTIØN subprogram is called by citing its name accompanied by one or more arguments in an arithmetic expression located in the calling program, a SUBRØUTINE subprogram is called by a CALL statement in the calling program; (2) whereas a FUNCTIØN subprogram must always return at least one datum to the calling program, a SUBRØUTINE subprogram does not have to return any datum to the calling program; and (3) whereas in a FUNCTIØN subprogram data are returned to the calling program via the FUNCTIØN subprogram name and possibly one or more of its dummy arguments, in a SUBRØUTINE subprogram if one or more data are returned, it is via one or more of the dummy arguments located in the SUBRØUTINE statement. Figure 7-7 illustrates the general form of the SUBRØUTINE subprogram statement.

```
cc  123456789...

    bbbbb  SUBRØUTINE sn(darg₁,darg₂,...,dargₙ)
```

where

bbbbb	represents an optional unsigned 1 though 5 integer number.
SUBRØUTINE	FORTRAN key word that distinguishes this statement from the other kinds of statements in the subprogram.
sn	represents the subprogram name. It must not appear in any other statement in the subprogram.
(	a special character that is a requirement of the FORTRAN language only if one or more dummy arguments follow it.
darg₁,darg₂,...,dargₙ	represents one or more optional dummy arguments, each of which can be either a variable, logical variable, array name, FORTRAN-supplied subprogram name, FUNCTIØN subprogram name, another SUBRØUTINE subprogram name, or an asterisk that denotes a return point specified by a statement number in the calling program. The dummy arguments must be separated by a comma. A subprogram name may or may not be accompanied by one or more of its arguments. Each symbolic name can be used only once in the statement. Each variable, logical variable, and array name can be enclosed in slashes.
)	a special character that is a requirement of the FORTRAN language only if one or more dummy arguments precede it.

Figure 7-7. The General Form of the SUBRØUTINE Subprogram Statement.

Similar to a FUNCTIØN subprogram, the statements composing a SUBRØUTINE subprogram should immediately follow the calling program. The SUBRØUTINE statement must be the first statement in the subprogram. Also, any kind of statement except a FUNCTIØN, another SUBRØUTINE, or BLØCK DATA statement may be located in the subprogram. If an IMPLICIT statement is located in the subprogram, it must immediately follow the SUBRØUTINE statement.

If one or more dummy arguments are used to return one or more datum to a calling program, each dummy argument must appear in the subprogram either (1) in the list portion of a READ statement, (2) as the symbolic name on the left side of the equal sign of either an arithmetic or logical statement, or (3) as an argument in a CALL statement.

The SUBRØUTINE statement is referenced by a CALL statement in the calling program. Figure 7-8 illustrates the general form of this statement:

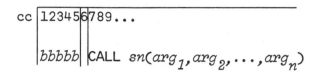

where

$bbbbb$ represents an unsigned 1 through 5 integer number that is required only if a transfer is made to this statement from another statement.

CALL   FORTRAN key word that distinguishes this statement from the other kinds of statements in the program.

sn represents the subprogram name.

(a special character that is a requirement of the FORTRAN language only if one or more arguments follow it.

$arg_1, arg_2, \ldots, arg_n$ represents one or more optical arguments, each of which can be either a literal, variable name, arithmetic or logical expression, array element, array name, FORTRAN-supplied subprogram name, FUNCTIØN subprogram name, SUBRØUTINE subprogram name, or $\&n$ where n is a calling program statement number, and be separated by a comma. Each symbolic name can be used only once.

)   a special character that is a requirement of the FORTRAN language only if one or more argu- precede it.

Figure 7-8.   The General Form of the CALL Statement.

The FUNCTIØN subprogram and the SUBRØUTINE subprogram are similar in five basic ways: (1) an argument in a CALL statement can transfer either itself or the datum stored under it to its corresponding dummy argument and/or can (except if the argument is a literal) have a datum returned from the called subprogram and stored under it, (2) the arguments accompanying the SUBRØUTINE subprogram name in the CALL statement and the dummy arguments accompanying the subprogram name in the SUBRØUTINE statement must agree in order, number, and type, (3) the symbolic name of an argument in a calling program can be either the same as or different than the symbolic name of its corresponding dummy argument, (4) an array name used as a dummy argument must be specified in either a DIMENSIØN or explicit specification statement in the program prior to any other statement that references it, and (5) the statement numbers and symbolic names used in a SUBRØUTINE subprogram are completely independent of those used in the calling program and those used in any other subprograms called by that calling program.

Figure 7-9 illustrates a CALL statement without arguments and Figure 7-10 illustrates the called SUBRØUTINE subprogram.

```
cc 123456 789...


          CALL TITLE
```

Figure 7-9.   An Illustration of the CALL Statement without Arguments.

```
cc 123456 789...



          SUBRØUTINE TITLE
          WRITE (6,1)
   1      FØRMAT ('1',T25,'SAMMY''S DEPARTMENT STØRE''S
          1FIRST QUARTER ENDING INVENTØRY')
          RETURN
          END
```

Figure 7-10.   The Called SUBRØUTINE Subprogram.

In the preceding illustrations, nothing is transferred either to the SUBRØUTINE subprogram or returned from it to the calling program. Rather, the computer transfers to the subprogram, prints SAMMY'S DEPARTMENT STØRE'S FIRST QUARTER ENDING INVENTØRY at the top of a page of printer printout, and then returns to the calling program.

Figure 7-11 illustrates a CALL statement with arguments in a calling program and Figure 7-12 illustrates the called SUBRØUTINE subprogram:

```
cc 123456 789...


          CALL PRICE(A,B)
```

Figure 7-11.   An Illustration of the CALL Statement with Arguments.

```
cc 123456 789...



          SUBRØUTINE PRICE(A,B)
          CØST = A*2.85+B
          B = CØST*4.
          RETURN
          END
```

Figure 7-12.   The Called SUBRØUTINE Subprogram.

In the preceding illustrations, the computer will transfer the number stored under the variable names A and B from the calling program to the called subprogram. It then executes the two arithmetic statements and returns the *new* number stored under the variable name B to the calling program.

The RETURN Statement   The use of both the RETURN and END statements in a SUBRØUTINE subprogram is the same as their use in a FUNCTIØN subprogram, except for one addition: it is possible to follow the key word RETURN with either an integer number or integer variable name with a number stored under it whose value, say *n*, denotes, counting from left to right, the *nth* statement number in the dummy argument list of the SUBRØUTINE subprogram.

Figure 7-13 illustrates the calling program and Figure 7-14 illustrates the called SUBRØUTINE subprogram having statement numbers as some of their arguments and dummy arguments:

```
cc  123456789...

        CALL SUBPRØ(I,J,K,&25,&50)
        NUMBER = I-J
        .
        .
        .
   25   NUMBER = I-K
        .
        .
        .
   50   NUMBER = J-K
        .
        .
        .
```

Figure 7-13. A Calling Program.

```
cc  123456789...

        SUBRØUTINE SUBPRØ(L,M,N,*,*,)
        .
        .
        .
   5    IF (Z) 10,20,30
   10   RETURN
   20   RETURN 1
   30   RETURN 2
        END
```

Figure 7-14. The Called Subprogram.

In the preceding illustrations, when the program statement assigned statement number 5 is executed, the computer will return to the program statement either immediately following the CALL statement or the statement assigned statement number 25 or 50, depending upon whether Z is negative, zero, or positive.

MULTIPLE ENTRY INTO A SUBPROGRAM

As previously discussed, the standard (normal) entry into a FUNCTIØN subprogram is made via the use of a subprogram name in an arithmetic expression of an arithmetic statement in a calling program. As also previously discussed, the standard entry into a SUBRØUTINE subprogram from a calling program is made via a CALL statement that refers to the subprogram name. In both of the above situations, entry into the called subprogram is made at the first executable statement following either the FUNCTIØN or SUBRØUTINE statement.

It is also possible to enter either a FUNCTIØN or a SUBRØUTINE subprogram by referencing an ENTRY statement in the called subprogram. In this situation, entry into the called subprogram is made at the first executable program statement following the ENTRY statement. Therefore it is possible, via the location of the ENTRY statement within the called subprogram, to "bypass" (not execute) several statements. Figure 7-15 illustrates the general form of this statement.

```
cc 123456789...

   bbbbb ENTRY sn(darg₁,darg₂,...,dargₙ)
```

where

bbbbb	represents an optional unsigned 1 through 5 integer number.
ENTRY	FORTRAN key word that distinguishes this statement from the other kinds of statements in the program.
sn	represents a symbolic name.
(	a special character that is a requirement of the FORTRAN language.
$darg_1, darg_2, \ldots, darg_n$	represents one or more dummy arguments, each of which must agree in order and type with its corresponding argument accompanying the symbolic name located in either the arithmetic expression of an arithmetic statement or the CALL statement in the calling program. The symbolic name of an argument and its corresponding dummy argument either may or may not be the same. One or more of the dummy arguments may be enclosed in slashes.
)	a special character that is a requirement of the FORTRAN language.

Figure 7-15.   The General Form of the ENTRY Statement.

An ENTRY statement is a non-executable program statement. As such, it does not affect the sequence of the execution of the program statements composing the subprogram in which it is located. An ENTRY statement cannot be located within the range of a DØ statement in the subprogram. The use of an ENTRY statement does not alter the rule that all statement functions in the subprogram must precede the first executable statement of the subprogram.

In the following illustrations,

```
cc 123456789...

      .
      .
      .
   RUG = TAB(A,B,C)
      .
      .
      .
   TØTAL = UNIT(D)*10
      .
      .
      .
```

Figure 7-16.   A Calling Program.

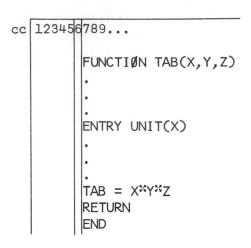

Figure 7-17. The Called Subprogram.

the FUNCTIØN subprogram named TAB is first entered at the first executable program statement after the FUNCTIØN statement (standard entry) and the number stored under each of the arguments A, B, and C is transferred to its corresponding dummy argument in the called subprogram. The subprogram is executed; when the RETURN statement is executed, execution of the statements in the subprogram is terminated and the computed number stored under the variable name TAB and control are returned to the calling program; and the number stored under TAB is stored under the variable name RUG. The next time the called subprogram named TAB is entered, entry occurs at the first executable program statement after the ENTRY statement. The number stored under the argument D in the calling program is transferred to the dummy argument X in the called subprogram and replaces the number stored under it. (With respect to using an ENTRY statement in a FUNCTIØN or SUBRØUTINE subprogram, each datum stored under an argument in a calling program must be transferred to the argument's corresponding dummy argument in the FUNCTIØN or SUBRØUTINE subprogram statement in the called subprogram *prior* to transferring a datum from the calling program to one of the dummy arguments in an ENTRY statement in the called subprogram.) No new numbers are transferred to the dummy arguments Y and Z. Thus, the number stored under Y and under Z will be changed only by operations in the subprogram. Assuming neither one of these two numbers are changed, the new number stored under the variable name TAB is computed by multiplying the new number stored under the variable name X times the unchanged number stored under the variable name Y times the unchanged number stored under the variable name Z. When the RETURN statement is executed, the new number stored under the variable name TAB will be returned to the calling program and stored under the variable name UNIT. This number will then be multiplied by the number 10., and the result stored under the variable name TØTAL.

THE USE OF SUBPROGRAM NAMES, WITH OR WITHOUT THEIR ARGUMENTS, AS ARGUMENTS

A FØRTRAN-supplied or FUNCTIØN subprogram name can be used as an argument in one of two possible ways: (1) it can be executed and the resultant datum transferred to the called subprogram or (2) it can be transferred to the called subprogram and the subprogram is executed during the execution of the called subprogram. Figure 7-18 illustrates the former possible way of using a subprogram name as an argument.

In the following illustration, the FUNCTIØN subprogram named PØS will be transferred the number stored under the argument Z. The subprogram will then be executed and a number returned and stored under

```
cc│ 123456789...
  │ │
  │ │ .
  │ │ .
  │ │ .
  │ │ X = 25.
  │ │ Y = 50.
  │ │ Z = 100.
  │ │ CALL RANK(X,Y,PØS(Z))
  │ │ .
  │ │ .
  │ │ .
```

Figure 7-18.   An Illustration of a Subprogram Name and Its Accompanying Argument Used as an Argument of Another Subprogram Name.

PØS. PØS becomes the third argument of the SUBRØUTINE subprogram named RANK. It, along with each number stored under the arguments X and Y, will then be transferred to the subprogram named RANK. Figure 7-19 illustrates the latter possible way of using another subprogram name as an argument:

```
cc│ 123456789...
  │ │
  │ │ EXTERNAL SQRT,JØB
  │ │ .
  │ │ .
  │ │ .
  │ │ A = 100.
  │ │ CALL WØRK(A,SQRT,JØB,B)
  │ │ .
  │ │ .
  │ │ .
```

```
cc│ 123456789...
  │ │
  │ │ SUBRØUTINE WØRK(A,SQRT,JØB,B)
  │ │ C = 10.5
  │ │ B = SQRT(A)+JØB(C)
  │ │ RETURN
  │ │ END
  │ │ FUNCTIØN JØB(C)
  │ │ .
  │ │ .
  │ │ .
  │ │ RETURN
  │ │ END
```

Figure 7-19.   An Illustration of a Subprogram Name Used as an Argument of Another Subprogram Name.

In the preceding illustration, the SUBRØUTINE subprogram named WØRK will be transferred the number stored under the argument A. When the second arithmetic statement in the subprogram is executed, the FORTRAN-supplied subprogram SQRT will be transferred the number stored under the argument A. The resultant number will replace SQRT(A). The FUNCTIØN subprogram named JØB will then be transferred the number stored under the argument C. The subprogram will be executed and the returned number will be stored under JØB. This number and the number stored under SQRT(A) will then be added together and the sum will be stored under the variable name B. Finally, the number stored under the variable name A (100.), the number returned from the FORTRAN-supplied subprogram SQRT and stored under SQRT(A), the number returned from the FUNCTIØN subprogram JØB and stored under JØB, and the number stored under the variable name B will be transferred through the dummy arguments A, SQRT, JØB, and B, respectively, to the calling program.

STATEMENT FUNCTIONS

A statement function is similar to a FUNCTIØN subprogram. However, it is not a subprogram because it is located in the same program unit that it references, whereas a called subprogram is not in the same program unit as the program unit calling it. A statement function specifies certain arithmetical and/or logical operations to be performed whenever that statement function name, accompanied by one or more arguments, appears in either an arithmetic or logical expression respectively of an arithmetic or logical statement in that program unit. All specification statements must precede all statement function statements, and all statement function statements must precede the first executable statement in the program unit. Figure 7-20 illustrates the general form of this statement.

```
cc  123456789...

    bbbbb  sfn(darg₁,darg₂,...,dargₙ) = expression
```

where

$bbbbb$ represents an optional unsigned 1 through 5 integer number.

sfn represents a statement function name.

$($ a special character that is a requirement of the FORTRAN language.

$darg_1, darg_2, \ldots, darg_n$ represents one or more dummy arguments, each of which must be a varaible name separated by a comma. There must be at least one dummy argument and each variable name can be used only once. Each variable name must have had either a number or true or false condition stored under it.

$)$ a special character that is a requirement of the FORTRAN language.

$=$ a special character that is a requirement of the FORTRAN language.

$expression$ represents either an arithmetic or logical expression that must not contain an array element. It must contain at least all of the dummy arguments.

Figure 7-20.   The General Form of the Statement Function Statement.

When a statement function name, immediately followed by its arguments, appears in either an arithmetic or logical expression located in the same program unit, the computer transfers each number and/or condition stored under each variable name, through its corresponding dummy argument, to its corresponding variable name in the arithmetic or logical expression of the statement function. The expression is then evaluated and the result, which assumes the type of the statement function name, is transferred through the statement function name and its accompanying dummy arguments to the referencing program statement and replaces the statement function name and its accompanying arguments in the arithmetic or logical expression.

Each variable name can be located more than once in the expression of the statement function statement. Also, the expression can include variable names that are not dummy arguments. Finally, the dummy argument variable names in a statement function statement are completely independent of the same variable names used in any other statement in the program unit. This includes another statement function statement located in the program unit. Thus, a dummy argument variable name used either by itself or as a dummy argument in one or more other statement function statements could each have a different number or condition stored under it.

The following is an illustration of the statement function statement:

```
cc | 123456789...

            SUM(A,B) = WAGE*HØURS-(A*X)-(A*B)
            WAGE = 2.50
            HØURS = 40.
            X = .05
            TAX = 4.3
            FICA = 2.4
            HØSP = 25.
            STØCK = 10.
     1      NET = SUM(TAX,FICA)-HØSP-STØCK
            .
            .
            .
```

In the preceding illustration the computer, when it executes the program statement assigned statement number 1, will transfer each number stored under the variable names TAX and FICA, through their corresponding dummy arguments A and B, to their corresponding arguments in the arithmetic expression of the statement function statement. The arithmetic expression will then be executed and the result transferred, through the statement function name and its accompanying dummy arguments on the left side of the equal sign, back to the program statement assigned statement number 1 where it replaces the statement function name and its accompanying arguments. The computer then continues to execute that program statement.

THE EXPLICIT SPECIFICATION STATEMENT

In certain situations, it may be desirable to specify the type of either a FUNCTIØN subprogram name or a statement function name. This may be accomplished through the use of an explicit specification statement. Figure 7-21 illustrates the general form of this statement:

```
cc | 123456789...

            Type  an_1, an_2, ..., an_n
```

where

> *Type* represents either the key word INTEGER, REAL,
> DØUBLE PRECISIØN, or LØGICAL.
>
> $an_1, an_2, \ldots, an_n$ represents one or more FUNCTIØN subprogram names
> and their accompanying argument(s) and/or state-
> ment function names and their accompanying
> argument(s).

Figure 7-21. The General Form of the Explicit Specification Statement.

ASSOCIATED PROGRAM STATEMENTS

There are three program statements that are commonly used in conjunction with one or more of the subprogram statements discussed thus far in this chapter. These are the EXTERNAL, CØMMØN, and EQUIVALENCE statements.

The EXTERNAL Statement   The EXTERNAL statement specifies that a subprogram name used as an argument, without its argument(s), by another subprogram is to be considered a subprogram name rather than a variable name. This statement is a specification statement and must precede the first executable statement in the program in which it appears. Figure 7-22 illustrates the general form of this statement:

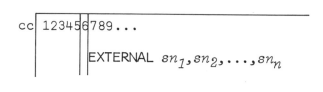

where

> EXTERNAL FORTRAN key word that distinguishes this statement
> from the other kinds of statements in the program.
>
> $sn_1, sn_2, \ldots, sn_n$ represents subprogram names, which, when written
> as an argument of another subprogram name without
> their arguments, are to be considered subprogram
> names rather than variable names.

Figure 7-22. The General Form of the EXTERNAL Statement.

The FORTRAN-supplied subprogram named SQRT in Figure 7-19 would have been considered a variable name, similar to variable names A and B, by the computer if the EXTERNAL statement had not been used to specify that it was a subprogram name.

The CØMMØN Statement   The CØMMØN statement is used when it is desirable to make one or more single storage spaces and/or arrays of storage spaces in the computer's memory simultaneously available to both a calling program and its one or more called subprograms. Thus, one or more datum can be read into the computer's memory and stored under either variable, logical variable, and/or array names by, say a main program, and be available for use by any of its called subprograms. A CØMMØN statement must be present in the calling program and each of its one or more called subprograms for the one or more storage spaces in the computer's memory to be simultaneously available to them.

The two primary advantages of using the CØMMØN statement instead of arguments and dummy arguments are that (1) it conserves computer memory space in that the designated memory space only has to be allocated once, even though it may be used by both a main program and one or more of its called subprograms; and (2) it eliminates the necessity of having to list the variable, logical variable, and/or array names as arguments in the calling program every time it is desirable to call a subprogram. A secondary advantage is that the main program will be executed faster due to the fact that the storage spaces designated by a CØMMØN statement are allocated during compilation of the program, whereas the storage spaces designated by arguments and dummy arguments are allocated during execution of the program.

The CØMMØN statement is a specification statement and thus must precede any statement function statements in the program. Also, a dummy argument cannot appear in this statement. Figure 7-23 illustrates the general form of this statement.

```
cc │123456│789...
   │      │
   │bbbbb │CØMMØN/ /or/vn₁/sn₁,sn₂,snₙ(in₁,in₂,in₃),...,/ /or
   │      │      /vnₙ/sn₁,sn₂,snₙ(inₙ,inₙ,inₙ)
```

where

bbbbb	represents an optional 1 through 5 integer number.
CØMMØN	FORTRAN key word that distinguishes this statement from the other kinds of statements in the program.
/ /,...,/ /	represents a blank common storage area. No characters, except one or more optional blanks, can be located between the pair of slashes.
/vn₁/,...,/vnₙ/	represents either a variable, logical variable, or array name, each of which must be separated by a comma.
sn₁, sn₂, snₙ	represents either a variable, logical variable, or array name, each of which must be separated by a comma.
(in₁,in₂,in₃,..., inₙ,inₙ,inₙ)	represents one, two, or three unsigned integer numbers enclosed in a pair of parentheses, each of which can be 1 through 7 characters in length, which specify the number of storage spaces to be allocated to the immediately preceding array name. If the immediately preceding *sn* is not an array name, this portion of the statement is not used. If there is more than one integer number, they must be separated by a comma. One, two, or three numbers are used, depending upon whether it is a one-, two-, or three-dimensional array. If the array is dimensioned earlier in the program in either a DIMENSIØN or explicit specification statement, it cannot be dimensioned again in a CØMMØN statement. (An array should be dimensioned in the statement in which it is first located in a program. The only exception to this is that an array that is a dummy argument in either a FUNCTIØN or SUBRØUTINE subprogram must first appear in a FUNCTIØN or SUBRØUTINE statement before it can appear in a statement that can dimension it.)

Figure 7-23. The General Form of the CØMMØN Statement.

There are two basic types of common storage areas: *blank* common and *labeled* common.

Blank Common   The use of a blank common storage area is particularly useful as a communications area in lengthy programs. In many instances, lengthy programs cannot be completely stored in the computer's memory because of the lack of enough storage space. Thus, they must be broken up into appropriate storable units. The first unit is stored in the computer's memory and executed; the second unit is then stored in the computer's memory and executed, etc. Throughout the execution of each of these units, any designated blank common storage area remains in one area of the computer's memory and the data stored in it by the first unit remains available to each succeeding unit. Thus, the blank common storage area provides a communication link among the program units.

A blank common storage area has no programmer-assigned name. Rather, it is specified in a CØMMØN statement by placing two slashes immediately prior to the variable, logical variable, and/or array names being assigned to the storage area. The two slashes can be omitted if the one or more symbolic names and/or array elements are the first ones following the key word CØMMØN. If one or more additional symbolic names and/or array elements are assigned to the storage area at another point in the CØMMØN statement, however, two slashes must immediately precede them.

The following is an illustration of the allocation of blank common storage area:

```
cc │1234567│89...
   │       │
   │       │CØMMØN A,B,C(10,10),D
```

In the preceding illustration, the variable names A and B, the two-dimensional array named C, and the variable name D are assigned, in that order, to the blank common storage area.

There can be only *one* blank common storage area in a program. It is possible to either increase or decrease the amount of allocated blank common storage area in different program units of a lengthy program. Finally, variables, logical variables, and array elements assigned to a blank common storage area cannot be assigned initial values.

Labeled Common   One or more labeled common storage areas, in contrast to the blank common storage area, should be used either whenever a program is capable of being completely stored in the computer's memory or as work areas and/or the communication of data within a program unit of a lengthy program that must be executed in two or more program units.

There can be many labeled common storage areas. Each labeled common storage area must have a name. Labeled common storage areas cannot be changed and as such must remain the same length as originally either implicitly or explicitly defined among program units of a lengthy program. Variable, logical variable, and array names can be assigned initial values by either a DATA and/or explicit specification statement, but only in a BLØCK DATA subprogram.

The following is an illustration of the allocation of a labeled common storage area:

```
cc │1234567│89...
   │       │
   │       │LØGICAL H
   │       │CØMMØN/ITEMS/X,Y,Z/TØTAL/D,T(100),S,H,U(35)
```

In the preceding illustration, the variable names X, Y, and Z are assigned, in that order, to the labeled common storage area named ITEMS and the variable name D, each of the array elements composing the single-dimensional array named T, the variable name S, the logical variable name H, and each of the array elements composing the array named U are assigned, in that order, to the labeled common storage area named TØTAL.

In summary, the following is an illustration of a CØMMØN statement designating both blank and labeled common storage areas.

```
cc 123456789...

      COMMON A,B,C/R/D,E,F//X,Y,Z
```

In the preceding illustration, the variable names A, B, C, X, Y and Z are assigned to the blank common storage area and the variable names D, E, and F are assigned to the labeled common storage area named R.

There can be more than one COMMON statement in a program. In such a situation, the computer allocates storage space for each variable, logical variable, and each of the array elements composing an array in the order in which they are assigned to either the blank or a particular labeled common storage area in the two or more COMMON statements. For example, the following two COMMON statements

```
cc 123456789...

      COMMON A,B,C/R/D,E/S/F/R/Q,U
      COMMON G,H/S/X,Y/R/P//W,T
```

have the same effect as the following single COMMON statement:

```
cc 123456789...

      COMMON A,B,C,G,H,W,T/R/D,E,Q,U,P/S/F,X,Y
```

In the preceding illustration, the computer assigns the variable names A, B, C, G, H, W, and T to the one allowable blank common storage area. It then assigns the variable names D, E, Q, U, and P and the variable names F, X, and Y in that order to their respective labeled common storage areas named R and S. As also indicated in the illustration, a labeled common storage area name can be used more than once in either the same COMMON statement or in more than one COMMON statement in a program.

An array assigned to either the blank or a particular labeled common storage area in a calling program and a called subprogram does not have to have the same symbolic name. The computer associates the corresponding array names by the order in which they appear in the COMMON statement. For example, the array names in the following calling program

```
cc 123456789...

          .
          .
          .
      COMMON/ABL/I,MIN(5,4)J,TNK(3,4)
      CALL BIC(...)
          .
          .
          .
```

could be written as follows in a called subprogram:

```
cc 123456789...

      SUBROUTINE BIC(...)
      COMMON/ABL/I,JOB(5,4),J,TNK(3,4)
```

A reference to the array element JØB (2,1) in the subprogram named BIC will cause the same number to be referenced as if the array element MIN (2,1) had been referenced in the calling program.

The storage of data in either the blank or a particular labeled common storage area is not limited to just one type of data. Any combination of data can be stored in either one of these two types of common storage areas. However, there must be agreement in type and byte length between a variable, logical variable, or array name in a calling program and its corresponding variable, logical variable, or array name in the called program. For example, the CØMMØN statements in the following calling program and its two called subprograms

```
cc 123456789...


       DØUBLE PRECISIØN A,B
       CØMMØN /ITEM/A/CØUNT/B/INCØM/I
```

                        Calling Program

```
cc 123456789...


       DØUBLE PRECISIØN C
       CØMMØN /ITEM/C/SIT/D/TØT/E/INCØM/J
```

                        Subprogram CALL1

```
cc 123456789...


       CØMMØN/WAGE/TØT(4)/INCØM/K
```

                        Subprogram CALL2

cause the computer to allocate 20 bytes in its memory for the main program and each of its two subprograms. Figure 7-24 is an illustration of this allocation in the computer's memory.

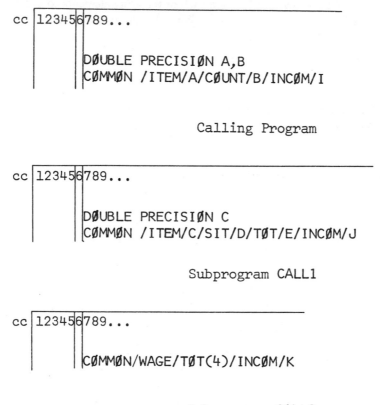

START	CØMMØN STORAGE AREA		END
ITEM A	CØUNT B		INCØM I

Calling Program

ITEM C	SIT D	SIT E	INCØM J

Subprogram CALL1

WAGE TØT(1)	WAGE TØT(2)	WAGE TØT(3)	WAGE TØT(4)	INCØM K

Subprogram CALL2

Figure 7-24. The Computer Memory Area Depicting the Use of a CØMMØN Statement in a Calling Program and Its Two Called Subprograms.

Because of agreement in type and byte length, the number stored under ITEM A can be retrieved by ITEM C and vice versa; and the number stored under INCØM I can be retrieved by either INCØM J or INCØM K and vice versa. However, because of nonagreement in byte length, no other such type of retrieval of a common number by either the main program or either one of its subprograms is possible. However, a number stored under either ITEM A or ITEM C will destroy any numbers stored in WAGE TØT(1) and WAGE TØT(2) and vice versa; and any number stored under CØUNT B will destroy any numbers stored under SIT D and TØT E and WAGE TØT(3) and WAGE TØT(4) and vice versa.

While it is not required, to increase execution efficiency the author suggests that when different types of data are designated for storage in the blank or a particular labeled common storage area they should be arranged in descending sequence according to length (the number of bytes allocated for a datum stored under either a variable or logical variable name or array element) in the CØMMØN statement. Normally, eight bytes are allocated for a double precision floating-point variable name or array element and four bytes are allocated for either an integer, single precision floating-point variable name, array element, or logical variable name. If this method of arranging the variable and array names in the blank or a common storage area is not feasible, then execution efficiency can be increased by appropriately inserting one or more dummy variable names of the required byte length to force proper alignment.

The EQUIVALENCE Statement   The EQUIVALENCE statement is also a means by which the storage space in the computer's memory allocated to either a main program and/or one or more of its called subprograms can be conserved. The use of this statement permits the same storage space in the computer's memory to be shared by two or more variable, logical variable names and/or array elements if the logic of a lengthy program composed of relatively independent units is such that they will not interfere with each other during execution of the program. It would also be desirable to use this statement if more than one symbolic name or array element was used in a program to represent the same datum. This might occur if two or more individuals were writing various units of a program.

The EQUIVALENCE statement is a specification statement and thus must precede any statement function statements in the program. Also, a dummy argument cannot appear in this statement. The EQUIVALENCE statement must not contradict either itself or any previously established equivalences in the program. Two symbolic names or array elements in either the blank or two or more labeled common storage areas cannot be made equivalent. However, a symbolic name or array element not in either the blank or a labeled common storage area can be made equivalent to a symbolic name or array element in either the blank or a labeled common storage area. Finally, like the CØMMØN statement, it is not required, but to increase execution efficiency it is recommended that when different types of symbolic names and array elements are being made equivalent, they should be arranged in descending sequence according to length. Figure 7-25 illustrates the general form of this statement.

```
cc  123456789...

    EQUIVALENCE (vn_1,vn_2,...,vn_n),(vn_1,vn_2,...,vn_n),...,
```

where

EQUIVALENCE	FORTRAN key word that distinguishes this statement from the other kinds of statements in the program.
(	a special character that is a requirement of the FORTRAN language.
$vn_1,vn_2,...,vn_n$	represents either variable names, logical variable names, or array elements which share the same storage space in the computer's memory.
)	a special character that is a requirement of the FORTRAN language.

Figure 7-25.   The General Form of the EQUIVALENCE Statement.

The following is an illustration of the EQUIVALENCE statement:

```
cc 123456789...

          EQUIVALENCE (A,B,C,D,E),(I,J,K,L)
```

In the preceding illustration, the variable names A, B, C, D, and E all share the same storage space and the variable names I, J, K, and L all share the same storage space in the computer's memory.

A subscript composed of two or three numbers accompanying an array name in an EQUIVALENCE statement specifies a normal ordered array element in either a two- or three-dimensional array. That is, in the following illustration RIG(3,2) specifies that particular array element in the two-dimensional array.

```
cc 123456789...


          DIMENSIØN RIG(5,4)
          EQUIVALENCE (H,RIG(3,2),S,T)
```

However, a subscript composed of only one number may specify a normal ordered array element in either a one-, two-, or three-dimensional array. For example, in the following illustration MIN(15) specifies the 15th storage space in the single-dimensional array.

```
cc 123456789...


          DIMENSIØN MIN(25)
          EQUIVALENCE (I,L,MIN(15),K)
```

In the following illustration, however, specification of the 6th normal ordered array element in a two-dimensional array may be written as either D(2,2) or D(6).

```
cc 123456789...


          DIMENSIØN D(4,5)
          EQUIVALENCE (X,D(2,2),Y)
```

```
cc 123456789...


          DIMENSIØN D(4,5)
          EQUIVALENCE (X,D(6),Y)
```

Both forms have the same meaning with respect to specifying the 6th array element.

If an array element not in the blank or a labeled common storage area is made equivalent to an array element in the blank or a labeled common storage area, it may implicitly equivalence the rest of the array elements in the array and in the process extend the size of the allocated common storage area. For example, the EQUIVALENCE statement in the following illustration

```
cc 123456789...


          CØMMØN X,Y,Z
          DIMENSIØN A(3)
          EQUIVALENCE (Y,A(1))
```

will cause the array element A(1) to share the same storage location as the variable name Y; array element A(2) to share the same storage location as the variable name Z; and the array element A(3) will cause the extension of the size of the blank common storage area A in the following manner:

```
X               (lowest location in the common storage area)
Y,A(1)
Z,A(2)
  A(3)          (highest location in the common storage area)
```

However, the size of the allocated common storage area cannot be extended so that array elements are added prior to the beginning of the established common storage area. For example, the EQUIV-ALENCE statement in the following illustration

```
cc│123456789...
  │
  │COMMON X,Y,Z
  │DIMENSION A(3)
  │EQUIVALENCE (Y,A(3))
```

is invalid because it would force the array element A(1) to precede the variable name X as follows:

```
  A(1)
X,A(2)          (lowest location in the common storage area)
Y,A(3)
Z               (highest location in the common storage area)
```

QUESTIONS

1. What is a subprogram? When would it be desirable to use a subprogram?
2. What is a calling program? What purpose does it serve?
3. What is the significant difference between a FORTRAN-supplied subprogram and a FUNCTION or SUBROUTINE subprogram?
4. Where must either a FUNCTION or SUBROUTINE statement be located in respectively a FUNCTION or SUBROUTINE subprogram?
5. What kind of statements can and cannot be located in a FUNCTION subprogram? In a SUB-ROUTINE subprogram?
6. How many arguments must transfer datum stored under them from a calling program to a FUNCTION subprogram and how many datum must be returned from the called FUNCTION subprogram to the calling program?
7. What three kinds of arguments must exist between the one or more arguments accompanying either the FUNCTION or SUBROUTINE subprogram name in a calling program and their corresponding dummy argument accompanying the subprogram name in the called subprogram?
8. Can the symbolic name of an argument in a calling program be different than the symbolic name of its corresponding dummy argument in the called subprogram?
9. Why can the same statement numbers and symbolic names be used in a calling program and each of its called FUNCTION or SUBROUTINE subprograms?
10. How does the computer know when an array name is used as a dummy argument in either a FUNCTION or SUBROUTINE statement?
11. Where must at least once a FUNCTION subprogram name and any dummy arguments accompanying a FUNCTION or SUBROUTINE name that are to return a datum to the calling program be located in the subprogram?
12. When a RETURN statement is executed in a FUNCTION or SUBROUTINE subprogram, what occurs?

13. What are the three principal differences between the two kinds of subprograms?
14. When a calling program calls either a FUNCTIØN or SUBRØUTINE subprogram, where does entry normally occur and where does entry occur if a reference is made in the calling program to an ENTRY statement in the called subprogram?
15. What are the two possible ways a subprogram name may be used as an argument?
16. Why isn't a statement function considered a subprogram?
17. What is the function of the EXTERNAL statement?
18. What is the function of the CØMMØN statement?
19. What is the function of the EQUIVALENCE statement?
20. How do the CØMMØN and EQUIVALENCE statements differ?

EXERCISES

1. Write a FUNCTIØN subprogram named TEST that computes the absolute value of several floating-point numbers stored in the computer's memory. After each absolute value has been calculated, return the number to the main program and calculate its square root. Then write both the original number and its square root.

2. Write a program that reads 25 employee punched cards, each containing an employee's identification number and weekly gross pay. Store the identification number in the array IDNR and the gross pay in the array GRØSS. Compute the amount of tax (the tax rate is 10%) via a statement function. Store the new pay in an array named NETPAY. After processing the last employee punched card, write each employee's identification number, gross pay, and net pay.

3. Write a main program that stores 4 floating-point numbers in an array named X and a SUBRØUTINE subprogram named TEST that computes the square root of these 4 numbers. After computing the square root of each of the 4 numbers, return to the main program and write each of the square roots. Both the main program and the called subprogram contain a labeled common storage area named A. The storage area in the main program contains the variable names A, B, C, and D; the storage area in the called subprogram contains an array named X, which is dimensioned 4 storage spaces. A FORTRAN statement in the main program should make the 4 array elements in the array X equivalent to the 4 variable names in the labeled common storage area.

4. Write a program that stores 4 floating-point numbers in an array named ITEM. Test each number to determine if it is either equal to or less than ten. If it is either equal to or less than ten, compute only the square of the number. If it is greater than ten, compute both the square and square root of the number. Perform all calculations in a FUNCTIØN subprogram named TEST. Differentiate between the two courses of action that can be taken in the called subprogram by the use of an ENTRY statement. Place the array ITEM in a labeled common storage area named A.

5. Write a program that stores 4 floating-point numbers in an array named ITEM, which is located in a labeled common storage area named A. Call a SUBRØUTINE subprogram named TEST and compute the square of each number. If the computed number is greater than ten, return to the calling program and compute its square root. If it is not, return to the calling program via a RETURN statement and do not compute its square root. Write each number, its square, and its square root (if any).

Chapter 8

ADDITIONAL FORTRAN STATEMENTS

The FORTRAN statements discussed in the first 7 chapters are the ones that will be most commonly used when writing a program. There are, however, several other less often used FORTRAN statements which, when writing a more complicated program, can in certain program situations be either more appropriately used in place of one or more of the already discussed statements or make either possible or easier the successful attainment of the objective of the program. Specifically, in many programming situations, the use of one or more of the following discussed statements results in a reduction in either programming time, program execution time, and/or computer memory storage space.

A DIFFERENT STYLE OF INPUT AND OUTPUT STATEMENTS

Up to this point, whenever the READ statement has been used to read data from one or more records of a data set located on a punch card reader or the WRITE statement has been used to write data into one or more records of a data set located on a printer, a specific data set reference number has been a component of each statement. The use of particular data set reference numbers presents no problem when the program is used in a computer installation that has assigned the same data set reference number to a data set that is located on either a card reader or a printer. However, as mentioned in Chapter 3 a particular data set reference number for a particular type of input or output device is assigned by the computer installation in which the device is located. Thus, an attempt could be made to execute a particular program in a computer installation that has assigned a *different* data set reference number to either the card reader and/or the printer. In such a situation, the program would not successfully execute.

There are many situations, however, when a particular program is written with the intention of it being executed in one or more computer installations that have possibly assigned different data set reference numbers to either the card reader, printer, and/or card punch. In order that the program may be readily usable in all of these computer installations, the following style of the READ, PRINT (this kind of statement is used instead of the WRITE statement when this style is used), and PUNCH (this kind of statement is used instead of the WRITE statement when this style is used and the data set is located on the card punch) statements may be used in place of the style of the READ and WRITE statement discussed in Chapter 3.

```
cc 123456789...

bbbbb READ n, list
        or
bbbbb PRINT n, list
        or
bbbbb PUNCH n, list
```

where

    bbbbb represents an unsigned 1 through 5 integer number that is required only if a transfer is made to this statement from another program statement.

READ
or PRINT FORTRAN key word that distinguishes this statement
or PUNCH from the other kinds of statements in the program.

    n represents the statement number of the FØRMAT statement that describes the particular form of the data being transferred either into or from the computer's memory.

    , a special character that is a requirement of the FORTRAN language.

list (for READ represents one or more variable, logical variable, statement) and/or array names, each of which must be separated by a comma. The data read from a record is stored in the computer's memory under these one or more variable, logical variable, and/or array names. The array name or names may be subscripted and these subscripts may be indexed.

    list represents one or more variable, logical variable, (for either the and/or array names, each of which must be separated PRINT or PUNCH by a comma. The datum stored under these one or statements) more variable names and/or array names is transferred from the computer's memory and written into one or more records. The array name or names may be subscripted and these subscripts may be indexed. The *list* is left blank if the FØRMAT statement designated by n contains only literal data.

Figure 8-1. The General Form of Another Style of the READ, PRINT and PUNCH Statements.

The elimination of the data set reference number from the three preceding statements makes it possible for a program to be executed on a different computer system with no reprogramming. In the following illustration,

```
cc 123456789...

      READ 1, A,B,C
        instead of
      READ (5,1) A,B,C
        or
      PRINT 1, A,B,C
        instead of
      WRITE (6,1) A,B,C
        or
      PUNCH 1, A,B,C
        instead of
      WRITE (7,1) A,B,C
```

the style of the READ, PRINT, and PUNCH statement may be used instead of the other style of the READ statement and the other style of the WRITE statement, respectively.

THE NAMELIST STATEMENT

The NAMELIST statement is a specification statement that provides the means to either read from or write into one or more records of a data set via the READ (i,n) or the WRITE (i,n) statements without using either the "list" portion of the statement or having the statement refer to a FØRMAT statement. Rather, the "n" portion of the statement refers to a specific NAMELIST name. Figure 8-2 illustrates the general form of this statement:

```
cc  123456789...

          NAMELIST /n₁/list₁/n₂/list₂/ ... /nₙ/listₙ
```

NAMELIST	FORTRAN key word that distinguishes this statement from the other kinds of statements in the program.
$/n_1/,/n_2/,...,/n_n/$	represents a NAMELIST name that is constructed according to the rules for constructing a variable name.
$list_1, list_2,...,list_n$	represents one or more variable and/or array names, each of which must be separated by a comma.

Figure 8-2.   The General Form of the NAMELIST Statement.

The following five rules must be considered when using a NAMELIST statement:

1. A NAMELIST name can appear in only one NAMELIST statement and can appear only once within that particular NAMELIST statement. Also, a NAMELIST name can only appear in READ and WRITE statements within the program.

2. A NAMELIST statement must precede any statement function and all executable statements.

3. A NAMELIST name cannot also be used as either a variable or array name in the program.

4. The same variable or array name may be located in more than one *list*.

5. A BACKSPACE statement cannot contain a data set reference number associated with a data set that is either read and/or written via a NAMELIST statement.

In the following illustration,

```
cc  123456789...

          DIMENSIØN I(5),M(3,2),NAM(7)
          NAMELIST /A/X,Y,I/INT/B,C,L,M,NAM
          READ (5,A)
          READ (5,INT)
          .
          .
          .
          WRITE (6,A)
          WRITE (6,INT)
```

a READ and WRITE statement each refers to the NAMELIST names A and INT.

Input Considerations   The data that is read from a data card via a READ statement must be punched in special form. The first character in each record to be read must be blank. The second character in the first record of a group of data records must be an ampersand (&), which must be immediately followed by the NAMELIST name. The NAMELIST name cannot contain any embedded blanks and must be immediately followed by a blank space. This name is followed by one or more datum, each of which must be separated by a comma (a comma is optional after the last datum). A datum is composed of three elements: (1) a variable or array name or an array element of an array name located in the *list* portion of the NAMELIST statement immediately following the NAMELIST name located in the READ statement, (2) an equal sign, and (3) depending upon whether it is preceded by either a variable name, array element, or array name, one or more data items, each of which must be separated by a comma. The end of a group of data records is indicated by &END. For example,

```
cc  123456789...

First data card    &A X=9.5,Y=5.2,I=3,92,164,17,5,&END
Second data card   &INT B=1.0,L=5,
Third data card    M(2,1)=27,M(3,2)=55,NAM=25,5*3,16,
Fourth data card   &END
```

when the first data record is read by the program statement READ (5,A) in the previous illustration, the number 5.2 will be stored under the variable name Y; the number 9.5 will be stored under the variable name X; and the numbers 3, 92, 164, 17, and 5 will be stored under the array elements I(1), I(2), I(3), I(4), and I(5) respectively. It should be noted that it is not necessary that the order of the symbolic names in the data card (Y and X) be the same as their order in the *list* portion of the NAMELIST statement (X and Y). When the second data record is read by the statement READ (5,INT), the number 1.0 will be stored under the variable name B; the number 5 will be stored under the variable name L; the number 27 will be stored under the array element M(2,1); the number 55 will be stored under the array element M(3,2); the number 25 will be stored under the array element NAM(1); the number 3 will be stored under the array elements NAM(2), NAM(3), NAM(4), NAM(5), and NAM(6); and the number 16 will be stored under the array element NAM(7). It should be noted that not all of the symbolic names located in the *list* portion of the NAMELIST statement must have a number stored under them; a number has not been stored under the variable name C and the array elements M(1,1), M(3,1), M(1,2), and M(2,2). Also, a repetition factor (*) may be used to store the same number under two or more array elements.

    A data item following an equal sign in a data card may be either integer, single or double precision floating-point, logical, literal data, or complex. If a data item is logical, it may be in the form T or .TRUE. and F or .FALSE..

    A symbolic name that has been made equivalent to a symbolic name located in a data record via an EQUIVALENCE statement cannot be substituted for that symbolic name in the *list* portion of the NAMELIST statement.

    While the *list* portion of the NAMELIST statement may contain symbolic names that are located in a CØMMØN statement, it cannot contain any dummy arguments.

Output Considerations   When data that has been stored via a NAMELIST statement is written, it is done so in the following form: the first record, beginning in the second position, contains an ampersand immediately followed by the NAMELIST name located in the WRITE statement; beginning with the second position of the second record and continuing through as many successive records as necessary, each time starting in the second position of the record, each datum that has been stored via a READ statement containing that particular NAMELIST name is written according to its type; the last record contains, again beginning in the second position, &END. Thus, execution of the WRITE (6,A) statement in the previous illustration would result in

```
        pp | 123456789...
           |
First record      | &A
Second record     | X=9.5,Y=5.2;I=3,92,164,17,5
Third record      | &END
```

being printed and execution of the WRITE (6,INT) statement would result in

```
        pp | 123456789...
           |
First record      | &INT
Second record     | B=10,L=5,M(2,1)=27,M(3,2)=55,NAM=25,5*3,16
Third record      | &END
```

being printed.

ADDITIONAL FORMAT CODES

The following is a discussion of two additional format codes. While useful in specific situations, their use is not often required because of the normally limited number of occurrences of these situations.

The Generalized (G) Format Code   This format code is a general purpose code used to either read from or write into one or more records of a data set integer, single or double precision floating-point, or logical data. Thus, it is especially useful for debugging a program. Figure 8-3 illustrates the general form of this format code.

```
cc | 123456789...
   |
   ccccc | FØRMAT (aGw.d)
```

a represents an optional unsigned integer number that specifies the number of times that particular format code is used each time the computer scans from the left to the right parenthesis of the FØRMAT statement. It may be omitted if the format code is to be used only once each time the computer scans from the left to the right parenthesis.

G specifies that either integer, single or double precision floating-point, or logical data compose the field of data.

w represents an unsigned integer number that specifies the number of characters in the field of data that are to be either read from or written into a record.

. is a necessary delimiter between w and d.

d represents an unsigned integer number that specifies the location of the decimal point within the floating-point number.

Figure 8-3. The General Form of the G Format Code.

Input Considerations   If the type of the variable name in the list portion of either the READ or WRITE statement is either integer or logical, the "." and d portions of the format code may be omitted; if these portions are not omitted, the computer will ignore their presence.

Output Considerations   The following three rules should be considered when printing an integer, single or double precision, or logical datum into a record:

1. If the type of number is either integer or logical, the "." and d portions of the format code may be omitted and the computer will print the number according to the rules for writing a number via either the I or L format codes.

2. If the type of the number, say n, is either single or double precision floating-point and the magnitude of the number is 0.1 n 10**d, the number is printed in the first 2-4 positions without a decimal exponent.

3. If the type of the number is either single or double precision floating-point and the magnitude of the number is either less than 0.1 or greater than 10**d, the number is printed with either an E or D decimal exponent, depending on the magnitude of w.

If the type of the number is either single or double precision floating-point, w must include a position for a decimal point, four positions for a decimal exponent and if the number is negative, a position for a minus sign.

The Hexadecimal (Z) Format Code   This format code is used to either read from or write into one or more records of a data set of hexadecimal data. Specifically, in certain situations it is desirable to read into a computer a number that is in hexadecimal form or store a specific pattern of binary characters under a symbolic name; in other situations it is desirable to print the number stored under a symbolic name in hexadecimal or binary form or to examine the pattern of binary characters composing a number stored under a symbolic name. Figure 8-4 illustrates the general form of this format code.

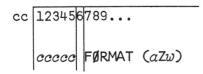

where

a represents an optional unsigned integer number that specifies the number of times that particular format code is used each time the computer scans from the left to the right parenthesis of the FØRMAT statement. It may be omitted if the format code is to be used only once each time the computer scans from the left to the right parenthesis.

Z   specifies that hexadecimal data compose the field of data.

w represents an unsigned integer number that specifies the number of characters in the field of data that are to be either read from or written into a record.

Figure 8-4.   The General Form of the Z Format Code.

Input Considerations   The computer scans a field of data from right to left. Leading, embedded, and trailing blanks in the field of data are replaced with zeros by the computer when the contents of the field of data are stored in its memory. Two hexadecimal characters are stored in one computer memory storage location (byte); thus, if a field of data contains an odd number of characters, a hexadecimal zero will be added to the left of the datum when it is stored in the computer's memory. If the computer memory storage area is not large enough to store all of the characters, the non-storable high-order characters will be truncated.

Output Considerations   If the number of characters in the computer memory storage area is less than w, the leftmost print positions are filled with blanks. However, if the number of characters in the computer memory storage area is greater than w, the leftmost characters are truncated and the rest of the number is printed.

THE PAUSE STATEMENT

This statement causes the computer to stop its execution of the program. However, unlike the STØP statement, this statement permits execution of the program to be restarted again at that point in the program. When the "start" key on the console typewriter is pressed, the computer will resume execution of the next executable program statement following the PAUSE statement. Figure 8-5 illustrates the general form of this statement.

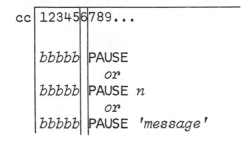

where

      bbbbb   represents an unsigned 1 through 5 integer number that is required only if a transfer is made to this statement from another program statement.

    PAUSE   FORTRAN key word that distinguishes this statement from the other kinds of statements in the program.

     n   represents an unsigned 1 through 5 integer number.

   'message'   represents literal data as discussed in Chapter 3 under the subtopic "Output Considerations," which is located under the topic "Literal Data and Apostrophes."

Figure 8-5.   The General Form of the PAUSE Statement.

One or more PAUSE statements may be located anywhere in the program prior to the END statement. When a PAUSE statement is executed, it is printed verbatim on the console typewriter's paper printout.

This statement should be used when it is desirable to interrupt execution of the program for some reason such as to correct an error or to provide more data. Since the computer operater must physically type the desired entry and restart execution of the program, the author suggests that this statement should not be used in a program unless the computer operator has been informed of the reason for its presence in the program and what action, if any, he is to take prior to restarting execution of the program.

THE DATA INITIALIZATION STATEMENT

In Chapter 3, the READ statement and in Chapter 4 the arithmetic and logical statements were discussed as a means of storing a datum under a symbolic name. In certain instances, however, it may be desirable to initially store a datum under a symbolic name without utilizing one of these three methods. In FORTRAN, this may be accomplished by means of the DATA initialization statement. Figure 8-6 illustrates the general form of this statement.

cc | 1 2 3 4 5 6 7 8 9 . . .

DATA $list_1/c_1{*}sn_1,c_2{*}sn_2,\ldots,c_n{*}sn_n/$, $list_n/c_n{*}sn_n$, $\ldots,c_n{*}sn_n$ /

where

DATA	FORTRAN key word that distinguishes this statement from the other kinds of statements in the program.
$list_1,\ldots,list_n$	represents one or more variable or array names, array elements, and/or logical variable names each of which must be separated by a comma. A dummy argument name may not be located in this portion of the statement.
/	a special character that is a requirement of the FORTRAN language.
,	a special character that is optional if more than one $list$ is present in the statement.
$c_1,\ldots,c_n$	represents an optional integer number that specifies the number of times the immediately following number, logical constant, or literal data is to be replicated.
*	a special character that is a requirement of the FORTRAN language if an optional integer number is used.
$sn_1,\ldots,sn_n$	represents one or more numbers (integer, single or double precision floating-point, complex, hexadecimal), logical constants, or literal data, each of which must be separated by a comma.
/	a special character that is a requirement of the FORTRAN language.
,	a special character that is optional if more than one $list$ is present in the statement.

Figure 8-6.   The General Form of the DATA Initialization Statement.

There must be a one-to-one ratio between the total number of specified and implied variable or array names, array elements, and/or logical variable names composing the *list* portion of a DATA initialization statement and the total number of numbers, logical variable names, and/or literal data, including any replication. Also, there must be *type* agreement between a specified or implied variable or array name, array element, or logical variable name located in the *list* portion of the statement and the datum that is to be stored under it, except in those instances when the datum is either literal or hexadecimal in nature.

To illustrate a fundamental use of the DATA statement, assume that the five variable names I, J, K, A, and B are to be assigned initial values of 0, 0, 0, 10.55, and 25.5. This can be accomplished by means of the following statement:

DATA I,J,K,A,B/0,0,0,10.55,25.5/

The computer will store, from left to right, the first number under the first variable name, the second number under the second variable name, etc.

The above same thing can also be accomplished in the following manner:

DATA I,J,K,A,B/3*0,10.55,25.5/

The computer will store a 0 under the leftmost three variable names (I,J,K), 10.55 under the variable name A, and 25.5 under the variable name B.

THE BLØCK DATA STATEMENT

In certain situations, it may be desirable to assign an initial datum to one or more variable names and/or array elements assigned to a common storage area. While it is not possible to assign an initial datum to either a variable or array element assigned to a blank common storage area, it is possible to do so in a labeled common storage area. However, a DATA, INTEGER, REAL, CØMPLEX, or LØGICAL statement may be used to assign an initial datum to either one or more variable names and/or array elements assigned to a labeled common storage area *only* if the statement is located in a BLØCK DATA subprogram. Figure 8-7 illustrates the general form of this statement.

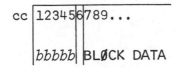

where

       bbbbb   represents an optional unsigned 1 through 5 integer number.

  BLØCK DATA   FORTRAN key word that distinguishes this statement from the other kinds of statements in the program.

Figure 8-7.   The General Form of the BLØCK DATA Statement.

The following four rules must be considered when using a BLØCK DATA subprogram:

1. The only statements that may be present in a BLØCK DATA subprogram are the

      IMPLICIT statement   LØGICAL statement
      CØMMØN statement   CØMPLEX statement
      INTEGER statement   DATA statement
      REAL statement   END statement

2. The BLØCK DATA statement must be the first statement in the subprogram. If an IMPLICIT statement is used in a BLØCK DATA subprogram, it must immediately follow the BLØCK DATA statement. If either a DATA, INTEGER, REAL, LØGICAL, and/or CØMPLEX statement is used to assign an initial datum to one or more variable names and/or array elements, it cannot precede the one or more CØMMØN statements which define those variable names and/or array elements.

3. A datum may be assigned to one or more variable names and/or array elements assigned to more than one labeled common storage area in a single BLØCK DATA subprogram.

4. Only one BLØCK DATA subprogram may be used to assign an initial datum to one or more variable names and/or array elements assigned to a particular labeled common storage area.

Assume it was desired to initialize the variable names I and J, which are assigned to a labeled common storage area, the number 4398 and the number 6572 respectively. The CØMMØN statement in the main program may be written as follows:

The CØMMØN statement in the subprogram may be written as follows:

```
cc 123456789...


          CØMMØN/NUMBER/I,J
```

The BLØCK DATA subprogram may be written as follows:

```
cc 123456789...


          BLØCK DATA
          CØMMØN/NUMBER/I,J
          DATA I,J/4398,6572/
```

THE IMPLICIT STATEMENT

The IMPLICIT statement is used when it is desirable to explicitly indicate the type of specific variable names appearing in the program. Figure 8-8 illustrates the general form of this specification statement.

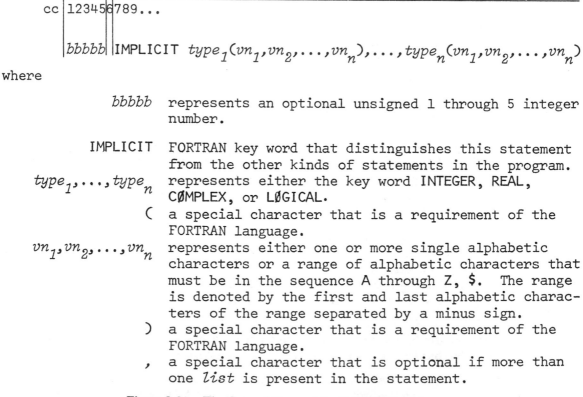

```
cc 123456789...


    bbbbb IMPLICIT  type_1(vn_1,vn_2,...,vn_n),...,type_n(vn_1,vn_2,...,vn_n)
```

where

bbbbb	represents an optional unsigned 1 through 5 integer number.
IMPLICIT	FORTRAN key word that distinguishes this statement from the other kinds of statements in the program.
$type_1,...,type_n$	represents either the key word INTEGER, REAL, CØMPLEX, or LØGICAL.
(	a special character that is a requirement of the FORTRAN language.
$vn_1,vn_2,...,vn_n$	represents either one or more single alphabetic characters or a range of alphabetic characters that must be in the sequence A through Z, $. The range is denoted by the first and last alphabetic characters of the range separated by a minus sign.
)	a special character that is a requirement of the FORTRAN language.
,	a special character that is optional if more than one *list* is present in the statement.

Figure 8-8.   The General Form of the IMPLICIT Statement.

The IMPLICIT statement must be the first statement in a main program and the second statement in a subprogram. There can only be one IMPLICIT statement per main program and subprogram. While the IMPLICIT statement overrides the predefined convention for specifying the particular type of a symbolic name (integer: I-N; single precision floating-point: A-H, Ø-Z, $), an explicit specification statement (INTEGER, REAL, DØUBLE PRECISIØN, CØMPLEX, and LØGICAL) overrides the IMPLICIT convention for specifying the particular type of a symbolic name.

In the following illustration,

```
cc 123456789...

        IMPLICIT INTEGER (A-D,F-H),REAL (I-K),LØGICAL (L,M,N)
```

all variable names beginning with the alphabetic characters A through D and F through H are declared integer variable names, all variable names beginning with the alphabetic characters I through K are declared single precision floating-point variable names, and all variable names beginning with the alphabetic characters L, M, and N are declared logical variable names. The type of all variable names beginning with the alphabetic characters E, Ø through Z, and $ is determined by the predefined convention.

THE CØMPLEX STATEMENT

The CØMPLEX statement, like the INTEGER, REAL, DØUBLE PRECISIØN, and LØGICAL statements, is an explicit specification statement. It is used when it is desirable to store a complex number under either a variable or array name, FUNCTIØN subprogram name, or statement function name.

Complex Numbers   In a mathematical textbook, a complex number is usually written in the form of a + ib where "a" and "b" are either single or double precision floating-point numbers and $_si_si = \sqrt[m]{-1}$. A complex number may, however, be written in vector form as (a,b), where "a" represents either a single or double precision floating-point number and "b" represents an imaginary part of the number. FORTRAN uses this latter technique of writing complex numbers.

Both the real and imaginary components must be either single or double precision floating-point numbers; they must be separated by a comma; and they must be enclosed in a set of parentheses. Either component may be positive, zero, or negative (if unsigned and nonzero, the component is assumed to be positive). The computer stores the two component numbers in successive storage locations.

The following are examples of *valid* complex numbers:

```
(5.7,-2.43)             (VALUE = 5.7 - 2.43i)
(-2.0E+03,.14E+02)      (VALUE = -2000. + 14.0i)
(24D+2,63D+3)           (VALUE = 2400. + 63000.i)
```

The following are examples of *invalid* complex numbers:

```
(15475,137.2)     (The real part is not either a single or double
                   precision floating-point number)
(9364.27,Z)       (A variable name cannot be used)
(3.6E3,.557D5)    (The real and imaginary parts differ in length)
```

The Use of the CØMPLEX Statement   When it is desirable to store a complex number under a symbolic name, a CØMPLEX statement must be used to explicitly indicate that this symbolic name will have this type of number stored under it. As a result, the first character of the symbolic name can be *any* alphabetic character. Figure 8-9 illustrates the general form of this specification statement.

```
cc 123456789...

        CØMPLEX sn₁(in₁,in₂,in₃),sn₂(in₁,in₂,in₃),...,snₙ(inₙ,inₙ,inₙ)
```

where

CØMPLEX FORTRAN key word that distinguishes this statement
        from the other kinds of statements in the program.

$sn_1, sn_2, \ldots, sn_n$ represents either a variable or array name, FUNCTIØN subprogram name, or statement function name.

$(in_1, in_2, in_3, \ldots,$
$\quad in_n, in_n, in_n)$ represents one, two, or three unsigned integer numbers each of which can be 1 through 7 characters in length, which specify the number of storage spaces to be allocated to the immediately preceding array name. If there is more than one integer number, they must be separated by a comma. One, two, or three numbers are used, depending upon whether it is a one-, two-, or three-dimensional array. If the immediately preceding sn is not an array name, this portion of the statement is omitted.

,   a special character that is required if more than one sn is present in the statement.

Figure 8-9.   The General Form of the CØMPLEX Statement.

In the following illustration,

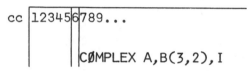

```
cc │123456789...
   │
   │ │ CØMPLEX A,B(3,2),I
```

A and I are declared to be complex variable names and B is declared to be a two-dimensional array composed of 6 complex elements.

THE LENGTH OF A SYMBOLIC NAME

The computer stores a character in the form of eight binary characters (1's and 0's) called bits. Eight successive bits are collectively called a byte, which is the smallest unit of length that may be referenced in FORTRAN. As illustrated in the following chart, a half-word is composed of two bytes; a full work is composed of two half-words; and a double word is composed of two full words.

Table 8-1:   The Standard and Optional Lengths for Each Type of Symbolic Name.

Double Word				
Full Word			Full Word	
Half-word		Half-word		
Byte	Byte			
8 bits				

Unless explicitly specified otherwise, the computer automatically allocates a particular type of symbolic name a specific (standard) number of bytes in its memory. Table 8-1 illustrates the standard and optional lengths (number of allocated bytes) for each type of symbolic name.

Type	Standard Length (bytes)	Optional Length (bytes)
INTEGER	4	2 (Short integer)
REAL	4	8 (Double precision floating-point)
LØGICAL	4	1 (Short logical)
CØMPLEX	8	16 (Double precision complex)

In certain situations, it may be desirable to explicitly specify an optional shorter length for a specific integer or logical symbolic name in order to conserve computer memory storage space or to explicitly specify an optional longer length for a specific real or complex symbolic name in order to obtain greater accuracy. This may be accomplished via three statements: (1) the IMPLICIT statement, (2) an explicit specification statement, and (3) the FUNCTIØN subprogram statement.

The IMPLICIT Statement   Except for the addition of the optional length specification to the statement, the general form and use of this statement is the same as that presented earlier in this chapter when this statement was discussed. Figure 8-10 illustrates the general form of this statement with the inclusion of the optional length specification:

```
cc 123456789...

   bbbbb IMPLICIT type₁*ls₁(vn₁,vn₂,...,vnₙ),...,typeₙ*lsₙ

                  (vn₁,·n₂,...,vnₙ)
```

where

$bbbbb$	represents an optional unsigned 1 through 5 integer number.
IMPLICIT	FORTRAN key word that distinguishes this statement from the other kinds of statements in the program.
$type_1,...,type_n$	represents either the key word INTEGER, REAL, CØMPLEX, or LØGICAL.
*	a special character that is a requirement of the FORTRAN language only if a length specification (ls) immediately follows it.
$ls_1,...,ls_n$	represents the optional length specification of the immediately preceding key word.
(	a special character that is a requirement of the FORTRAN language.
$vn_1,vn_2,...,vn_n$	represents either one or more single alphabetic characters or a range of alphabetic characters that must be in the sequence A through Z, $. The range is denoted by the first and last alphabetic characters of the range separated by a minus sign.
)	a special character that is a requirement of the FORTRAN language.
,	a special character that is optional if more than one $list$ is present in the statement.

Figure 8-10.   The General Form of the IMPLICIT Statement with the Optional Length Specification.

In the following illustration

```
cc 123456789...

         IMPLICIT INTEGER*2(A,B),REAL*8(I)
```

all variable names beginning with the alphabetic characters A and B are declared integer variable names with 2 bytes allocated to each variable name; and all variable names beginning with the alphabetic character I are declared double precision floating-point variable names with 8 bytes allocated to each variable name.

The Explicit Statement   An explicit specification statement has two options: (1) length specification and (2) initial data assignment. Either one or both of these options may be used concurrently in the statement. The appropriate general form of this statement is presented and discussed in Chapters 2, 6, 7, and the CØMPLEX statement in this chapter. Figure 8-11 illustrates the complete general form of this statement:

```
cc | 123456789...


   | Type*ls sn_1*ls_1(in_1,in_2,in_3)/c_1*sn_1,c_2*sn_2,...,

   |     c_n*sn_n/,...,sn_n*ls_n(in_1,in_2,in_3)/c_n*sn_n,

   |     c_n*sn_n,...,c_n*sn_n/
```

where

$Type$ represents either the key word INTEGER, REAL, CØMPLEX, or LØGICAL.

  *   a special character that is a requirement of the FORTRAN language only if a length specification (ls) immediately follows it.

ls represents the optional length specification of the immediately preceding key word. Unless explicitly specified otherwise in the statement, each symbolic name in the statement is declared to be that length and thus allocated that many storage locations.

$sn_1,...,sn_n$ represents either a variable, array, logical variable, FUNCTIØN subprogram, or statement function name.

  *   a special character that is a requirement of the FORTRAN language only if a length specification (ls) immediately follows it.

$ls_1,...,ls_n$ represents the optional length specification of the immediately preceding variable, array, logical variable, FUNCTIØN subprogram, or statement function name.

(in_1,in_2,in_3) represents optional one, two, or three unsigned integer numbers each of which can be 1 through 7 characters in length, which specify the number of bytes to be allocated to the immediately preceding array name. If there is more than one integer number, they must be separated by a comma. One, two, or three numbers are used, depending upon whether it is a one-, two-, or three-dimensional array. If the immediately preceding symbolic name is not an array name, this portion of the statement is omitted. If this statement is located in either a FUNCTIØN or SUBRØUTINE subprogram, one, two, or three integer variable names, each being of standard length, may be used in place of an unsigned integer number provided that the array name is a dummy argument.

$/c_1 \text{*} sn_1, c_2 \text{*} sn_2, \ldots,$
$c_n \text{*} sn_n /, \ldots, /c_n \text{*} sn_n,$
$c_n \text{*} sn_n, \ldots, c_n \text{*} sn_n /$

represents an optional initial assignment of one or more datum to one or more symbolic names. The general use of this portion of the statement is similar to this portion in the DATA statement. A dummy argument may not be assigned an initial datum.

, a special character that is optional if more than one symbolic name is present in the statement.

Figure 8-11. The Complete General Form of an Explicit Specification Statement.

An explicit specification statement that initializes a symbolic name must be preceded by any other explicit specification statements containing that symbolic name. If initial data are assigned to an array in an explicit specification statement, the number of storage locations that are to be allocated to the array must also be specified either in the same statement or in a preceding DIMENSIØN or CØMMØN statement. While a statement function name may appear in an explicit specification statement, it cannot be assigned an initial datum.

In the following illustration,

```
cc 123456789...

       INTEGER*2 CØUNT/10/,WEIGHT,TAG
```

the variable names CØUNT, WEIGHT, and TAG are declared to be integer in type. In addition, each variable name is allocated 2 bytes and the variable name CØUNT is initialized to the number 10.

In the following illustration,

```
cc 123456789...

       REAL KAT(4,3)/3*2.5,9*4.1/,ITEM*2,TEST(3,4)
```

the variable names KAT, ITEM, and TEST are declared to be single precision floating-point in type. In addition, the variable name KAT is initialized to the number 2.5 in its first 3 storage spaces, and the number 4.1 in its next 9 storage spaces; the variable name ITEM is allocated 2 bytes; and the variable name TEST is allocated 12 storage spaces.

It should be noted that while the DØUBLE PRECISIØN statement may be used to declare one or more variable or array names, logical variable names, FUNCTIØN subprogram names, and/or statement function names as being double precision floating-point, it cannot be used if an initial datum is to be assigned to a symbolic name located in the statement. Since the use of the key word and optional length specification REAL*8 results in the same number of bytes being allocated as the use of the DØUBLE PRECISIØN statement, the former statement and optional length specification may be used instead of the latter statement, especially when it is desirable to assign an initial datum to a symbolic name located in the statement. Also, since the key word DØUBLE PRECISIØN cannot be used in an IMPLICIT statement, the key word and optional length specification REAL*8 may be used to accomplish the same desired result with respect to the allocation of 8 bytes to one or more symbolic names. Finally, an optional length specification cannot be used in a DØUBLE PRECISIØN statement; each symbolic name located in the statement is allocated 8 bytes.

When an array is dimensioned in a DØUBLE PRECISIØN statement, the number of storage spaces to be allocated to an array may be either partly or totally specified via the following two forms: (1) as indicated in Chapter 6 by means of an unsigned integer number and (2) by a symbolic name with a length specification of 4 bytes.

The FUNCTIØN Statement   Except for the addition of the optional length specification to the statement, the general form and use of this statement is the same as that presented during the discussion of this statement in Chapter 7. Figure 8-12 illustrates the general form of this statement with the inclusion of the optional length specification.

```
cc │123456789...
   │
   │bbbbb│ Type FUNCTIØN sn*ls(darg₁,darg₂,...,dargₙ)
```

where

$bbbbb$	represents an optional unsigned 1 through 5 integer number.
$Type$	represents either the optional key word INTEGER, REAL, DØUBLE PRECISIØN, CØMPLEX, or LØGICAL.
FUNCTIØN	FORTRAN key word that distinguishes this statement from the other kinds of statements in the program.
sn	represents the subprogram name. Either it or one or more of its accompanying dummy arguments must appear at least once within the subprogram either (1) in the $list$ of a READ statement, (2) as the variable name on the left side of the equal sign of either an arithmetic or logical statement, (3) as an argument in a CALL statement, or (4) as an argument in a FORTRAN-supplied subprogram statement.
*	a special character that is a requirement of the FORTRAN language only if a length specification (ls) immediately follows it.
ls	represents the optional length specification of the immediately preceding subprogram name. It may be included optionally only when $Type$ is specified in the statement. However, it cannot be used when $Type$ is the key word DØUBLE PRECISIØN.
(	a special character that is a requirement of the FORTRAN language.
$darg_1,darg_2,...,darg_n$	represents one or more dummy arguments, each of which must be either a variable or array name, another FUNCTIØN subprogram, or SUBRØUTINE subprogram name and be separated

```
                                        by a comma.  There must be at least one dummy
                                        argument and each symbolic name can be used
                                        only once.
                                    )   a special character that is a requirement of
                                        the FORTRAN language.
```

Figure 8-12. The General Form of the FUNCTIØN Statement with the Optional Length Specification.

In Chapter 7, it was stated during the discussion of FUNCTIØN subprograms that the one or more arguments accompanying the FUNCTIØN subprogram name in the calling program and their corresponding dummy arguments accompanying the subprogram name in the FUNCTIØN statement located in the called subprogram must agree in order, number, and type. In addition, there must be agreement in length specification. That is, the length of the arguments in the calling program must be the same as the length of their corresponding dummy argument in the called subprogram. Therefore, if an argument in the calling program is specified to be its optional length, that length must also be specified for its corresponding dummy argument in the called subprogram.

In the following illustration,

```
cc  123456789...


    INTEGER FUNCTIØN FNC*2(M,N)
    .
    .
    .
    FNC = M*N
    .
    .
    .
    RETURN
    END
```

the FUNCTIØN subprogram named FNC is declared to be type INTEGER; also, two storage locations are allocated to it.

QUESTIONS

1. When is it desirable to use either a READ, PRINT, or PUNCH statement with a data set reference number?
2. What is the function of the NAMELIST statement?
3. What is the function of the PAUSE statement?
4. How do the PAUSE and STØP statement differ?
5. What is the function of the DATA initialization statement?
6. How may a number or condition be assigned to more than one operand in the preceding *list* portion of the DATA initialization statement?
7. What is the function of a BLØCK DATA statement?
8. What is the function of the IMPLICIT specification statement?
9. What is the function of the CØMPLEX specification statement?
10. What is the standard and optional length (bytes) of an INTEGER, REAL, LØGICAL, and CØMPLEX symbolic name?

EXERCISES

1.   Write a program that stores 10 employee identification numbers in a two-dimensional array named ID and each employee's weekly gross pay in an array named GRØSS. Compute each employee's federal tax—use 10% if the employee's gross pay is either equal to or less than $200.00 and 15% if it is greater than $200.00—and store it in an array named FEDTAX. Store each employee's identification number, gross pay, federal tax, and net pay. Use the A format code to read the identification numbers. Make all variable names real mode through the use of an IMPLICIT statement. (Remember, though, that subscripts must be integer and thus you will have to explicitly declare their mode.)

2.   Write a program to store 4 floating-point numbers under the variable names A, B, C, and D via a NAMELIST statement. Calculate the square root of each number stored under the variable names A and B and store it under the variable names E and F respectively. Calculate the absolute value of each number stored under the variable names C and D and store them under the variable names G and H respectively. Write each of the original numbers and their respective associated number. Place the variable names E, F, G, and H in the NAMELIST statement.

3.   Write a program to read one or more numbers and determine the magnitude of each number. If its magnitude is less than zero, temporarily stop execution of the program and write the message NEG; if its magnitude is greater than 500, temporarily stop execution of the program and write the message 10001.

4.   Write a program to read a one- or two-character employee identification number ranging from 1 through 25 and his gross pay. Use a blank punch card to terminate reading. In a called FUNCTIØN subprogram named MATCH, compute the tax, which is 10% if the employee's gross pay is $200.00 or less and 15% if it is not, and return the employee's net pay to the calling program. Write each employee's identification number, gross pay, tax, and net pay. The main program and the called subprogram contain a labeled common storage area named A, which contains the arrays GRØSS, FEDTAX, NET, and RATE. The first three of these arrays is dimensioned 25 storage spaces. Initialize the array elements of the arrays GRØSS, FEDTAX, and NET to zero and the first array element of the array RATE to .10 and the second array element of this array to .15.

Chapter 9

TAPE AND DISK STATEMENTS

The discussion of the FORTRAN language in the first 8 chapters has assumed, when applicable, that the data to be processed was read from punched cards and the information resulting from the processing was printed by a printer. There are situations, however, such as the processing and storing of large amounts of data, when it is desirable to store the data on and read the data from either a magnetic tape or disk. For this reason, a discussion of applicable tape and disk statements is presented in this chapter.

MAGNETIC TAPE

The storage of one or more records on or the retrieval of one or more records from a magnetic tape may only be accomplished sequentially. For this reason, the process of writing records on and the process of reading records from a magnetic tape is called *sequential-access*.

There are seven statements associated with magnetic tape. They are: (1) WRITE (i,n) *list*, (2) READ (i,n) *list*, (3) WRITE (i) *list*, (4) READ (i) *list*, (5) BACKSPACE, (6) REWIND, and (7) END FILE.

Input and Output Statements   Magnetic tape input and output statements do not provide a method of designating which specific record is to be either written or read. Rather, each time a WRITE or READ statement is encountered one or more records are either sequentially written on or read from a magnetic tape. Because of this inability to designate a specific record, it is both difficult to skip one or more records and it takes as long to skip a record as it does to either write or read a record.

A magnetic tape is always moving in the forward direction while a record is being written on it and as a result the data composing a record is written along the length of the magnetic tape. Similarly, a magnetic tape is always moving in the forward direction while a record is being read from it. The minimum size of a record written on a magnetic tape is 18 record columns (bytes).

There are two basic types of magnetic tape WRITE and READ statements: formatted and unformatted.

Formatted WRITE and READ Statements   These two statements are used in those situations where one or more records being written on a magnetic tape are to be at some later date read, possibly processed, and written on an output device such as a printer. Figure 9-1 illustrates the general form of these two statements.

```
cc 123456789...

   bbbbb WRITE (i,n) list

and

   bbbbb READ (i,n) list
```

Figure 9-1. The General Form of the Formatted WRITE and READ Statements.

Each of the statements in the above illustration has the same general form and possesses the same capabilities as the WRITE and READ statements discussed in Chapter 3. The only difference is the data set reference number. (Data set reference number 8 will be associated with a data set that is being either written on or read from a magnetic tape.)

The formatted WRITE statement is used to write one or more records, which are stored in the computer's memory, on a magnetic tape. This statement must always reference a FØRMAT statement. The following is an illustration of this statement:

```
cc 123456789...


     WRITE (8,1) I,J,K,L
   1 FØRMAT (I5,T16,I5)
```

In the preceding illustration, the WRITE statement causes two records, each 20 record columns in length, to be written on a magnetic tape.

The formatted READ statement is used to read one or more records which were written on a magnetic tape via a formatted WRITE statement. The one or more records are transferred to the computer's memory. Like the formatted WRITE statement, it must always reference a FØRMAT statement. The following is an illustration of this statement:

```
cc 123456789...


     READ (8,1,END=99) I,J,K,L
   1 FØRMAT (I5,T16,I5)          .
```

In the preceding illustration, the READ statement causes two records, each 20 columns in length, to be read from a magnetic tape.

Unformatted WRITE and READ Statements   These two statements are used in those situations where one or more records being written on a magnetic tape are to be at some later date read, processed, and *rewritten* on a magnetic tape by the computer rather than read, possibly processed, and written on an output device such as a printer. An example of such a situation would be an intermediate data set. The primary advantage of using these two statements instead of the formatted WRITE and READ statements in such situations is the increased speed with which these two statements are executed. A secondary advantage of using these two statements is that the writing of a FØRMAT statement each time is avoided. Figure 9-2 illustrates the general form of these statements:

```
cc 123456789...


   bbbbb WRITE (i) list

and

   bbbbb READ (i) list
```

Figure 9-2. The General Form of the Unformatted WRITE and READ Statements.

The only difference between the formatted WRITE and READ statements and the preceding WRITE and READ statements is that the two preceding statements do *not* refer to a FØRMAT statement.

The unformatted WRITE statement is used to write one or more records, which are stored in the computer's memory, on a magnetic tape. The following is an illustration of this statement:

```
cc  123456789...



            WRITE (8) A,B,C,X,Y,Z
```

In the preceding illustration, the WRITE statement causes a record composed of each single precision floating-point number stored under the variable names A, B, C, X, Y, and Z to be written on a magnetic tape. Since there is no FØRMAT statement to serve as the basis for determining the number of record columns that compose the record, unless specified otherwise, four record columns are required to store an integer and single precision floating-point number and a logical constant and eight record columns are required to store a double precision floating-point number. Thus, the record containing the above six single precision floating-point numbers is composed of 24 record columns.

The unformatted READ statement is used to read one or more records which were written on a magnetic tape by an unformatted WRITE statement. The one or more records are transferred from the magnetic tape to the computer's memory. The following is an illustration of this statement:

```
cc  123456789...



            READ (8,END=99) A,B,C,X,Y,Z,
```

In the preceding illustration, the READ statement causes one record composed of 24 record columns to be read from a magnetic tape and transferred to the computer's memory.

When the unformatted READ statement is used, the number of record columns composing the magnetic tape record being read must be equal to the number of record columns required for the variable, logical variable, and/or array names located in the *list* portion of the statement. An unequal match causes an abnormal termination of the program. Also, special care must be taken to make sure that the type of the variable, logical variable, and/or array names located in the *list* of the READ statement is the same type as the corresponding variable, logical variable, and/or array names located in the *list* portion of the WRITE statement that wrote the record on the magnetic tape.

Magnetic Tape Control Statements   Up to this point, the discussion has centered around the process of writing on and reading from a magnetic tape. The following is a discussion of the four statements that are available to control either the forward or backward movement of a magnetic tape.

Forward Movement of a Magnetic Tape   A magnetic tape can be moved forward one or more records by the use of either a READ (*i,n*) list statement or a READ (*i*) statement. For example, assume that it is desirable to read the fourth record residing on a magnetic tape. Depending upon whether a formatted or unformatted WRITE statement was used to write the record on magnetic tape, either the statements in the following illustration

```
cc  123456789...



            READ (8,1,END=99) A,B,C,D
     1      FØRMAT (F5.2)
```

or the statements in the following illustration may be used:

```
cc 123456789...


     READ (8) A
     READ (8) B
     READ (8) C
     READ (8) D
```

In the two preceding illustrations, the first 3 records are read and a single precision floating-point number stored under the variable names A, B, and C respectively. However, the number stored under each of these three variable names will not be used. The fourth record is then read and the desired single precision floating-point number stored under the variable name D.

With respect to the first of the preceding illustrations, an important point to remember is that an entire record is read, whether or not data stored in every record column of the record is read, each time the computer scans from the left parenthesis to the right parenthesis. And, of course, with respect to the second of the preceding illustrations, an entire record is read by each READ statement.

If a situation requires many records to be skipped, either one of the READ statements can be used in a DØ loop. For example, assume that it was desirable to use the data composing the fiftieth record written on magnetic tape.

```
cc 123456789...


       DØ 2 I = 1,50
  2    READ (8,1,END=99) J
  1    FØRMAT (I3)
```

In the preceding illustration, the computer reads and destroys the integer number read from the first 49 records. Thus, in effect, the first 49 records have been skipped.

The BACKSPACE Statement   This statement causes the computer to backspace one record each time it is executed. If, however, the magnetic tape is positioned at the first record, execution of this statement has no effect. Figure 9-3 illustrates the general form of this statement.

```
cc 123456789...

bbbbb  BACKSPACE in
```

where

bbbbb	represents an unsigned 1 through 5 integer number that is required only if a transfer is made to this statement from another program statement.
BACKSPACE	FORTRAN key word that distinguishes this statement from the other kinds of statements in the program.
in	represents either an unsigned integer number or variable name with an unsigned integer number stored under it that is the data set reference number associated with a data set stored on magnetic tape.

Figure 9-3.   The General Form of the BACKSPACE Statement.

In the following illustration, the BACKSPACE statements cause the computer to backspace 3 records.

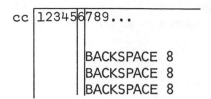

```
cc 123456789...


       BACKSPACE 8
       BACKSPACE 8
       BACKSPACE 8
```

Similar to skipping forward many records via the DØ statement, in those situations where it is necessary to backspace many records to a desired record, the DØ statement can be used. The statements below cause the computer to backspace 10 records.

```
cc 123456789...



       DØ 1 I = 1,10
 1     BACKSPACE 8
```

The REWIND Statement   This statement causes the computer to rewind the magnetic tape to the first record on the tape. Figure 9-4 illustrates the general form of this statement.

```
cc 123456789...


 bbbbb REWIND in
```

where

bbbbb	represents an unsigned 1 through 5 integer number that is required only if a transfer is made to this statement from another program statement.
REWIND	FORTRAN key word that distinguishes this statement from the other kinds of statements in the program.
in	represents either an unsigned integer number or variable name with an unsigned integer number stored under it that is the data set reference number associated with a data set stored on magnetic tape.

Figure 9-4.   The General Form of the REWIND Statement.

In the following illustration, the REWIND statement

```
cc 123456789...


       REWIND 8
```

causes the computer to rewind, from its present position, to the beginning of the first record on the tape. If, however, the magnetic tape is positioned at the first record, execution of this statement has no effect. A subsequent WRITE statement, which references this data set, will cause the computer to begin writing data in the first record on the tape; whereas a subsequent READ statement which references this data set will cause the computer to begin reading data from the first record on the tape.

The END FILE Statement   This statement causes the computer to write an end-of-file mark, which is an 80 record-column record. This mark indicates to the computer that the last record of the file has either been written on or read from the magnetic tape. Figure 9-5 illustrates the general form of this statement.

```
cc  1234567 89...

    bbbbb  END FILE in
```

where

  bbbbb represents an unsigned 1 through 5 integer number that is required only if a transfer is made to this statement from another program statement.

END FILE FORTRAN key word that distinguishes this statement from the other kinds of statements in the program.

   in represents either an unsigned integer number or variable name with an unsigned integer number stored under it that is the data set reference number associated with a data set stored on magnetic tape.

Figure 9-5.   The General Form of the END FILE Statement.

In the following illustration, the END FILE statement

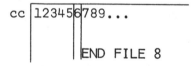

causes the computer to write an end-of-file mark on a magnetic tape.

  If the END= option is used in the READ statement, the reading of an end-of-file mark causes the computer to proceed to the program statement assigned the statement number immediately following the equal sign. If the END= option is not used in the READ statement, however, the reading of an end-of-file mark causes an abnormal termination of the program.

MAGNETIC DISK

  The storage of one or more records on or the retrieval of one or more records from a magnetic disk is accomplished through one of the following processes:

  1. *Sequential Access*   This process, like magnetic tape sequential access, involves either the sequential storage on or retrieval of one or more records.

  2. *Direct Access*   This process involves random accessibility by the computer (the ability to proceed directly to any point on a disk with equal accessibility) and either the sequential or random storage on or retrieval of one or more records.

  3. *Indexed Sequential*   This process combines the sequential access and direct access processes. It involves either the sequential or random storage on or retrieval of one or more records by means of an index composed of a unique, common *key* field of each record. This index is established by the operating system of the computer. Each of these fields is equated to the actual address of the record containing that field.

A major distinction between magnetic tape and magnetic disk with respect to either the storage on or retrieval of one or more records is the ability to designate specific records on a magnetic disk. Two other distinctions are:

1. The minimum size of a record written on magnetic disk may be 1 record column (byte).

2. The END= option is illegal as the term "end-of-file" is meaningless in a direct-access file. The ERR= option may, however, be used.

There are four statements associated with magnetic disk. They are: (1) DEFINE FILE $i(m,r,f,v)$; (2) WRITE $(i'r,n)$ *list*; (3) READ $(i'r,n)$ *list*; and (4) FIND $(i'r)$.

The DEFINE FILE Statement   This statement describes the characteristics of one or more data sets associated with a data set reference number located in the statement. As such, it must precede any of the other program statements associated with a magnetic disk that refer to a data set associated with a data set reference number located in the statement. The DEFINE FILE statement is a specification statement and thus precedes any statement function statements in the program. Figure 9-6 illustrates the general form of this statement.

```
cc  123456789...

    bbbbb  DEFINE FILE i₁(m₁,r₁,f₁,v₁), i₂(m₂,r₂,f₂,v₂),

                       i₃(m₃,r₃,f₃,v₃),...
```

where

bbbbb	represents an optional unsigned 1 through 5 integer number.
DEFINE FILE	FORTRAN key word that distinguishes this statement from the other kinds of statements in the program.
i	represents an unsigned integer number that is a data set reference number.
(	a special character that is a requirement of the FORTRAN language.
m	represents an unsigned integer number that specifies the number of records in the data set associated with the data set reference number by i.
r	represents an unsigned integer number that specifies the maximum size of each record in the data set represented by i. The length of a record is measured by counting either the number of characters, storage locations, or storage units composing it, depending upon the form of the data set as specified by f.
f	represents either the format alphabetic character E, U, or L where E specifies that the data is to be either written on or read from the data set in a form specified by a FØRMAT statement. The maximum record size is r record columns (bytes). U specifies that the data set is either written on or read from the data set without reference to a FØRMAT statement. The maximum size is r storage units (words). L specifies that the data set is either written on or read from the data set

either with or without reference to a FØRMAT statement. The maximum record size is r storage locations (bytes).

v represents a variable name called an *associated variable* name. At the conclusion of either a write or read operation, it designates the record number of the next record in the data set; at the conclusion of a find operation, it designates the record number of the record found.

)   a special character that is a requirement of the FORTRAN language.

,   a special character that is optional if more than one data set is described in the statement.

Figure 9-6. The General Form of the DEFINE FILE Statement.

The DEFINE FILE statement in the following illustration

```
cc | 123456789...
   |
   | DEFINE FILE 3(10,80,E,I),9(20,35,U,J),4(25,50,L,K)
```

describes the characteristics of three data sets. The data set associated with data set reference number 3 is composed of 10 records; the maximum size of each record in the data set is 80 record columns; the data is to be either written on or read from the data set in a form specified by a FØRMAT statement; at the conclusion of either a write or read operation, the number stored under the associated variable name I will designate the record number of the next record in the data set. The data set associated with data set reference number 9 is composed of 20 records; the maximum size of each record in the data set is 35 words; the data is to be either written on or read from the data set without reference to a FØRMAT statement; at the conclusion of either a write or read operation, the number stored under the associated variable name J will designate the record number of the next record in the data set. The data set associated with data set reference number 4 is composed of 25 records; the maximum size of each record in the data set is 50 record columns; the data is to be either written on or read from the data set either with or without reference to a FØRMAT statement; at the conclusion of either a write or read operation, the number stored under the associated variable name K will designate the record number of the next record in the data set.

The WRITE (*i'r,n*) *list* Statement   This statement causes the computer to transfer from its memory the data stored under the variable, logical variable, and/or array names located in the *list* portion of the statement and write it on a magnetic disk. Like the sequential-access WRITE statement, this statement also possesses the same capabilities as the WRITE statement discussed in Chapter 3. Figure 9-7 illustrates the general form of this statement.

```
cc | 123456789...
   |
   | bbbbb | WRITE (i'r,n) list
```

where

bbbbb   represents an unsigned 1 through 5 integer number that is required only if a transfer is made to this statement from another program statement.

WRITE   FORTRAN key word that distinguishes this statement from the other kinds of statements in the program.

(a special character that is a requirement of the FORTRAN language.

    i   represents either an unsigned integer number or integer variable name with an unsigned integer number stored under it that is the data set reference number associated with a particular data set that is to be stored on a magnetic disk.

    '   a special character that is a requirement of the FORTRAN language.

    r   represents an integer expression. Its current value specifies the record number of the first logical record to be written in the data set associated with the data set reference number represented by *i*.

    ,   a special character that is a requirement of the FORTRAN language.

    n   represents a statement number of the FØRMAT statement that describes the particular form of the data transferred from the computer's memory. If a FØRMAT statement is not used, *n* is not used.

)   a special character that is a requirement of the FORTRAN language.

 list   represents one or more variable, logical variable, and/or array names, each of which must be separated by a comma. The data stored under these one or more variable names and/or array names is transferred from the computer's memory and written into one or more records composing the data set associated with the data set reference number represented by *i*. The array name or names may be subscripted and these subscripts may be indexed. The *list* is left blank if the FØRMAT statement designated by *n* contains only literal data.

Figure 9-7. The General Form of the WRITE Statement.

In the following illustration, the WRITE statement

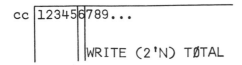

```
cc 123456789...

        WRITE (9'I,1) MIN,NUM
```

causes the computer to write each integer number stored in its memory under the variable names MIN and NUM in the data set located on a magnetic disk associated with data set reference number 9. The specific record in which the data will be written is designated by the integer number stored under the associated variable name I. The data will be transferred to a magnetic disk in the form specified by the FØRMAT statement assigned statement number 1.

Similarly, in the following illustration the WRITE statement

```
cc 123456789...

        WRITE (2'N) TØTAL
```

causes the computer to write the single precision floating-point number stored in its memory under the variable name TØTAL into the data set located on a magnetic disk associated with data set reference number 2. The specific record in which the number will be written is designated by the number stored under the associated variable name N. The absence of a statement number reflects the fact that the number will be transferred to a magnetic disk without reference to a FØRMAT statement.

The READ (*i'r,n*) *list* **Statement**   This statement causes the computer to read from a magnetic disk the data stored under the variable, logical variable, and/or array names located in the *list* portion of the statement and transfer it to its memory. Like the sequential-access READ statement, this statement also possesses the same capabilities as the READ statement discussed in Chapter 3. Figure 9-8 illustrates the general form of this statement.

```
cc 123456789...


    bbbbb READ (i'r,n) list
```

where

>   *bbbbb*   represents an unsigned 1 through 5 integer number that is
>   required only if a transfer is made to this statement from
>   another program statement.
>
>   READ   FORTRAN key word that distinguishes this statement from the
>   other kinds of statements in the program.
>
>   (a special character that is a requirement of the FORTRAN
>   language.
>
>   *i*   represents either an unsigned integer number or integer
>   variable name with an unsigned integer number stored under
>   it that is the data set reference number associated with a
>   particular data set that is stored on a magnetic disk.
>
>   '   a special character that is a requirement of the FORTRAN
>   language.
>
>   *r*   represents an integer expression. Its current value speci-
>   fies the record number of the first logical record to be
>   read in the data set associated with the data set reference
>   number represented by *i*.
>
>   ,   a special character that is a requirement of the FORTRAN
>   language.
>
>   *n*   represents a statement number of the FØRMAT statement that
>   describes the particular form of the data transferred from
>   a magnetic disk. If a FØRMAT statement is not used, *n* is
>   not used.
>
>   )   a special character that is a requirement of the FORTRAN
>   language.
>
>   *list*   represents one or more variable, logical variable, and/or
>   array names, each of which must be separated by a comma.
>   The data read from a record of the particular data set
>   designated by *i* is stored in the computer's memory under
>   these one or more variable, logical variable, and/or array
>   names. The array name or names may be subscripted and these
>   subscripts may be indexed.

Figure 9-8.   The General Form of the READ Statement.

In the following illustration, the READ statement

causes the computer to read from the data set associated with data set reference number 3 each number stored on a magnetic disk under the variable names A and B and transfer them to its memory. The specific record of the data set that will be read is designated by the number stored under the associated variable name LN. The data will be transferred to the computer's memory in the form specified by the FØRMAT statement assigned statement number 5.

Similarly, in the following illustration the READ statement

```
cc  12345 6 789...



        READ (1'M) RATE
```

causes the computer to read from the data set associated with data set reference number 1 each number stored on a magnetic disk under the variable name RATE and transfer it to its memory. The specific record of the data set that will be read is designated by the number stored under the associated variable name M. The absence of a statement number reflects the fact that the number will be transferred to its memory without reference for a FØRMAT statement.

The Format Alphabetic Characters As indicated in the discussion of the DEFINE FILE statement, the length of a record either written on or read from a magnetic disk is dependent upon which one of the three possible format alphabetic characters is located in the DEFINE FILE statement that contains the same data set reference number as the one located in either the WRITE or READ statement.

If the format alphabetic character E is located in the DEFINE FILE statement, the record length is measured in record columns (bytes). A record column contains one character.

The statements

```
cc  12345 6 789...



        DEFINE FILE 9(25,35,E,I)
        WRITE (9'I,1) MINT,TØT
  1     FØRMAT (I4,'THE TØTAL AMØUNT IS',1X,F5.2)
```

cause the computer to write a record of a data set associated with data set reference number 9. The specific record written in is designated by the number stored under the associated variable name I. As specified by the FØRMAT statement, data will be written in 29 record columns of the record.

The statements

```
cc  12345 6 789...



        DEFINE FILE 3(5,15,E,N)
        READ (3'N,2) A,B,C
  1     FØRMAT (F3.1,F2.2,F5.4)
```

cause the computer to read a record of a data set associated with data set reference number 3. As specified by the FØRMAT statement, data will be read from 10 record columns of the record. The specific record read from is designated by the number stored under the associated variable name N.

If the format alphabetic character U is located in the DEFINE FILE statement, the record length is measured in storage units (words). Unless specified otherwise, one storage unit is required to store a number under either an integer, single precision floating-point, or logical variable name and two storage units are required to store a number under a double precision floating-point variable name.

The statements

```
cc | 123456789...


        DEFINE FILE 9(10,16,U,L)
        DØUBLE PRECISIØN A
        WRITE (9'L) A,I
```

cause the computer to write each number stored in its memory under the variable names A and I in a record of a data set associated with data set reference number 9. The specific record written is designated by the number stored under the associated variable name L. Data will be written in 3 storage units of the record.

The statements

```
cc | 123456789...


        LØGICAL H
        DEFINE FILE 1(1,20,U,NM)
        READ (1'NM) H,X,Y,Z
```

cause the computer to read the datum stored in a record of a data set associated with data set reference number 1 under the symbolic names H, X, Y, and Z. The specific record read is designated by the number stored under the associated variable name NM. Data will be read from 4 storage units of the record.

If the format alphabetic character L is located in the DEFINE FILE statement, the record length is measured in storage locations (bytes). Unless specified otherwise, if either the WRITE or READ statement does refer to a FØRMAT statement, one storage location is required for each record column specified by the FØRMAT statement. And unless specified otherwise, if either the WRITE or READ statement does not refer to a FØRMAT statement, four storage locations are required by each integer, single precision floating-point, and logical variable name and eight storage locations are required by each double precision floating-point variable name located in the *list* portion of the statement.

The statements

```
cc | 123456789...


        DEFINE FILE 9(25,15,L,N)
        LØGICAL J
        WRITE (9'N,1) I,J,K
1       FØRMAT (I5,L4,I5)
```

cause the computer to write a record of a data set associated with data set reference number 9. The specific record written in is designated by the number stored under the associated variable name N. As specified by the FØRMAT statement, data will be written in 14 storage locations of the record.

The statements

```
cc | 123456789...


        DEFINE FILE 2(5,20,L,I)
        DØUBLE PRECISIØN A
        READ (2'I) A,B,C
```

cause the computer to read a record of a data set associated with data set reference number 2. The specific record read from is designated by the number stored under the associated variable name I. Data will be read from 16 storage locations of the record.

The Associated Variable Name   The use of the associated variable name is illustrated in the following four illustrations.

```
cc  123456789...


        DEFINE FILE 15(35,20,E,J)
        J = 1
        WRITE (15'J,3) A,B,C
    3   FØRMAT (F4.1,F3.2,F7.1)
```

In the preceding illustration, the computer will write the number stored under the variable names A, B, and C in the first record (J = 1) of the data set associated with data set reference number 15. At the conclusion of the operation, the number 1 stored under the associated variable name J will be automatically replaced by the number 2. Thus, the next time the WRITE statement is executed, assuming the number under J is not replaced by another number via another statement in the program, the data will be written in the second record of the data set.

In this illustration,

```
cc  123456789...


        DEFINE FILE 4(20,20,U,M)
        M = 5
    1   READ (4'M+5) I,J
```

the computer will read each of the numbers stored under the variable names I and J from the tenth record (M+5) of the data set associated with data set reference number 4. At the conclusion of the operation, the number 10 stored under the associated variable name M will be automatically replaced by the number 11. Thus, the next time this READ statement is executed, assuming the number stored under M is not replaced by another number via another statement in the program, the data will be read from the sixteenth record of the data set.

In the following illustration,

```
cc  123456789...


        DEFINE FILE 9(100,10,L,MIN)
        DIMENSIØN WAGE(100)
        MIN = 1
        DØ 2 I = 1,100
    1   FØRMAT (F5.2)
        WRITE (9'MIN,1) WAGE(I)
    2   CØNTINUE
```

the computer will write a number in each of the 100 array elements of the array named WAGE. Each number will be written in a record of a data set associated with data set reference number 9.

Finally, in the following illustration

```
cc 123456789...

      DEFINE FILE 6(100,11,E,I)
      DØ 3 J = 1,100
      READ (5,1,END=99) ITEM,CØST
  1   FØRMAT (I5,F5.2)
      WRITE (6'ITEM,2) CØST
  2   FØRMAT (T6,F6.2)
  3   CØNTINUE
```

the ease with which data can be updated throughout a data set is shown. The data set associated with data set reference number 6 contains 100 records, each of which contains the item number and cost of a particular item. The 100 records are stored on a disk by item number. The statements in the above illustration update the data set by reading the new cost of an item and writing that cost into the record designated by the item number. Thus, the data cards can be in any order. Although the associated variable I is not referred to by the WRITE statement, after each WRITE operation its value designates the record number of the record following the record into which data was written.

The FIND Statement   This statement is used to reduce the time it takes the computer to read a record of a data set located on a magnetic disk. Its usefulness lies in the fact that the computer can simultaneously continue to execute one or more of the following statements in the program while it is seeking the specific record of a data set. Thus, the time required to execute the program is reduced. There is no time saved, however, in using this statement prior to a writing operation. Figure 9-9 illustrates the general form of this statement.

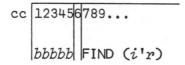

where

   bbbbb   represents an unsigned 1 through 5 integer number that is required only if a transfer is made to this statement from another program statement.

   FIND   FORTRAN key word that distinguishes this statement from the other kinds of statements in the program.

   (a special character that is a requirement of the FORTRAN language.

   i   represents either an unsigned integer number or integer variable name with an unsigned integer number stored under it that is the data set reference number associated with a particular data set that is stored on a magnetic disk.

   '   a special character that is a requirement of the FORTRAN language.

   r   represents an integer expression. Its current value specifies the record number of the first record to be read in the data set associated with the data set reference number represented by *i*.

)   a special character that is a requirement of the FORTRAN language.

Figure 9-9.   The General Form of the FIND Statement.

The FIND statement in the following illustration

```
cc 123456789...

   DEFINE FILE 3(25,20,E,I)
   .
   .

   FIND (3'K)
   .
   .
   .

   READ (3'K,1) X,Y,Z
 1 FØRMAT (3F.2)
   .
   .
   .
```

causes the computer to begin seeking the record of the data set associated with data set reference number 3 designated by the number stored under the variable name K. Simultaneously, it will continue to execute the one or more program statements located between the FIND and READ statements. When the computer executes the READ statement, it will either already have found the desired record and will be ready to immediately read it or if it has not yet found the record, the time it has spent so far doing so reduces the time by that amount that it would now have to spend seeking that record if the FIND statement had not been used. Such factors as the number and kinds of statements that must be executed between the FIND and READ statements, the speed of the computer, and the location of the record being sought on the magnetic disk determine whether or not the computer will have had time to find the desired record prior to executing the READ statement. At the conclusion of the FIND operation, the number stored under the variable name K will replace the number stored under the associated variable name I.

QUESTIONS

1. Why is the process of writing records on and the process of reading records from a magnetic tape called sequential-access?
2. What may be the minimum size of a record written on magnetic tape?
3. When is a formatted WRITE or READ statement used and when is an unformatted WRITE or READ statement used?
4. What is the function of the BACKSPACE statement?
5. What is the function of the REWIND statement?
6. What is the function of the END FILE statement?
7. What does an end-of-file mark indicate?
8. Why is the process of writing records on and the process of reading records from a magnetic disk called direct-access?
9. What major distinction exists between the sequential-access and direct-access methods with respect to designating specific records?
10. What may be the minimum size of a record written on magnetic disk?
11. What is the function of the DEFINE FILE statement?
12. What is the function of the FIND statement?

EXERCISES

1. Read 5 five-character integer numbers from a data card into an array named NN. Determine the square of each number and store the square in the corresponding array element of an array named

NNN, i.e., the square of NN(1) is stored in the array element NNN(1) etc. After each data card is read and each of the 5 numbers squared, write each of the numbers and its square onto a tape unit assigned data set reference number 8. Each number is to be immediately followed by its square, i.e., NN(1), NNN(1), NN(2), NNN(2), etc. The 10 numbers are to compose 1 record. After all of the data cards are read, processed, and written on magnetic tape, they are to be read from the magnetic tape and printed by the printer. The number of data cards is unknown.

2.   An unknown number of data cards, each containing information for a delivery made by the XYZ trucking company, are to be read. Each data card contains the following three integer numbers: (1) a two-character account number ranging from 01 to 10, (2) a number representing total miles driven, and (3) a number representing gross tonnage. The cost per delivery is to be determined. The charge is $1.00 per ton per mile. After the cost of a delivery is determined, write the account number, the gross tonnage, the number of miles hauled, and the delivery cost into a record located on a tape unit assigned data set reference number 8. After all of the data cards have been read, read the 4 numbers from each record; as each record is being read write the gross tonnage, the total number of miles, and the total cost into a two-dimensional array named ACCT that is dimensioned (10,3), i.e., for account number 01 store the total gross tonnage in (1,1), the total number of miles in (1,2) and the total cost in (1,3) etc. A grand total of the gross tonnage, total number of miles, and delivery costs is to be determined. After the grand totals are determined, the last three records are to be printed. After these three records are printed, each customer's record is to be printed.

3.   One hundred data cards have been dropped and completely mixed-up with respect to their sequence. Each data card contains a three-character sequence number ranging from 001 to 100 and a five-character integer number. You are to read the deck of data cards, square the integer number, and write the number and its square on to a magnetic disk so that the two numbers will be in the record position indicated by the card's sequence number. After all of the data cards are processed, new data cards containing the sequence number, the number, and its square are to be punched. The disk unit is to be assigned data set reference number 92 and the data may be either formatted or unformatted.

4.   The XYZ company needs to process its monthly charges. The company has 10 customers with account numbers ranging from 01 to 10. The charges have been accumulated for 4 weeks, with five work-days per week. A charge card is made out each day for each customer's account. Read the charge cards for the four-week period, determine the cost charged to each account each day at a rate of $4.00 per hour, and write each daily account record with the associated cost onto a disk unit assigned data set reference number 8. Also maintain a weekly total of costs charged to each account as well as a grand total of hours and costs charged to each account. At the end of each week, write onto a record of a disk unit assigned data set reference number 9 the total hours and total costs for that week, each account number, and the total costs for that account to date. Then print a weekly summary of each account's charges per day, the account total up to that date of the month, and the total hours and costs for that week.

Appendix A

AN INTRODUCTION TO THE IBM 29 CARD PUNCH

This appendix is a brief discussion of both the operation of the IBM 29 Card Punch and the use of the various functional control switches and keys and punching keys.

All functional control keys are blue with white printing; all punching keys are gray with black printing. Only the information concerning the specific functional control switched and keys and punching keys that the reader will need to understand and apply to punch most program statements and data into punch cards is presented. For a more in-depth discussion of the IBM 29 Card Punch, the reader should refer to a copy of *Reference Manual IBM 29 Card Punch*, Reference Number GA24-3332-6.

TO PREPARE THE CARD PUNCH FOR OPERATION

1. Flip the Main Line Switch, which is located directly beneath the right side of the machine cabinet (Figure A-1), to the "on" position. There is no warm-up period necessary before the machine is operative.
2. Place up to approximately 500 punch cards in the Card Hopper, which is located on the upper right side of the machine (Figure A-1). Even though the reader may desire to use no more than 1 punch card, the author suggests that a minimum of 2 punch cards be placed in the Card Hopper at a time.

    The punch cards are placed into the Card Hopper 9 edge down and face forward. They are held in place by a pressure plate. This plate should be pushed back until the pressure plate can slide back no further. Then release the back portion of the pressure plate and the pressure plate should lock in place. Next, place the punch cards in the Card Hopper. After the punch cards have been placed in the Card Hopper, release the pressure plate by again squeezing the two-piece top portion of the pressure plate and allowing the pressure plate to slowly slide toward the punch cards until it stops at the back of the last punch card placed in the Card Hopper.

    The punch cards, when the FEED functional control key (Figure A-3, #35) is pressed, are fed from the front of the Card Hopper.
3. Flip the PRINT functional control switch (Figure A-2) to the "on" position. This permits the printing of each card column as it is either being punched or duplicated. Whether the reader desires to also flip the AUTO FEED functional control switch (Figure A-2), which permits the feeding of punch cards from the Card Hopper automatically after the first two punch cards have been manually fed, to the "on" position is optional. If the reader has had little experience with this card punch machine, the author suggests that he leave this switch in the "off" position.

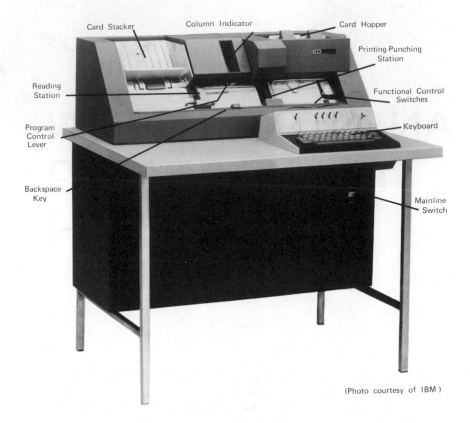

Card Stacker Column Indicator Card Hopper

Printing-Punching
Station

Reading
Station

Functional Control
Switches

Program
Control
Lever

Keyboard

Backspace
Key

Mainline
Switch

(Photo courtesy of IBM)

Figure A-1

Functional Switches

Keyboard

(Photo courtesy of IBM)

Figure A-2

The AUTO SKIP–DUP, TWO, PROG SEL, and L PRINT functional control switches (Figure A-2) should be rendered inoperative by flipping the Program Control Lever, which is located at the bottom of the Program Unit (Figure A-1), to the right, thus raising the Starwheels.

TO PREPARE THE CARD PUNCH FOR PUNCHING A PUNCH CARD

4. By pressing the FEED functional control key, a punch card is lowered from the Card Hopper to the Printing-Punching Station, which is located immediately beneath the Card Hopper (Figure A-1).

5. By pressing the REG (Figure A-3, #37) functional control key, the first punch card located in the Printing-Punching Station is registered and thus placed in position to be punched beginning with the first card column.

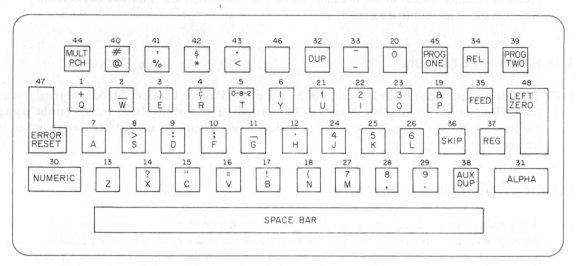

Figure A-3

TO PUNCH THE PUNCH CARD

6. Any punching key (Figure A-3) having two character symbols illustrated on it may be thought of as similar to a typewriter key with two character symbols illustrated on it in reference to its operation. The keyboard is in ALPHA mode (Figure A-3, #31) during its normal mode of operation and thus any punching key—and the DUP functional control key—that is pressed with a two character symbol illustrated on it will punch into and print on (assuming the PRINT functional control switch is in the "on" position) the particular card column indicated by the Column Indicator, which is located at the base of the Program Drum holder (Figure A-1), the illustrated lower level character.

   Any punching key pressed with only one character symbol illustrated on it will punch and print (assuming the same situation as described above) the illustrated character into the particular card column indicated by the Column Indicator.

7. To punch an upper level illustrated character when the card punch is in ALPHA mode, the reader must press the NUMERIC functional control key (Figure A-3, #30) prior to pressing the punching key illustrating the desired character.

8. The Column Indicator indicates the card column under the punching and/or reading head that will be either read and/or punched the next time either a punching key or the DUP functional control key is pressed.

9. If during the punching of a punch card, the reader desires to skip one or more punch cards columns, this can be accomplished by pressing the Space Bar (Figure A-3). Each time the Space Bar is pressed, the punch cards in both the Printing-Punching and Reading Stations (Figure A-1) progress forward one card column.

10. If the reader desires to punch a character in more or more card columns of a punch card that have already passed the Print-Punching heads, he can back the punch card up to the desired card column

or columns by pressing the Backspace functional control key, which is located just below the card bed (Figure A-1), between the punching and the reading heads. As long as the Backspace Key is held down, any registered punch cards at either the Printing-Punching and/or Reading Stations and the Program Drum will backspace one card column at a time until card column 1 is reached.

TO MOVE THE COMPLETED PUNCH CARD FROM THE PRINTING-PUNCHING STATION TO THE READING STATION

11.   When the punching of the punch card in the Printing-Punching Station is completed, the reader should press the REL functional control key (Figure A-3, #34). This key moves the punch card in the Printing-Punching Station to the Reading Station and the punch card in the Reading Station (if any) into position to move into the Card Stacker.

THE READING STATION

12.   The Reading Station is located directly to the left of the Printing-Punching Station. Through use of the DUP functional control key (Figure A-3), either all or part of the data punched on the punch card located in the Reading Station can be duplicated on the punch card that has been registered in the Printing-Punching Station.

DUPLICATING PUNCH CARD DATA

13.   If the reader desires to duplicate either all or part of the data punched on a punch card located in the Reading Station on to a punch card that has been registered in the Printing-Punching Station, he must press the DUP functional control key. Consecutive columns of data punched in the punch card in the Reading Station will continue to be duplicated as long as the DUP functional control key is pressed.

      If the reader should desire to change one or more characters punched in particular card columns of a punch card being duplicated, continue duplicating and/or spacing until the Column Indicator indicates each card column the reader desires to change the character punched in it; then, using the previously discussed procedures, press the punching key illustrating the desired character.

THE TERMINAL LOCATION OF THE PUNCHED CARDS

14.   The Card Stacker is located on the upper left side of the Card Punch (Figure A-1). Like the Card Hopper, it can hold up to approximately 500 punched cards. The punched cards are stacked at an angle, 12 edge down and face backward, and are held in position by a card weight. When the punched cards are removed, they are in the same sequence as they were punched.

TERMINATING OPERATION OF THE CARD PUNCH

15.   When punching is completed, all punch cards that left the Card Hopper but are not in the Card Stacker can be moved to the Card Stacker by flipping the CLEAR functional control switch (Figure A-2) to the "on" position until all the punch cards have cleared the card bed.
16.   Remove all punch cards from the Card Hopper by using the same basic process that was used to originally place them in the Card Hopper.
17.   Remove all punched cards from the Card Stacker.
18.   The Card Punch is turned off by flipping the Main Line Switch to the "off" position.

A LIST OF THE FORTRAN IV KEY WORDS

.AND.	EQUIVALENCE	.ØR.
ASSIGN	ERR	
AT	EXTERNAL	PAUSE
		PRINT
BACKSPACE	.FALSE.	PUNCH
BLØCK DATA	FIND	
	FØRMAT	READ
CALL	FUNCTIØN	REAL
CHARACTER		RETURN
CØMMØN	.GE.	REWIND
CØMPLEX	GENERIC	
CØNTINUE	GØ TØ	STØP
	.GT.	SUBCHK
DATA		SUBRØUTINE
DEBUG	IF	SUBTRACE
DEFINE FILE	IMPLICIT	
DIMENSIØN	INIT	TRACE
DISPLAY	INTEGER	TRACE ØFF
DØ		TRACE ØN
DØUBLE PRECISIØN	.LE.	.TRUE.
	LØGICAL	UNIT
END	.LT.	
END FILE		WAIT
ENTRY	NAMELIST	WRITE
.EQ.	.NE.	
	.NØT.	

PROGRAM DEBUGGING

Unfortunately, most computer programs do not successfully execute the first time they are read into the computer by means of an input device. Rather, many computer programs contain one or more errors of three possible types of program errors the first several times they are read into the computer. The process of detecting and correcting these program errors is called "debugging."

The following is a brief discussion, in the order of their detection, of each of these three types of errors:

1. *Syntax Errors*   A syntax error indicates that a program statement is not formed according to the rules of the FORTRAN language. For instance, a key word may be misspelled or a required delimiter may be missing. This type of error is detected during compilation of the source program by the FORTRAN compiler program. The FORTRAN compiler program indicates its discovery of these errors to the programmer through the printing on the printer printout of appropriate diagnostic error messages.

2. *Execution Errors*   Execution errors are detected during execution of the object program; that is, after the source program has been compiled into an object program and the computer begins to execute the object program. An execution error indicates that, for example, an attempt was made to divide a number by zero or a calculated number exceeds the memory storage capacity of the computer for that particular type of number. This type of error is also indicated by the printing on the printer printout of appropriate diagnostic error messages.

3. *Logical Errors*   Logical errors indicate that the computer program does not correctly express the problem it is attempting to solve and thus the results are incorrect. For example, a program statement may be executed out of sequence or the program may transfer to the incorrect program statement under certain conditions. This type of error is the most difficult to discover as it is not detected by the computer and thus no diagnostic error messages are printed on the printer printout.

The IBM System/360 and System/370 computers generally have available one or more of the following four FORTRAN compilers to execute FORTRAN IV programs: (1) FORTRAN G, (2) FORTRAN H, (3) WATFOR, and (4) WATFIV. The first two compilers are provided by IBM and the last two by the

University of Waterloo, Waterloo, Ontario, Canada. The following is a brief description of some of the major features of each of these compilers:

FORTRAN G and H Compilers

1. The FORTRAN G compiler requires less computer memory storage than the FORTRAN H compiler.

2. The FORTRAN G compiler compiles a source program considerably faster than the FORTRAN H compiler.

3. The FORTRAN G compiler provides better overall efficiency for program debugging and the compilation and execution of short programs.

4. The FORTRAN H compiler executes an object program faster than the FORTRAN G compiler.

5. The FORTRAN G and H compilers permit the punching of an object program deck.

6. The FORTRAN G and H compilers will accept either a source or object program deck and provide various options such as a program memory map.

THE DEBUG FACILITY

The debug facility is a programming aid that enables a person to locate any syntax errors in a FORTRAN source program (main program or subprogram). This facility provides the options for (1) tracing the compilation flow within a program, (2) tracing the compilation flow between a main program and one or more subprograms, (3) displaying the number stored under one or more variable or array names, and (4) checking the validity of subscripts.

The debug facility consists of a DEBUG specification statement, an AT debug packed identification statement, and three executable statements (TRACE ØN, TRACE ØFF, DISPLAY). These statements, alone or in combination with the program statements, are used to state the desired debugging operations for either a main program or a subprogram.

This debug facility is available only under either the IBM operating System/360 with the FORTRAN IV (G), FORTRAN IV (G1), and Code and Go FORTRAN compilers or the Disk Operating System/360 with the DOS FORTRAN IV compiler.

When the debug facility is to be used in either a main program or a subprogram, the arrangement of the program is as follows: (1) the source program statements (excluding the END statement), (2) a DEBUG specification statement, (3) one or more debug packets, and (4) an END statement.

The program statements that compose a debugging operation must be grouped in one or more debug packets. A debug packet is composed of one or more executable debug facility statements and/or source program statements. It must be immediately preceded by an AT debug packet identification statement. A debug packet is terminated by either another AT debug packet identification statement or an END statement.

The following programming factors must be considered when preparing a debug packet:

1. Any DØ loops initiated within a debug packet must be wholly contained within that packet.

2. Statement numbers within a debug packet must be unique. They must be different from statement numbers within other debug packets and within the source program being debugged.

3. An error in a source program should not be corrected with a debug packet; when the debug packet is removed, the error should remain in the source program.

4. The following statements cannot appear in a debug packet:

SUBRØUTINE	IMPLICIT
FUNCTIØN	BLØCK DATA
ENTRY	statement function

5. A transfer cannot be made from a statement located in the source program being debugged to a program statement located in a debug packet to a statement located in the source program. In addition, a debug packet may contain a RETURN, STØP, or CALL EXIT statement.

The following is a discussion of each debug facility program statement:

DEBUG Specification Statement   This specification statement establishes the conditions for operation of the debug facility and designates debugging operations that apply to the entire main program or subprogram (such as subscript checking). There must be one DEBUG statement for each main and subprogram to be debugged, and it must immediately precede the first debug packet in the main or subprogram. Figure C-1 illustrates the general form of this specification statement.

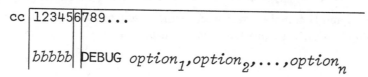

where

bbbbb   represents an optional unsigned 1 through 5 integer number.

DEBUG   FORTRAN key word that distinguishes this statement from the other kinds of statements in the program.

option   UNIT (i) where i is a data set reference number. All debugging output is placed in this data set, called the debug output data set. If this option is not specified, any debugging output is printed by the printer. The same debug output data set must be used throughout the main program or subprogram.

SUBCHK   ($an_1, an_2, \ldots, an_n$) where an is an array name. The validity of the subscripts used with the named arrays is checked by comparing the subscript combination with the size of the array. If the subscript exceeds its dimension bounds, a message is placed in the debug output data det. Program execution continues, using the incorrect subscript. If the list of array names is omitted, *all* arrays in the program are checked for valid subscript usage. If the entire option is omitted, no arrays are checked for valid subscripts.

TRACE   This option must be in the DEBUG specification statement of each source program or subprogram for which tracing is desired. If this option is omitted, there can be no display of program flow by statement number within the program. Even when this option is used, a TRACE ON statement must appear in the first debug packet in which tracing is desired.

INIT   ($sn_1, sn_2, \ldots, sn_n$) where sn is a variable or array name that is to be displayed in the debug output data set only when either the number stored under the variable name or one or more numbers stored under the array name

change. If *sn* is a variable name, the name and number
are displayed whenever the variable name is assigned a
new number in either an arithmetic or logical assignment, READ, or assigned GØ TØ statement. If *sn* is an
array name, the changed array element is displayed.
If the list of variable and/or array names is omitted,
a display occurs whenever the number of a variable name
or an array element is changed. If the entire option
is omitted, no display occurs when numbers change.

SUBTRACE This option specifies that the name of the subprogram is to be displayed whenever it is entered. The
message RETURN is to be displayed whenever execution of
the subprogram is completed.

Figure C-1.   The General Form of the DEBUG Specification Statement.

If there is more than one option in a DEBUG specification statement, they may be in any order and each
must be separated by a comma.

The AT Debug Packet Identification Statement   This statement identifies the beginning of a debug packet
and indicates the point in the source program at which debugging is to begin. There may be one or more
debug packets following a main program or a subprogram. An AT statement must be the first statement in
each debug packet. Figure C-2 illustrates the general form of this identification statement.

```
cc│123456789...
  │
  │bbbbb│AT sn
```

where

bbbbb   represents an optional unsigned 1 through 5 integer number.

AT   FORTRAN key word that distinguishes this statement from the
other kinds of statements in the program.

sn   represents a statement number assigned to an executable
statement in the source program or subprogram to be debugged.

Figure C-2.   The General Form of the AT Debug Packet Identification Statement.

The debugging operations specified within the debug packet are performed prior to the execution of
the program statement assigned to the statement number located in the AT debug packet identification
statement.

The TRACE ØN Statement   This statement initiates the display of source program flow by statement
number. Each time a program statement assigned a statement number is executed, a statement number is
written on the debug output data set. When this statement is used, the option TRACE must be used in the
DEBUG specification statement. Figure C-3 illustrates the general form of this statement.

```
cc│123456789...
  │
  │bbbbb│TRACE ØN
```

where

    bbbbb   represents an optional unsigned 1 through 5 integer number.
TRACE ∅N   FORTRAN key word that distinguishes this statement from
            the other kinds of statements in the program.

Figure C-3. The General Form of the TRACE ∅N Statement.

The TRACE ∅N statement takes effect for a specific debug packet immediately prior to the execution of the program statement assigned the statement number located in the AT debug packet identification statement. Tracing continues through any level of transfer to and return from a subprogram. However, if a transfer is made to either the main program or a subprogram in which the TRACE option is not used, tracing is terminated and thus any statement numbers assigned to program statements within it are not written on the debug output data set. The statement continues in effect until a TRACE ∅FF statement is executed. This statement may not appear as the conditional part of a logical IF statement.

The TRACE ∅FF Statement   This statement terminates the tracing and writing of statement numbers when the program statement assigned to it is executed on the debug output data set. Figure C-4 illustrates the general form of this statement.

```
cc 123456789...

   bbbbb TRACE ∅FF
```

where

    bbbbb   represents an optional unsigned 1 through 5 integer number.
TRACE ∅FF   FORTRAN key word that distinguishes this statement from
           the other kinds of statements in the program.

Figure C-4. The General Form of the TRACE ∅FF Statement.

The TRACE ∅FF statement may appear anywhere within a debug packet. However, it cannot appear as the conditional part of a logical IF statement.

The DISPLAY Statement   This statement causes data to be displayed in a NAMELIST output format. It eliminates the need for either a F∅RMAT or NAMELIST and WRITE statements to display the results of a debugging operation. The effect of this statement is the same as the following two program statements:

```
cc 123456789...

      NAMELIST /n/list
      WRITE (i,n)
```

Figure C-5 illustrates the general form of this statement.

```
cc 123456789...

   bbbbb DISPLAY list
```

where

    bbbbb   represents an optional unsigned 1 through 5 integer number.

Example 2   165

> DISPLAY   FORTRAN key word that distinguishes this statement from
>   the other kinds of statements in the program.
> *list*   represents a series of variable and/or array names, each
>   of which must be separated by a comma.

Figure C-5.   The General Form of the DISPLAY Statement.

Array elements cannot appear in the *list* portion of the statement. If the statement appears in a SUBRØUTINE subprogram, *n* cannot be a dummy argument of the subprogram. This statement cannot appear as the conditional part of a logical IF statement.

Three examples of the use of the debug facility follow.

EXAMPLE 1

```
cc 123456789...

       INTEGER A,B,C
       .
       .
       .
1      C = A*B
2      IF (C) 10,20,30
       .
       .
       .
       DEBUG
       AT 2
       DISPLAY C,A,B
       END
```

In the preceding example, when the program statement assigned statement number 2 is encountered by the computer the number stored under each of the variable names C, A, and B located in the program statement assigned statement number 1 are printed by the printer. If statement number 2 in the AT statement was to be replaced by statement number 1, the number stored under each of the variable names immediately prior to the execution of the program statement assigned statement number 1 would be printed by the printer.

EXAMPLE 2

```
cc 123456789...

       DIMENSIØN TØTAL(100), SUBTØT(100)
       .
       .
       .
       DØ 2 I = 1,100
1      TØTAL(I) = TØTAL(I)+SUBTØT(I)
2      CØNTINUE
3      X = Y+Z
       .
       .
       .
       DEBUG
       AT 3
       DISPLAY TØTAL
       END
```

In the preceding example, when the program statement assigned statement number 3 is encountered by the computer the number stored under the array named TØTAL at the completion of the DØ loop will be printed by the printer. If statement number 3 in the AT statement was to be replaced by statement number 1, the number that had been stored under an array element composing the array named TOTAL immediately prior to each time the computer encountered the program statement assigned statement number 2 would be printed by the printer.

EXAMPLE 3

```
cc  123456789...


1      W = 5.2
2      J = 100
3      X = Y*25.
4      DØ 5 I = 1,3
       .
       .
       .
5      CØNTINUE
6      Y = X/W
7      Z = Y+2.5
       STØP
       .
       .
       .
       DEBUG  TRACE
C      DEBUG  PACKET  NUMBER  1
       AT 1
       TRACE ØN
C      DEBUG  PACKET  NUMBER  2
       AT 4
       TRACE ØFF
       DØ 8 I = 1,5
       .
       .
       .
8      CØNTINUE
       TRACE ØN
C      DEBUG  PACKET  3
       AT 7
       TRACE ØFF
       END
```

In the preceding example, when the program statement assigned statement number 1 is encountered by the computer tracing will begin as indicated by debug packet number 1. When the program statement assigned statement number 4 is encountered, tracing will stop as indicated by the TRACE ØFF statement in debug packet number 2. There will be no tracing during execution of the DØ loop in debug packet number 2. However, tracing will resume immediately after execution of the DØ loop is completed, which is immediately prior to leaving debug packet number 2. When the program statement assigned statement number 7 is encountered, debug packet number 3 is executed which causes tracing to stop. The statement numbers that will have been printed by the printer are 1, 2, 3, 4, 5, 5, 5, and 6; statement numbers 7 and 8 will not be printed.

WATFOR AND WATFIV COMPILERS

1. The WATFOR and WATFIV compilers compile source programs faster but execute object programs slower than the FORTRAN G and H compilers.

2. The WATFOR and WATFIV compilers more efficiently and effectively compile and execute either short or average length FORTRAN programs than the FORTRAN G and H compilers.

3. The WATFOR and WATFIV compilers, as contrasted with the FORTRAN G and H compilers, skip the "load and go" steps and begin program execution immediately after program compilation'.

4. Except for those FORTRAN-supplied library subprograms, such as SIN and COS, WATFOR and WATFIV compilers cannot call for library subprograms.

5. The WATFOR and WATFIV compilers are more efficient and effective for debugging FORTRAN programs that the FORTRAN G and H compilers because they provide both more intelligible diagnostic error messages and detect many kinds of program errors that are not detected by FORTRAN G and H compilers.

6. The WATFOR and WATFIV compilers will only accept a source program deck.

7. WATFOR does not provide for any program options whereas WATFIV does provide for certain program options.

8. WATFOR and WATFIV, as contrasted with FORTRAN G and H compilers, are incore compilers; that is, the WATFOR and WATFIV compiler is completely located in the computer's memory at the same time the object program is located in the computer's memory. Thus, assuming an equal amount of available computer memory, a WATFOR or WATFIV compiler cannot compile as large a source program as a FORTRAN G or H compiler.

As previously mentioned, the WATFOR and WATFIV compilers provide efficient and effective diagnostic error messages. A complete list of the diagnostic error messages provided by each of these compilers follows.

WATFOR DIAGNOSTIC ERROR MESSAGES[1]

```
'ASSIGN STATEMENTS AND VARIABLES'
AS-2    'ATTEMPT TO REDEFINE AN ASSIGNED VARIABLE IN AN ARITHMETIC
            STATEMENT'
AS-3    'ASSIGNED VARIABLE USED IN AN ARITHMETIC EXPRESSIØN'
AS-4    'ASSIGNED VARIABLE CANNØT BE HALF WØRD INTEGER'
AS-5    'ATTEMPT TO REDEFINE AN ASSIGN VARIABLE IN AN INPUT LIST'


'BLØCK DATA STATEMENTS'
BD-0    'EXECUTABLE STATEMENT IN BLØCK DATA SUBPRØGRAMME'
BD-1    'IMPRØPER BLØCK DATA STATEMENT'


'CARD FØRMAT AND CØNTENTS'
CC-0    'CØLUMNS 1-5 ØF CØNTINUATION CARD NØT BLANK'
            PRØBABLE CAUSE – STATEMENT PUNCHED TØ LEFT ØF CØLUMN 7
CC-1    'TØØ MANY CØNTINUATIØN CARDS (MAXIMUM ØF 7)'
```

WATFOR

[1]WATFOR error messages have been reproduced by permission from "1360 WATFOR Implementation Guide," Computer Centre, University of Waterloo, Waterloo, Ontario, Canada, February 1968.

CC-2   'INVALID CHARACTER IN FØRTRAN STATEMENT '$' INSERTED IN SØURCE
            LISTING'
CC-3   'FIRST CARD ØF A PRØGRAMME IS A CØNTINUATIØN CARD'
            PRØBABLE CAUSE - STATEMENT PUNCHED TØ LEFT ØF CØLUMN 7
CC-4   'STATEMENT TØØ LØNG TØ CØMPILE (SCAN-STACK ØVERFLØW)'
CC-5   'BLANK CARD ENCØUNTERED'
CC-6   'KEYPUNCH USED DIFFERS FRØM KEYPUNCH SPECIFIED ØN JØB CARD'
CC-7   'FIRST CHARACTER ØF STATEMENT NØT ALPHABETIC'
CC-8   'INVALID CHARACTER(S) CØNCATENTATED WITH FØRTRAN KEYWØRD'
CC-9   'INVALID CHARACTERS IN CØL 1-5.   STATEMENT NUMBER IGNØRED'
            PRØBABLE CAUSE - STATEMENT PUNCHED TØ LEFT OF CØLUMN 7

'CØMMØN'
CM-0   'VARIABLE PREVIØUSLY PLACED IN CØMMØN'
CM-1   'NAME IN CØMMØN LIST PREVIØUSLY USED AS ØTHER THAN VARIABLE'
CM-2   'SUBPRØGRAMME PARAMETER APPEARS IN CØMMØN STATEMENT'
CM-3   'INITIALIZING ØF CØMMØN SHØULD BE DØNE IN A BLØCK DATA
            SUBPRØGRAMME'
CM-4   'ILLEGAL USE OF BLØCK NAME'

'FØRTRAN TYPE CØNSTANTS'
CN-0   'MIXED REAL *4, REAL * 8 IN CØMPLEX CØNSTANT'
CN-1   'INTEGER CØNSTANT GREATER THAN 2,147,483,647 (2**31-1)'
CN-2   'EXPØNENT ØVERFLØW ØR UNDERFLØW CØNVERTING CØNSTANT IN SØURCE
            STATEMENT'
CN-3   'EXPØNENT ØN REAL CØNSTANT GREATER THAN 99'
CN-4   'REAL CØNSTANT HAS MØRE THAN 16 DIGITS, TRUNCATED TØ 16'
CN-5   'INVALID HEXADECIMAL CØNSTANT'
CN-6   'ILLEGAL USE ØF DECIMAL PØINT'
CN-8   'CØNSTANT WITH E-TYPE EXPØNENT HAS MØRE THAN 7 DIGITS,
            ASSUME D-TYPE'
CN-9   'CØNSTANT ØR STATEMENT NUMBER GREATER THAN 99999'

'CØMPILER ERRØRS'
CP-0   'DETECTED IN PHASE RELØC'
CP-1   'DETECTED IN PHASE LINKR'
CP-2   'DUPLICATE PSEUDØ STATEMENT NUMBERS'
CP-4   'DETECTED IN PHASE ARITH'
CP-5   'CØMPILER INTERRUPT'

'DATA STATEMENT'
DA-0   'REPLICATIØN FACTØR GREATER THAN 32767, ASSUME 32767'
DA-1   'NØN-CØNSTANT IN DATA STATEMENT'
DA-2   'MØRE VARIABLES THAN CØNSTANTS IN DATA STATEMENT'
DA-3   'ATTEMPT TØ INITIALIZE A SUBPRØGRAMME PARAMETER IN A DATA
            STATEMENT'
DA-4   'NØN-CØNSTANT SUBSCRIPTS IN A DATA STATEMENT INVALID IN /360
            FØRTRAN'
DA-5   '/360 FØRTRAN DØES NØT HAVE IMPLIED DØ IN DATA STATEMENT'
DA-6   'NØN-AGREEMENT BETWEEN TYPE ØF VARIABLE AND CØNSTANT IN DATA
            STATEMENT
DA-7   'MØRE CØNSTANTS THAN VARIABLES IN DATA STATEMENT'
DA-8   'VARIABLE PREVIØUSLY INITIALIZED, LATEST VALUE USED' CHECK
            CØMMØN/EQUIVALENCED VARIABLES
DA-9   'INITIALIZING BLANK CØMMØN NØT ALLØWED IN /360 FØRTRAN'

DA-A   'INVALID DELIMITER IN CØNSTANT LIST PØRTIØN ØF DATA STATEMENT'
DA-B   'TRUNCATIØN ØF LITERAL CØNSTANT HAS ØCCURRED'

'DIMENSIØN STATEMENTS'
DM-0   'NØ DIMENSIØNS SPECIFIED FØR A VARIABLE IN A DIMENSIØN STATEMENT'
DM-1   'ØPTIØNAL LENGTH SPECIFICATIØN IN DIMENSIØN STATEMENT IS ILLEGAL'
DM-2   'INITIALIZATIØN IN DIMENSIØN STATEMENT IS ILLEGAL'
DM-3   'ATTEMPT TØ RE-DIMENSIØN A VARIABLE'
DM-4   'ATTEMPT TØ DIMENSIØN AN INITIALIZED VARIABLE'

'DØ LØØPS'
DØ-0   'ILLEGAL STATEMENT USED AS ØBJECT ØF DØ'
DØ-1   'ILLEGAL TRANSFER INTØ THE RANGE ØF A DØ-LØØP'
DØ-2   'ØBJECT ØF A DØ STATEMENT HAS ALREADY APPEARED'
DØ-3   'IMPRØPERLY NESTED DØ-LØØPS'
DØ-4   'ATTEMPT TØ REDEFINE A DØ-LØØP PARAMETER WITHIN RANGE ØF LØØP'
DØ-5   'INVALID DØ-LØØP PARAMETER'
DØ-6   'TØØ MANY NESTED DØ'S (MAXIMUM OF 20)'
DØ-7   'DØ-PARAMETER IS UNDEFINED ØR ØUTSIDE RANGE'
DØ-8   'THIS DØ LØØP WILL TERMINATE AFTER FIRST TIME THROUGH'
DØ-9   'ATTEMPT TØ REDEFINE A DØ-LØØP PARAMETER IN AN INPUT LIST'

'EQUIVALENCE AND/ØR CØMMØN'
EC-0   'TWØ EQUIVALENCED VARIABLES APPEAR IN CØMMØN'
EC-1   'CØMMØN BLØCK HAS DIFFERENT LENGTH THAN IN A PREVIØUS SUBPRØGRAMME'
EC-2   'CØMMØN AND/ØR EQUIVALENCE CAUSES INVALID ALIGNMENT.   EXECUTIØN
           SLØWED'   REMEDY – ØRDER VARIABLES IN DESCENDING ØRDER BY LENGTH
EC-3   'EQUIVALENCE EXTENDS CØMMØN DØWNWARDS'
EC-7   'CØMMØN/EQUIVALENCE STATEMENT DØES NØT PRECEDE PREVIØUS USE ØF
           VARIABLE'
EC-8   'VARIABLE USED WITH NØN-CØNSTANT SUBSCRIPT IN CØMMØN/EQUIVALENCE
           LIST'
EC-9   'A NAME SUBSCRIPTED IN AN EQUIVALENCE STATEMENT WAS NØT DIMENSIØNED

'END STATEMENTS'
EN-0   'NØ END STATEMENT IN PRØGRAMME -- END STATEMENT GENERATED'
EN-1   'END STATEMENT USED AS STØP STATEMENT AT EXECUTIØN'
EN-2   'IMPRØPER END STATEMENT'
EN-3   'FIRST STATEMENT ØF SUBPRØGRAMME IS END STATEMENT'

'EQUAL SIGNS'
EQ-6   'ILLEGAL QUANTITY ØN LEFT ØF EQUAL SIGN'
EQ-8   'ILLEGAL USE ØF EQUAL SIGN'
EQ-A   'MULTIPLE ASSIGNMENT STATEMENTS NØT IN /360 FØRTRAN'

'EQUIVALENCE STATEMENTS'
EV-0   'ATTEMPT TØ EQUIVALENCE A VARIABLE TØ ITSELF'
EV-1   'ATTEMPT TØ EQUIVALENCE A SUBPRØGRAMME PARAMETER'
EV-2   'LESS THAN 2 MEMBERS IN AN EQUIVALENCE LIST'
EV-3   'TØØ MANY EQUIVALENCE LISTS (MAX = 255)'
EV-4   'PREVIØUSLY EQUIVALENCED VARIABLE RE-EQUIVALENCED INCØRRECTLY'

'PØWERS AND EXPØNENTIATIØN'
EX-0   'ILLEGAL CØMPLEX EXPØNENTIATIØN'
EX-2   'I**J WHERE I=J=0'
EX-3   'I**J WHERE I=0,J.LT.0'

EX-6 '0.0**Y WHERE Y.LE.0.0'
EX-7 '0.0**J WHERE J=0'
EX-8 '0.0**J WHERE L.LT.0'
EX-9 'X**Y WHERE X.LT.0.0,NE.0.0'

'ENTRY STATEMENT'

WATFOR

EY-0 'SUBPRØGRAMME NAME IN ENTRY STATEMENT PREVIØUSLY DEFINED'
EY-1 'PREVIØUS DEFINITIØN ØF FUNCTIØN NAME IN AN ENTRY IS INCØRRECT
EY-2 'USE ØF SUBPRØGRAMME PARAMETER INCØNSISTENT WITH PREVIØUS ENTRY PØINT'
EY-3 'ARGUMENT NAME HAS APPEARED IN AN EXECUTABLE STATEMENT' BUT WAS NØT A SUBPRØGRAMME PARAMETER
EY-4 'ENTRY STATEMENT NØT PERMITTED IN MAIN PRØGRAMME'
EY-5 'ENTRY PØINT INVALID INSIDE A DØ-LØØP'
EY-6 'VARIABLE WAS NØT PREVIØUSLY USED AS A PARAMETER - PARAMETER ASSUMED'

'FØRMAT'

SØME FØRMAT ERRØR MESSAGES GIVE CHARACTERS IN WHICH ERRØR WAS DETECTED

FM-0 'INVALID CHARACTER IN INPUT DATA'
FM-2 'NØ STATEMENT NUMBER ØN A FØRMAT STATEMENT'
FM-5 'FØRMAT SPECIFICATIØN AND DATA TYPE DØ NØT MATCH'
FM-6 'INCØRRECT SEQUENCE ØF CHARACTERS IN INPUT DATA'
FM-7 'NØN-TERMINATING FØRMAT'

WATFOR

FT-0 'FIRST CHARACTER ØR VARIABLE FØRMAT NØT A LEFT PARENTHESIS'
FT-1 'INVALID CHARACTER ENCØUNTERED IN FØRMAT'
FT-2 'INVALID FØRM FØLLØWING A SPECIFICATIØN'
FT-3 'INVALID FIELD ØR GRØUP CØUNT'
FT-4 'A FIELD ØR GRØUP CØUNT GREATER THAN 255'
FT-5 'NØ CLØSING PARENTHESIS ØN VARIABLE FØRMAT'
FT-6 'NØ CLØSING QUØTE IN A HØLLERITH FIELD'
FT-7 'INVALID USE ØF CØMMA'
FT-8 'INSUFFICIENT SPACE TØ CØMPILE A FØRMAT STATEMENT (SCAN-STACK ØVERFLØW)
FT-9 'INVALID USE ØF P SPECIFICATIØN'
FT-A 'CHARACTER FØLLØWS CLØSING RIGHT PARENTHESIS'
FT-B 'INVALID USE ØF PERIØD (.)'
FT-C 'MØRE THAN THREE LEVELS ØF PARENTHESES'
FT-D 'INVALID CHARACTER BEFØRE A RIGHT PARENTHESIS'
FT-E 'MISSING ØR ZERØ LENGTH HØLLERITH ENCØUNTERED'
FT-F 'NØ CLØSING RIGHT PARENTHESIS'

WATFOR

'FUNCTIØNS AND SUBRØUTINES'

FN-0 'NØ ARGUMENTS IN A FUNCTIØN STATEMENT'
FN-3 'REPEATED ARGUMENT IN SUBPRØGRAMME ØR STATEMENT FUNCTIØN DEFINITIØN'
FN-4 'SUBSCRIPTS ØN RIGHT HAND SIDE ØF STATEMENT FUNCTIØN' PRØBABLE CAUSE - VARIABLE TØ LEFT ØF = NØT DIMENSIØNED
FN-5 'MULTIPLE RETURNS ARE INVALID IN FUNCTIØN SUBPRØGRAMMES'
FN-6 'ILLEGAL LENGTH MØDIFIER IN TYPE FUNCTIØN STATEMENT'
FN-7 'INVALID ARGUMENT IN ARITHMETIC ØR LØGICAL STATEMENT FUNCTIØN'
FN-8 'ARGUMENT ØF SUBPRØGRAMME IS SAME AS SUBPRØGRAMME NAME'

'GØ TØ STATEMENTS'
GØ-0   'STATEMENT TRANSFERS TØ ITSELF ØR A NØN-EXECUTABLE STATEMENT'
GØ-1   'INVALID TRANSFER TØ THIS STATEMENT'
GØ-2   'INDEXED ØF CØMPUTED 'GØTØ' IS NEGATIVE; ZERØ ØR UNDEFINED'
GØ-3   'ERRØR IN VARIABLE ØF 'GØ TØ' STATEMENT'
GØ-4   'INDEX ØF ASSIGNED 'GØ TØ' IS UNDEFINED ØR NØT IN RANGE'

'HØLLERITH CØNSTANTS'
HØ-0   'ZERØ LENGTH SPECIFIED FØR H-TYPE HØLLERITH'
HØ-1   'ZERØ LENGTH QUØTE-TYPE HØLLERITH'
HØ-2   'NØ CLØSING QUØTE ØR NEXT CARD NØT CØNTINUATION CARD'
HØ-3   'HØLLERITH CØNSTANT SHØULD APPEAR ØNLY IN CALL STATEMENT'
HØ-4   'UNEXPECTED HØLLERITH ØR STATEMENT NUMBER CØNSTANT'

'IF STATEMENTS (ARITHMETIC AND LØGICAL)'
IF-0   'STATEMENT INVALID AFTER A LØGICAL IF'
IF-3   'ARITHMETIC ØR INVALID EXPRESSIØN IN LØGICAL IF'
IF-4   'LØGICAL, CØMPLEX, ØR INVALID EXPRESSIØN IN ARITHMETIC IF'

'IMPLICIT STATEMENT'
IM-0   'INVALID MØDE SPECIFIED IN AN IMPLICIT STATEMENT'
IM-1   'INVALID LENGTH SPECIFIED IN AN IMPLICIT ØR TYPE STATEMENT'
IM-2   'ILLEGAL APPEARANCE ØF $ IN A CHARACTER RANGE'
IM-3   'IMPRØPER ALPHABETIC SEQUENCE IN CHARACTER RANGE'
IM-4   'SPECIFICATIØN MUST BE SINGLE ALPHABETIC CHARACTER, 1ST CHARACTER
       USED'
IM-5   'IMPLICIT STATEMENT DØES NØT PRECEDE ØTHER SPECIFICATIØN STATEMENTS'
IM-6   'ATTEMPT TØ ESTABLISH THE TYPE ØF A CHARACTER MØRE THAN ØNCE'
IM-7   '360/ FØRTRAN ALLØWS ØNE IMPLICIT STATEMENT PER PRØGRAMME'
IM-8   'INVALID ELEMENT IN IMPLICIT STATEMENT'
IM-9   'INVALID DELIMITER IN IMPLICIT STATEMENT'

'INPUT/ØUTPUT'
IØ-0   'MISSING CØMMA IN I/Ø LIST OF I/Ø ØR DATA STATEMENT'
IØ-2   'STATEMENT NUMBER IN I/Ø STATEMENT NØT A FØRMAT STATEMENT NUMBER'
IØ-3   'FØRMATTED LINE TØØ LØNG FØR I/Ø DEVICE (RECØRD LENGTH EXCEEDED)'
IØ-6   'VARIABLE FØRMAT NØT AN ARRAY NAME'
IØ-8   'INVALID ELEMENT IN INPUT LIST ØR DATA LIST'
IØ-9   'TYPE ØF VARIABLE UNIT NØT INTEGER IN I/Ø STATEMENTS'
IØ-A   'HALF-WØRD INTEGER VARIABLE USED AS UNIT IN I/Ø STATEMENTS'
IØ-B   'ASSIGNED INTEGER VARIABLE USED AS UNIT IN I/Ø STATEMENTS'
IØ-C   'INVALID ELEMENT IN AN ØUTPUT LIST'
IØ-D   'MISSING ØR INVALID UNIT IN I/Ø STATEMENT'
IØ-E   'MISSING ØR INVALID FØRMAT IN READ/WRITE STATEMENT'
IØ-F   'INVALID DELIMITER IN SPECIFICATIØN PART ØF I/Ø STATEMENT'
IØ-G   'MISSING STATEMENT NUMBER AFTER END= ØR ERR='
IØ-H   '/360FØRTRAN DØESN'T ALLØW END/ERR RETURNS IN WRITE STATEMENTS'
IØ-J   'INVALID DELIMITER IN I/Ø LIST'
IØ-K   'INVALID DELIMITER IN STØP, PAUSE, DATA, ØR TAPE CØNTRØL STATEMENT'

'JØB CØNTRØL CARDS'
JB-1   'JØB CARD ENCØUNTERED DURING CØMPILATIØN'
JB-2   'INVALID ØPTIØN(S) SPECIFIED ØN JØB CARD'
JB-3   'UNEXPECTED CØNTRØL CARD ENCØUNTERED DURING CØMPILATIØN'

WATFOR

'JØB TERMINATIØN'
KØ-0   'JØB TERMINATED IN EXECUTIØN BECAUSE ØF CØMPILE TIME ERRØR'
KØ-1   'FIXED-PØINT DIVISIØN BY ZERØ'
KØ-2   'FLØATING-PØINT DIVISIØN BY ZERØ'
KØ-3   'TØØ MANY EXPØNENT ØVERFLØWS'
KØ-4   'TØØ MANY EXPØNENT UNDERFLØWS'
KØ-5   'TØØ MANY FIXED-PØINT ØVERFLØWS'
KØ-6   'JØB TIME EXCEEDED'
KØ-7   'CØMPILER ERRØR - INTERRUPTIØN AT EXECUTIØN TIME, RETURN TØ SYSTEM'
KØ-8   'INTEGER IN INPUT DATA IS TØØ LARGE (MAXIMUM IS 2147483647)

'LØGICAL ØPERATIØN'
LG-2   '. NØT . USED AS A BINARY ØPERATØR'

'LIBRARY RØUTINES'
LI-0   'ARGUMENT ØUT ØF RANGE DGAMMA ØR GAMMA, (1.382E-76 .LT. X .LT. 57.57)'
LI-1   'ABSØLUTE VALUE ØF ARGUMENT .GT. 174.673, SINH, CØSH, DSINH, DCØSH'
LI-2   'SENSE LIGHT ØTHER THAN 0,1,2,3,4 FØR SLITE ØR 1,2,3,4 FØR SLITET'
LI-3   'REAL PØRTIØN ØF ARGUMENT .GT. 174.673, CEXP ØR CDEXP'
LI-4   'ABS(AIMAG(Z)).GT. 174.673 FØR CSIN, CCØS, CDSIN ØR CDCØS ØF Z'
LI-5   'ABS(REAL(Z)).GE. 3.537E15 FØR CSIN, CCØS, CDSIN ØR CDCØS ØF Z'
LI-6   'ABS(AIMAG(Z)) .GE. 3.537E15 FØR CEXP ØR CDEXP ØF Z'
LI-7   'ARGUMENT .GT. 174.673, EXP ØR DEXP'
LI-8   'ARGUMENT IS ZERØ, CLØG, CLØG10, CDLØG ØR CDLG10'
LI-9   'ARGUMENT IS NEGATIVE ØR ZERØ, ALØG, ALØG10, DLØG ØR DLØG1Ø'
LI-A   'ABS(X) .GE. 3.537E15 FØR SIN, CØS, DSIN ØR DCØS ØF X'
LI-B   'ABSØLUTE VALUE ØF ARGUMENT .GT. 1 FØR ARSIN, ARCØS, DARSIN ØR
          DARCØS
LI-C   'ARGUMENT IS NEGATIVE, SQRT ØR DSQRT'
LI-D   'BØTH ARGUMENTS ØF DATAN2 ØR ATAN2 ARE ZERØ'
LI-E   'ARGUMENT TØØ CLØSE TØ A SINGULARITY, TAN, CØTAN, DTAN ØR DCØTAN'
LI-F   'ARGUMENT ØUT ØF RANGE DLGAMA ØR ALGAMA. (0.0 .LT. X .LT. 4.29E73)'
LI-G   'ABSØLUTE VALUE ØF ARGUMENT .GE. 3.537E15, TAN, CØTAN, DTAN, DCØTAN'
LI-H   'FEWER THAN TWØ ARGUMENTS FØR ØNE ØF MIN0, MIN1, AMIN0, ETC.'

WATFOR

'MIXED MØDE'
MD-2   'RELATIØNAL ØPERATØR HAS A LØGICAL ØPERAND'
MD-3   'RELATIØNAL ØPERATØR HAS A CØMPLEX ØPERAND'
MD-4   'MIXED MØDE - LØGICAL WITH ARITHMETIC'
MD-6   'WARNING - SUBSCRIPT IS CØMPLEX. REAL PART USED'

'MEMØRY ØVERFLØW'
MØ-0   'SYMBØL TABLE ØVERFLØWS ØBJECT CØDE. SØURCE ERRØR CHECKING CØNTINUES'
MØ-1   'INSUFFICIENT MEMØRY TØ ASSIGN ARRAY STØRAGE. JØB ABANDØNED'
MØ-2   'SYMBØL TABLE ØVERFLØWS CØMPILER. JØB ABANDØNED'
MØ-3   'DATA AREA ØF SUBPRØGRAMME TØØ LARGE --SEGMENT SUBPRØGRAMME'
MØ-4   'GETMAIN CANNØT PRØVIDE BUFFER FØR WATLIB'

WATFOR

'NAMELIST'
NA-0   'MULTIPLY DEFINED NAMELIST NAME'
NA-1   'NAMELIST NØT IMPLEMENTED'

'PARENTHESES'
PC-0   'UNMATCHED PARENTHESES'
PC-1   'INVALID PARENTHESIS CØUNT'

'PAUSE, STØP STATEMENTS'
PS-0   'STØP WITH ØPERATØR MESSAGE NØT ALLØWED. SIMPLE STØP ASSUMED'
PS-1   'PAUSE WITH ØPERATØR MESSAGE NØT ALLØWED. TREATED AS CØNTINUE'

'RETURN STATEMENT'
RE-0   'FIRST CARD ØF SUBPRØGRAMME IS A RETURN STATEMENT'
RE-1   'RETURN I, WHERE I IS ZERØ, NEGATIVE ØR TØØ LARGE'
RE-2   'MULTIPLE RETURN NØT VALID IN FUNCTIØN SUBPRØGRAMME'
RE-3   'VARIABLE IN MULTIPLE RETURN IS NØT A SIMPLE INTEGER VARIABLE'
RE-4   'MULTIPLE RETURN NØT VALID IN MAIN PRØGRAMME'

'ARITHMETIC AND LØGICAL STATEMENT FUNCTIØNS'
    PRØBABLE CAUSE ØF SF ERRØRS - VARIABLE ØN LEFT ØF = WAS NØT DIMENSIØNED
SF-1   'PREVIØUSLY REFERENCED STATEMENT NUMBER ØN STATEMENT FUNCTIØN'
SF-2   'STATEMENT FUNCTIØN IS THE ØBJECT ØF A LØGICAL IF STATEMENT'
SF-3   'RECURSIVE STATEMENT FUNCTIØN, NAME APPEARS ØN BØTH SIDES ØF ='
SF-5   'ILLEGAL USE ØF A STATEMENT FUNCTIØN'

'SUBPRØGRAMMES'
SR-0   'MISSING SUBPRØGRAMME'
SR-2   'SUBPRØGRAMME ASSIGNED DIFFERENT MØDES IN DIFFERENT PRØGRAMME
        SEGMENTS'
SR-4   'INVALID TYPE ØF ARGUMENT IN SUBPRØGRAMME REFERENCE'
SR-5   'SUBPRØGRAMME ATTEMPTS TØ REDEFINE A CØNSTANT, TEMPØRARY ØR DØ
        PARAMETER'
SR-6   'ATTEMPT TØ USE SUBPRØGRAMME RECURSIVELY'
SR-7   'WRØNG NUMBER ØF ARGUMENTS IN SUBPRØGRAMME REFERENCE'
SR-8   'SUBPRØGRAMME NAME PREVIØUSLY DEFINED -- FIRST REFERENCE USED'
SR-9   'NØ MAIN PRØGRAMME'
SR-A   'ILLEGAL ØR BLANK SUBPRØGRAMME NAME'

'SUBSCRIPTS'
SS-0   'ZERØ SUBSCRIPT ØR DIMENSIØN NØT ALLØWED'
SS-1   'SUBSCRIPT ØUT ØF RANGE'
SS-2   'INVALID VARIABLE ØR NAME USED FØR DIMENSIØN'

'STATEMENTS AND STATEMENT NUMBERS'
ST-0   'MISSING STATEMENT NUMBER'
ST-1   'STATEMENT NUMBER GREATER THAN 99999'
ST-3   'MULTIPLY DEFINED STATEMENT NUMBER'
ST-4   'NØ STATEMENT NUMBER ØN STATEMENT FØLLØWING TRANSFER STATEMENT'
ST-5   'UNDECØDEABLE STATEMENT'
ST-7   'STATEMENT NUMBER SPECIFIED IN A TRANSFER IS A NØN-EXECUTABLE
        STATEMENT'
ST-8   'STATEMENT NUMBER CØNSTANT MUST BE IN A CALL STATEMENT'
ST-9   'STATEMENT SPECIFIED IN A TRANSFER STATEMENT IS A FØRMAT STATEMENT'
ST-A   'MISSING FØRMAT STATEMENT'

'SUBSCRIPTED VARIABLES'
SV-0   'WRØNG NUMBER ØF SUBSCRIPTS'
SV-1   'ARRAY NAME ØR SUBPRØGRAMME NAME USED INCØRRECTLY WITHØUT LIST'
SV-2   'MØRE THAN 7 DIMENSIØNS NØT ALLØWED'
SV-3   'DIMENSIØN TØØ LARGE'
SV-4   'VARIABLE WITH VARIABLE DIMENSIØNS IS NØT A SUBPRØGRAMME PARAMETER'

SV-5   'VARIABLE DIMENSIØN NEITHER SIMPLE INTEGER VARIABLE NØR S/P
          PARAMETER'

'SYNTAX ERRØRS'
SX-0   'MISSING ØPERATØR'
SX-1   'SYNTAX ERRØR-SEARCHING FØR SYMBØL, NØNE FØUND'
SX-2   'SYNTAX ERRØR-SEARCHING FØR CØNSTANT, NØNE FØUND'
SX-3   'SYNTAX ERRØR-SEARCHING FØR SYMBØL ØR CØNSTANT, NØNE FØUND'
SX-4   'SYNTAX ERRØR-SEARCHING FØR STATEMENT NUMBER, NØNE FØUND'
SX-5   'SYNTAX ERRØR-SEARCHING FØR SIMPLE INTEGER VARIABLE, NØNE FØUND'
SX-C   'ILLEGAL SEQUENCE ØF ØPERATØRS IN EXPRESSIØN'
SX-D   'MISSING ØPERAND ØR ØPERATØR'

'I/Ø ØPERATIØNS'
UN-0   'CØNTRØL CARD ENCØUNTERED ØN UNIT 5 DURING EXECUTIØN'
              PROBABLE CAUSE - MISSING DATA ØR IMPRØPER FØRMAT STATEMENTS
UN-1   'END ØF FILE ENCØUNTERED'
UN-2   'I/Ø ERRØR'
UN-3   'DATA SET REFERENCED FØR WHICH NØ DD CARD SUPPLIED'
UN-4   'REWIND, ENDFILE, BACKSPACE REFERENCES UNIT 5, 6, 7'
UN-5   'ATTEMPT TØ READ ØN UNIT 5 AFTER IT HAS HAD END-ØF-FILE'
UN-6   'UNIT NUMBER IS NEGATIVE, ZERØ, GREATER THAN 7 ØR UNDEFINED'
UN-7   'TØØ MANY PAGES'
UN-8   'ATTEMPT TØ DØ SEQUENTIAL I/Ø ØN A DIRECT ACCESS FILE'
UN-9   'WRITE REFERENCES 5 ØR READ REFERENCES 6, 7'
UN-A   'ATTEMPT TØ READ MØRE DATA THAN CØNTAINED IN LØGICAL RECØRD'
UN-B   'TØØ MANY PHYSICAL RECØRDS IN A LØGICAL RECØRD. INCREASE RECØRD
          LENGTH.'

'UNDEFINED VARIABLES'
UV-0   'UNDEFINED VARIABLE - SIMPLE VARIABLE'
UV-1   'UNDEFINED VARIABLE - EQUIVALENCED, CØMMØNED, ØR DUMMY PARAMETER'
UV-2   'UNDEFINED VARIABLE - ARRAY MEMBER'
UV-3   'UNDEFINED VARIABLE - ARRAY NAME WHICH WAS USED AS A DUMMY
          PARAMETER'
UV-4   'UNDEFINED VARIABLE - SUBPRØGRAMME NAME USED AS DUMMY PARAMETER'
UV-5   'UNDEFINED VARIABLE - ARGUMENT ØF THE LIBRARY SUBPRØGRAMME NAMED'
UV-6   'VARIABLE FØRMAT CØNTAINS UNDEFINED CHARACTER(S)'

'VARIABLE NAMES'
VA-0   'ATTEMPT TØ REDEFINE TYPE ØF A VARIABLE NAME'
VA-1   'SUBRØUTINE NAME ØR CØMMØN BLØCK NAME USED INCØRRECTLY'
VA-2   'VARIABLE NAME LØNGER THAN SIX CHARACTERS. TRUNCATED TØ SIX'
VA-3   'ATTEMPT TØ REDEFINE THE MØDE ØF A VARIABLE NAME'
VA-4   'ATTEMPT TØ REDEFINE THE TYPE ØF A VARIABLE NAME'
VA-6   'ILLEGAL USE ØF A SUBRØUTINE NAME'
VA-8   'ATTEMPT TØ USE A PREVIØUSLY DEFINED NAME AS FUNCTIØN ØR ARRAY'
VA-9   'ATTEMPT TØ USE A PREVIØUSLY DEFINED NAME AS A STATEMENT FUNCTIØN'
VA-A   'ATTEMPT TØ USE A PREVIØUSLY DEFINED NAME AS A SUBPRØGRAMME NAME'
VA-B   'NAME USED AS A CØMMØN BLØCK PREVIØUSLY USED AS A SUBPRØGRAMME NAME'
VA-C   'NAME USED AS SUBPRØGRAMME PREVIØUSLY USED AS A CØMMØN BLØCK NAME'
VA-D   'ILLEGAL DØ-PARAMETER, ASSIGNED ØR INITIALIZED VARIABLE IN
          SPECIFICATIØN'
VA-E   'ATTEMPT TØ DIMENSIØN A CALL-BY-NAME PARAMETER'

WATFOR

'EXTERNAL STATEMENT'
XT-0   'INVALID ELEMENT IN EXTERNAL LIST'
XT-1   'INVALID DELIMITER IN EXTERNAL STATEMENT'
XT-2   'SUBPRØGRAMME PREVIØUSLY EXTERNALLED'

WATFIV DIAGNOSTIC ERROR MESSAGES[2]

'ASSEMBLER LANGUAGE SUBPRØGRAMS'
AL-0   'MISSING END CARD ØN ASSEMBLY LANGUAGE ØBJECT DECK'
AL-1   'ENTRY-PØINT ØR CSECT NAME IN AN ØBJECT DECK WAS PREVIØUSLY DEFINED.
         FIRST DEFINITIØN USED'

'BLØCK DATA STATEMENTS'
BD-0   'EXECUTABLE STATEMENTS ARE ILLEGAL IN BLØCK DATA SUBPRØGRAMS'
BD-1   'IMPRØPER BLØCK DATA STATEMENT'

'CARD FØRMAT AND CØNTENTS'
CC-0   'COLUMNS 1-5 ØF CØNTINUATIØN CARD ARE NØT BLANK. PRØBABLE CAUSE:
         STATEMENT PUNCHED TØ LEFT ØF CØLUMN 7'
CC-1   'LIMIT ØF 5 CØNTINUATIØN CARDS EXCEEDED'
CC-2   'INVALID CHARACTER IN FØRTRAN STATEMENT. A '$' WAS INSERTED IN THE
         SØURCE LISTING'
CC-3   'FIRST CARD ØF A PRØGRAM IS A CØNTINUATIØN CARD. PRØBABLE CAUSE:
         STATEMENT PUNCHED TØ LEFT ØF CØLUMN 7'
CC-4   'STATEMENT TØØ LØNG TØ CØMPILE (SCAN-STACK ØVERFLØW)'
CC-5   'A BLANK CARD WAS ENCØUNTERED'
CC-6   'KEYPUNCH USED DIFFERS FRØM KEYPUNCH SPECIFIED ØN JØB CARD'
CC-7   'THE FIRST CHARACTER ØF THE STATEMENT WAS NØT ALPHABETIC'
CC-8   'INVALID CHARACTER(S) ARE CØNCATENATED WITH THE FØRTRAN KEYWØRD'
CC-9   'INVALID CHARACTERS IN CØLUMNS 1-5. STATEMENT NUMBER IGNØRED.
         PRØBABLE CAUSE: STATEMENT PUNCHED TØ LEFT ØF COLUMN 7'

'CØMMØN'
CM-0   'THE VARIABLE IS ALREADY IN CØMMØN'
CM-1   'ØTHER CØMPILERS MAY NØT ALLØW CØMMØNED VARIABLES TØ BE INITIALIZED
         IN ØTHER THAN A BLØCK DATA SUBPRØGRAM'
CM-2   'ILLEGAL USE ØF A CØMMØN BLØCK ØR NAMELIST NAME'

'FØRTRAN TYPE CØNSTANTS'
CN-0   'MIXED REAL*4,REAL*8 IN CØMPLEX CØNSTANT; REAL*8 ASSUMED FØR BØTH'
CN-1   'AN INTEGER CØNSTANT MAY NØT BE GREATER THAN 2,147,483,647 (2**31-1)'
CN-2   'THE EXPØNENT ØF A REAL CØNSTANT IS GREATER THAN 99, THE MAXIMUM'
CN-3   'A REAL CØNSTANT HAS MØRE THAN 16 DIGITS. IT WAS TRUNCATED TØ 16'
CN-4   'INVALID HEXADECIMAL CØNSTANT'
CN-5   'ILLEGAL USE ØF A DECIMAL PØINT'
CN-6   'CØNSTANT WITH MØRE THAN 7 DIGITS BUT E-TYPE EXPØNENT, ASSUMED TØ BE
         REAL *4'
CN-7   'CØNSTANT ØR STATEMENT NUMBER GREATER THAN 99999'
CN-8   'AN EXPØNENT ØVERFLØW ØR UNDERFLØW ØCCURRED WHILE CØNVERTING A
         CØNSTANT IN A SØURCE STATEMENT'

[2]WATFIV error messages have been reproduced by permission from "1360 WATFIV Implementation Guide," Department of Applied Analysis and Computer Centre, University of Waterloo, Waterloo, Ontario, Canada, September 1969.

'CØMPILER ERRØRS'
CP-0   'CØMPILER ERRØR - LANDR/ARITH'
CP-1   'CØMPILER ERRØR. LIKELY CAUSE: MØRE THAN 255 DØ STATEMENTS'
CP-4   'CØMPILER ERRØR - INTERRUPT AT CØMPILE TIME, RETURN TØ SYSTEM'

'CHARACTER VARIABLE'
CV-0   'A CHARACTER VARIABLE IS USED WITH A RELATIØNAL ØPERATØR'
CV-1   'LENGTH ØF A CHARACTER VALUE ØN RIGHT ØF EQUAL SIGN EXCEEDS THAT
            ØN LEFT. TRUNCATIØN WILL ØCCUR'
CV-2   'UNFØRMATTED CØRE-TØ-CØRE I/Ø NØT IMPLEMENTED'

'DATA STATEMENT'
DA-0   'REPLICATIØN FACTØR IS ZERØ ØR GREATER THAN 32767. IT IS ASSUMED
            TØ BE 32767'
DA-1   'MØRE VARIABLES THAN CØNSTANTS'
DA-2   'ATTEMPT TØ INITIALIZE A SUBPRØGRAM PARAMETER IN A DATA STATEMENT'
DA-3   'OTHER COMPILERS MAY NØT ALLØW NØN-CØNSTANT SUBSCRIPTS IN DATA
            STATEMENTS'
DA-4   'TYPE ØF VARIABLE AND CØNSTANT DØ NØT AGREE (MESSAGE ISSUED ØNCE
            FØR AN ARRAY)'
DA-5   'MØRE CØNSTANTS THAN VARIABLES'
DA-6   'A VARIABLE WAS PREVIØUSLY INITIALIZED. THE LATEST VALUE IS USED.
            CHECK CØMMØNED AND EQUIVALENCED VARIABLES'
DA-7   'ØTHER CØMPILERS MAY NØT ALLØW INITIALIZATIØN ØF BLANK CØMMØN'
DA-8   'A HØLLERITH CØNSTANT HAS BEEN TRUNCATED'
DA-9   'ØTHER CØMPILERS MAY NØT ALLØW IMPLIED DØ-LØØPS IN DATA STATEMENTS'

'DEFINE FILE STATEMENTS'
DF-0   'THE UNIT NUMBER IS MISSING'
DF-1   'INVALID FØRMAT TYPE'
DF-2   'THE ASSØCIATED VARIABLE IS NØT A SIMPLE INTEGER VARIABLE'
DF-3   'NUMBER ØF RECØRDS ØR RECØRD SIZE IS·ZERØ ØR GREATER THAN 32767'

'DIMENSIØN STATEMENTS'
DM-0   'NØ DIMENSIØNS ARE SPECIFIED FØR A VARIABLE IN A DIMENSIØN
            STATEMENT'
DM-1   'THE VARIABLE HAS ALREADY BEEN DIMENSIØNED'
DM-2   'CALL-BY-LØCATIØN PARAMETERS MAY NØT BE DIMENSIØNED'
DM-3   'THE DECLARED SIZE ØF ARRAY EXCEEDS SPACE PRØVIDED BY CALLING
            ARGUMENT'

DØ LØØPS'
DØ-0   'THIS STATEMENT CANNØT BE THE ØBJECT ØF A DØ-LØØP'
DØ-1   'ILLEGAL TRANSFER INTØ THE RANGE ØF A DØ-LØØP'
DØ-2   'THE ØBJECT ØF THIS DØ-LØØP HAS ALREADY APPEARED'
DØ-3   'IMPRØPERLY NESTED DØ-LØØPS'
DØ-4   'ATTEMPT TØ REDEFINE A DØ-LØØP PARAMETER WITHIN THE RANGE ØF THE
            LØØP'
DØ-5   'INVALID DØ-LØØP PARAMETER'
DØ-6   'ILLEGAL TRANSFER TØ A STATEMENT WHICH IS INSIDE THE RANGE OF A
            DØ-LØØP'
DØ-7   'A DØ-LØØP PARAMETER IS UNDEFINED ØR ØUT ØF RANGE'
DØ-8   'BECAUSE ØF ØNE ØF THE PARAMETERS, THIS DØ-LØØP WILL TERMINATE AFTER
            THE FIRST TIME THRØUGH'
DØ-9   'A DØ-LØØP PARAMETER MAY NØT BE REDEFINED IN AN INPUT LIST'

WATFIV

WATFIV

WATFIV

DØ-A   'ØTHER CØMPILERS MAY NØT ALLØW THIS STATEMENT TØ END A DØ-LØØP'

'EQUIVALENCE AND/ØR CØMMØN'
EC-0   'EQUIVALENCED VARIABLE APPEARS IN A CØMMØN STATEMENT'
EC-1   'A CØMMØN BLØCK HAS A DIFFERENT LENGTH THAN IN A PREVIØUS
            SUBPRØGRAM: GREATER LENGTH USED'
EC-2   'CØMMØN AND/ØR EQUIVALENCE CAUSES INVALID ALIGNMENT. EXECUTIØN
            SLØWED. REMEDY: ØRDER VARIABLES BY DECREASING LENGTH'
EC-3   'EQUIVALENCE EXTENDS CØMMØN DØWNWARDS'
EC-4   'A SUBPRØGRAM PARAMETER APPEARS IN A CØMMØN ØR EQUIVALENCE
            STATEMENT'
EC-5   'A VARIABLE WAS USED WITH SUBSCRIPTS IN AN EQUIVALENCE STATEMENT
            BUT HAS NØT BEEN PRØPERLY DIMENSIØNED'

'END STATEMENTS'
EN-0   'MISSING END STATEMENTS: END STATEMENT GENERATED'
EN-1   'AN END STATEMENT WAS USED TØ TERMINATE EXECUTIØN'
EN-2   'AN END STATEMENT CANNØT HAVE A STATEMENT NUMBER. STATEMENT NUMBER
            IGNØRED'
EN-3   'END STATEMENT NØT PRECEDED BY A TRANSFER'

'EQUAL SIGNS'
EQ-0   'ILLEGAL QUANTITY ØN LEFT ØF EQUAL SIGN'
EQ-1   'ILLEGAL USE ØF EQUAL SIGN'
EQ-2   'ØTHER CØMPILERS MAY NØT ALLØW MULTIPLE ASSIGNMENT STATEMENTS'
EQ-3   'MULTIPLE ASSIGNMENT IS NØT IMPLEMENTED FØR CHARACTER VARIABLES'

'EQUIVALENCE STATEMENTS'
EV-0   'ATTEMPT TØ EQUIVALENCE A VARIABLE TØ ITSELF'
EV-2   'A MULTI-SUBSCRIPTED EQUIVALENCE VARIABLE HAS BEEN INCØRRECTLY
            RE-EQUIVALENCED. REMEDY: DIMENSIØN THE VARIABLE FIRST'

'PØWERS AND EXPØNENTIATIØN'
EX-0   'ILLEGAL CØMPLEX EXPØNENTIATIØN'
EX-1   'I**J WHERE I=J=0'
EX-2   'I**J WHERE I=0,J .LT. 0'
EX-3   '0.0**Y WHERE Y .LE. 0.0'
EX-4   '0.0**J WHERE J=0'
EX-5   '0.0**J WHERE J .LT. 0'
EX-6   'X**Y WHERE X .LT. 0.0,Y .NE. 0.0'

'ENTRY STATEMENT'
EY-0   'ENTRY-PØINT NAME WAS PREVIØUSLY DEFINED'
EY-1   'PREVIØUS DEFINITIØN ØF FUNCTIØN NAME IN AN ENTRY IS INCØRRECT'
EY-2   'THE USAGE ØF A SUBPRØGRAM PARAMETER IS INCØNSISTENT WITH A
            PREVIØUS ENTRY-PØINT'
EY-3   'A PARAMETER HAS APPEARED IN A EXECUTABLE STATEMENT BUT IS NØT A
            SUBPRØGRAM PARAMETER'
EY-4   'ENTRY STATEMENTS ARE INVALID IN THE MAIN PRØGRAM'
EY-5   'ENTRY STATEMENT INVALID INSIDE A DØ-LØØP'

'FØRMAT'
    SØME FØRMAT ERRØR MESSAGES GIVE CHARACTERS IN WHICH ERRØR WAS DETECTED
FM-0   'IMPRØPER CHARACTER SEQUENCE ØR INVALID CHARACTER IN INPUT DATA'
FM-1   'NØ STATEMENT NUMBER ØN A FØRMAT STATEMENT'

WATFIV

FM-2   'FØRMAT CØDE AND DATA TYPE DØ NØT MATCH'
FM-4   'FØRMAT PRØVIDES NØ CØNVERSIØN SPECIFICATIØN FØR A VALUE IN I/O
         LIST'
FM-5   'AN INTEGER IN THE INPUT DATA IS TØØ LARGE. (MAXIMUM = 2,147,
         483,647 = 2**31-1)'
FM-6   'A REAL NUMBER IN THE INPUT DATA IS ØUT ØF MACHINE RANGE (1.E-78,
         1.E+75)'
FM-7   'UNREFERENCED FØRMAT STATEMENT'
FT-0   'FIRST CHARACTER ØF VARIABLE FØRMAT IS NØT A LEFT PARENTHESIS'
FT-1   'INVALID CHARACTER ENCØUNTERED IN FØRMAT'
FT-2   'INVALID FØRM FØLLØWING A FØRMAT CØDE'
FT-3   'INVALID FIELD ØR GRØUP CØUNT'
FT-4   'A FIELD ØR GRØUP CØUNT GREATER THAN 255'
FT-5   'NØ CLØSING PARENTHESIS ØN VARIABLE FØRMAT'
FT-6   'NØ CLØSING QUØTE IN A HØLLERITH FIELD'
FT-7   'INVALID USE ØF CØMMA'
FT-8   'FØRMAT STATEMENT TØØ LØNG TØ CØMPILE (SCAN-STACK ØVERFLØW)'
FT-9   'INVALID USE ØF P FØRMAT CØDE'
FT-A   'INVALID USE ØF PERIOD (.)'
FT-B   'MØRE THAN THREE LEVELS ØF PARENTHESIS'
FT-C   'INVALID CHARACTER BEFØRE A RIGHT PARENTHESIS'
FT-D   'MISSING ØR ZERØ LENGTH HØLLERITH ENCØUNTERED'
FT-E   'NØ CLØSING RIGHT PARENTHESIS'
FT-F   'CHARACTERS FØLLØW CLØSING RIGHT PARENTHESIS'
FT-G   'WRØNG QUØTE USED FØR KEY-PUNCH SPECIFIED'
FT-H   'LENGTH ØF HØLLERITH EXCEEDS 255'

'FUNCTIØNS AND SUBRØUTINES'
FN-1   'A PARAMETER APPEARS MØRE THAN ØNCE IN A SUBPRØGRAM ØR STATEMENT
             FUNCTIØN DEFINITIØN'
FN-2   'SUBSCRIPTS ØN RIGHT-HAND SIDE ØF STATEMENT FUNCTIØN. PRØBABLE
             CAUSE: VARIABLE TØ LEFT ØF EQUAL SIGN NØT DIMENSIØNED'
FN-3   'MULTIPLE RETURNS ARE INVALID IN FUNCTIØN SUBPRØGRAMS'
FN-4   'ILLEGAL LENGTH MØDIFIER'
FN-5   'INVALID PARAMETER'
FN-6   'A PARAMETER HAS THE SAME NAME AS THE SUBPRØGRAM'

'GØ TØ STATEMENT'
GØ-0   'THIS STATEMENT CØULD TRANSFER TØ ITSELF'
GØ-1   'THIS STATEMENT TRANSFERS TØ A NØN-EXECUTABLE STATEMENT'
GØ-2   'ATTEMPT TØ DEFINE ASSIGNED GØ TØ INDEX IN AN ARITHMETIC STATEMENT'
GØ-3   'ASSIGNED GØ TØ INDEX MAY BE USED ØNLY IN ASSIGNED GØ TØ AND
             ASSIGN STATEMENTS'
GØ-4   'THE INDEX ØF AN ASSIGNED GØ TØ IS UNDEFINED ØR ØUT ØF RANGE, ØR
             INDEX ØF CØMPUTED GØ TØ IS UNDEFINED'
GØ-5   'ASSIGNED GØ TØ INDEX MAY NØT BE AN INTEGER*2 VARIABLE'

'HØLLERITH CØNSTANTS'
HØ-0   'ZERØ LENGTH SPECIFIED FØR H-TYPE HØLLERITH'
HØ-1   'ZERØ LENGTH QUØTE-TYPE HØLLERITH'
HØ-2   'NØ CLØSING QUØTE ØR NEXT CARD NØT A CØNTINUATION CARD'
HØ-3   'UNEXPECTED HØLLERITH ØR STATEMENT NUMBER CØNSTANT'

WATFIV

WATFIV

'IF STATEMENTS (ARITHMETIC AND LØGICAL)'
IF-0   'AN INVALID STATEMENT FØLLØWS THE LØGICAL IF'
IF-1   'ARITHMETIC ØR INVALID EXPRESSIØN IN LØGICAL IF'
IF-2   'LØGICAL, CØMPLEX, ØR INVALID EXPRESSIØN IN ARITHMETIC IF'

'IMPLICIT STATEMENT'
IM-0   'INVALID DATA TYPE'
IM-1   'INVALID ØPTIØNAL LENGTH'
IM-3   'IMPRØPER ALPHABETIC SEQUENCE IN CHARACTER RANGE'
IM-4   'A SPECIFICATIØN IS NØT A SINGLE CHARACTER. THE FIRST CHARACTER
            IS USED'
IM-5   'IMPLICIT STATEMENT DØES NØT PRECEDE ØTHER SPECIFICATIØN STATEMENTS'
IM-6   'ATTEMPT TØ DECLARE THE TYPE ØF A CHARACTER MØRE THAN ØNCE'
IM-7   'ØNLY ØNE IMPLICIT STATEMENT PER PRØGRAM SEGMENT ALLØWED. THIS ØNE
            IGNØRED'

'INPUT/ØUTPUT'
IØ-0   'I/Ø STATEMENT REFERENCES A STATEMENT WHICH IS NØT A FØRMAT
            STATEMENT'
IØ-1   'A VARIABLE FØRMAT MUST BE AN ARRAY NAME'
IØ-2   'INVALID ELEMENT IN INPUT LIST ØR DATA LIST'
IØ-3   'ØTHER CØMPILERS MAY NØT ALLØW EXPRESSIØNS IN ØUTPUT LISTS'
IØ-4   'ILLEGAL USE ØF END= ØR ERR= PARAMETERS'
IØ-5   'INVALID UNIT NUMBER'
IØ-6   'INVALID FØRMAT'
IØ-7   'ØNLY CØNSTANTS, SIMPLE INTEGER*4 VARIABLES, AND CHARACTER
            VARIABLES ARE ALLØWED AS UNIT'
IØ-8   'ATTEMPT TØ PERFØRM I/Ø IN A FUNCTIØN WHICH IS CALLED IN AN ØUTPUT
            STATEMENT'
IØ-9   'UNFØRMATTED WRITE STATEMENT MUST HAVE A LIST'

'JØB CØNTRØL CARDS'
JB-0   'CØNTRØL CARD ENCØUNTERED DURING CØMPILATIØN:
            PRØBABLE CAUSE: MISSING $ ENTRY CARD'
JB-1   'MIS-PUNCHED JØB ØPTIØN'

'JØB TERMINATIØN'
KØ-0   'SØURCE ERRØR ENCØUNTERED WHILE EXECUTING WITH RUN=FREE'
KØ-1   'LIMIT EXCEEDED FØR FIXED-PØINT DIVISIØN BY ZERØ'
KØ-2   'LIMIT EXCEEDED FØR FLØATING-PØINT DIVISIØN BY ZERØ'
KØ-3   'EXPØNENT ØVERFLØW LIMIT EXCEEDED'
KØ-4   'EXPØNENT UNDERFLØW LIMIT EXCEEDED'
KØ-5   'FIXED-PØINT ØVERFLØW LIMIT EXCEEDED'
KØ-6   'JØB-TIME EXCEEDED'
KØ-7   'CØMPILER ERRØR - EXECUTIØN TIME: RETURN TØ SYSTEM'
KØ-8   'TRACEBACK ERRØR. TRACEBACK TERMINATED'

'LØGICAL ØPERATIØNS'
LG-0   '.NØT. WAS USED AS A BINARY ØPERATØR'

'LIBRARY RØUTINES'
LI-0   'ARGUMENT ØUT ØF RANGE DGAMMA ØR GAMMA. (1.382E-76 .LT. X .LT. 57.57)'

LI-1   'ABSØLUTE VALUE ØF ARGUMENT .GT. 174.673, SINH, CØSH, DSINH, DCØSH'
LI-2   'SENSE LIGHT ØTHER THAN 0, 1, 2, 3, 4 FØR SLITE ØR 1, 2, 3, 4 FØR
            SLITET'
LI-3   'REAL PØRTIØN ØF ARGUMENT .GT. 174.673, CEXP ØR CDEXP'
LI-4   'ABS(AIMAG(Z)) .GT. 174.673 FØR CSIN, CCØS, CDSIN ØR CDCØS ØF Z'
LI-5   'ABS(REAL(Z)) .GE. 3.537E15 FØR CSIN, CCØS, CDSIN ØR CDCØS ØF Z'
LI-6   'ABS(AIMAG(Z)) .GE. 3.537E15 FØR CEXP ØR CDEXP ØF Z'
LI-7   'ARGUMENT .GT. 174.673, EXP ØR DEXP'
LI-8   'ARGUMENT IS ZERØ, CLØG, CLØG10, CDLØG ØR CDLG10'
LI-9   'ARGUMENT IS NEGATIVE ØR ZERØ, ALØG, ALØG10, DLØG ØR DLØG10'
LI-A   'ABS(X) .GE. 3.537E15 FØR SIN, CØS, DSIN ØR DCØS ØF X'
LI-B   'ABSØLUTE VALUE ØF ARGUMENT .GT. 1. FØR ARSIN, ARCØS, DARSIN ØR
            DARCØS'
LI-C   'ARGUMENT IS NEGATIVE, SQRT ØR DSQRT'
LI-D   'BØTH ARGUMENTS ØF DATAN2 ØR ATAN2 ARE ZERØ'
LI-E   'ARGUMENT TØØ CLØSE TØ A SINGULARITY, TAN, CØTAN, DTAN ØR DCØTAN'
LI-F   'ARGUMENT ØUT ØF RANGE, DLGAMA ØR ALGAMA. (0.0 .LT. X .LT. 4.29F73)'
LI-G   'ABSØLUTE VALUE ØF ARGUMENT .GE. 3.537E15, TAN, CØTAN, DTAN, DCØTAN'
LI-H   'LESS THAN TWØ ARGUMENTS FØR ØNE ØF MIN0, MIN1, AMIN0, ETC.'

'MIXED MØDE'
MD-0   'RELATIØNAL ØPERATØR HAS LØGICAL ØPERAND'
MD-1   'RELATIØNAL ØPERATØR HAS CØMPLEX ØPERAND'
MD-2   'MIXED MØDE - LØGICAL ØR CHARACTER WITH ARITHMETIC'
MD-3   'ØTHER CØMPILERS MAY NØT ALLØW SUBSCRIPTS ØF TYPE CØMPLEX, LØGICAL
            ØR CHARACTER'

'MEMØRY ØVERFLØW'
MØ-0   'INSUFFICIENT MEMØRY TØ CØMPILE THIS PRØGRAM. REMAINDER WILL BE
            ERRØR CHECKED ØNLY'
MØ-1   'INSUFFICIENT MEMØRY TØ ASSIGN ARRAY STØRAGE. JØB ABANDØNED'
MØ-2   'SYMBØL TABLE EXCEEDS AVAILABLE SPACE. JØB ABANDØNED'
MØ-3   'DATA AREA ØF SUBPRØGRAM EXCEEDS 24K -- SEGMENT SUBPRØGRAM'
MØ-4   'INSUFFICIENT MEMØRY TØ ALLØCATE CØMPILER WØRK AREA ØR WATLIB
            BUFFER'

'NAMELIST STATEMENTS'
NL-0   'NAMELIST ENTRY MUST BE A VARIABLE, NØT A SUBPRØGRAM PARAMETER'
NL-1   'NAMELIST NAME PREVIØUSLY DEFINED'
NL-2   'VARIABLE NAME TØØ LØNG'
NL-3   'VARIABLE NAME NØT FØUND IN NAMELIST'
NL-4   'INVALID SYNTAX IN NAMELIST INPUT'
NL-6   'VARIABLE INCØRRECTLY SUBSCRIPTED'
NL-7   'SUBSCRIPT ØUT ØF RANGE'

'PARENTHESES'
PC-0   'UNMATCHED PARENTHESIS'
PC-1   'INVALID PARENTHESIS NESTING IN I/Ø LIST'

'PAUSE, STØP STATEMENTS'
PS-0   'ØPERATØR MESSAGES NØT ALLØWED: SIMPLE STØP ASSUMED FØR STØP,
            CØNTINUE ASSUMED FØR PAUSE'

'RETURN STATEMENT'
RE-1   'RETURN I, WHERE I IS ØUT ØF RANGE ØR UNDEFINED'
RE-2   'MULTIPLE RETURN NØT VALID IN FUNCTIØN SUBPRØGRAM'
RE-3   'VARIABLE IS NØT A SIMPLE INTEGER'
RE-4   'A MULTIPLE RETURN IS NØT VALID IN THE MAIN PRØGRAM'

'ARITHMETIC AND LØGICAL STATEMENT FUNCTIØNS'
    PRØBABLE CAUSE ØF SF ERRØRS - VARIABLE ØN LEFT ØF = WAS NØT DIMENSIØNED
SF-1   'A PREVIØUSLY REFERENCED STATEMENT NUMBER APPEARS ØN A STATEMENT
            FUNCTIØN DEFINITIØN'
SF-2   'STATEMENT FUNCTIØN IS THE ØBJECT ØF A LØGICAL IF STATEMENT'
SF-3   'RECURSIVE STATEMENT FUNCTIØN DEFINITIØN: NAME APPEARS ØN BØTH SIDES
            ØF EQUAL SIGN. LIKELY CAUSE: VARIABLE NØT DIMENSIØNED'
SF-4   'A STATEMENT FUNCTIØN DEFINITIØN APPEARS AFTER THE FIRST EXECUTABLE
            STATEMENT'
SF-5   'ILLEGAL USE ØF A STATEMENT FUNCTIØN NAME'

'SUBPRØGRAMS'
SR-0   'MISSING SUBPRØGRAM'
SR-1   'SUBPRØGRAM REDEFINES A CØNSTANT, EXPRESSIØN, DØ-PARAMETER ØR
            ASSIGNED GØ TØ INDEX'
SR-2   'THE SUBPRØGRAM WAS ASSIGNED DIFFERENT TYPES IN DIFFERENT PRØGRAM
            SEGMENTS'
SR-3   'ATTEMPT TO USE A SUBPRØGRAM RECURSIVELY'
SR-4   'INVALID TYPE ØF ARGUMENT IN REFERENCE TØ A SUBPRØGRAM'
SR-5   'WRØNG NUMBER ØF ARGUMENTS IN A REFERENCE TØ A SUBPRØGRAM'
SR-6   'A SUBPRØGRAM WAS PREVIØUSLY DEFINED. THE FIRST DEFINITIØN IS USED'
SR-7   'NØ MAIN PRØGRAM'
SR-8   'ILLEGAL ØR MISSING SUBPRØGRAM NAME'
SR-9   'LIBRARY PRØGRAM WAS NØT ASSIGNED THE CØRRECT TYPE'
SR-A   'METHØD FØR ENTERING SUBPRØGRAM PRØDUCES UNDEFINED VALUE FØR
            CALL-BY-LØCATIØN PARAMETER'

'SUBSCRIPTS'
SS-0   'ZERØ SUBSCRIPT ØR DIMENSIØN NØT ALLØWED'
SS-1   'ARRAY SUBSCRIPT EXCEEDS DIMENSIØN'
SS-2   'INVALID SUBSCRIPT FØRM'
SS-3   'SUBSCRIPT IS ØUT ØF RANGE'

'STATEMENTS AND STATEMENT NUMBERS'
ST-0   'MISSING STATEMENT NUMBER'
ST-1   'STATEMENT NUMBER GREATER THAN 99999'
ST-2   'STATEMENT NUMBER HAS ALREADY BEEN DEFINED'
ST-3   'UNDECØDEABLE STATEMENT'
ST-4   'UNNUMBERED EXECUTABLE STATEMENT FØLLØWS A TRANSFER'
ST-5   'STATEMENT NUMBER IN A TRANSFER IS A NØN-EXECUTABLE STATEMENT'
ST-6   'ØNLY CALL STATEMENTS MAY CØNTAIN STATEMENT NUMBER ARGUMENTS'
ST-7   'STATEMENT SPECIFIED IN A TRANSFER STATEMENT IS A FØRMAT STATEMENT'
ST-8   'MISSING FØRMAT STATEMENT'
ST-9   'SPECIFICATIØN STATEMENT DØES NØT PRECEDE STATEMENT FUNCTIØN
            DEFINITIØNS OR EXECUTABLE STATEMENTS'
ST-A   'UNREFERENCED STATEMENT FØLLØWS A TRANSFER'

WATFIV

'SUBSCRIPTED VARIABLES'
SV-0   'THE WRØNG NUMBER ØF SUBSCRIPTS WERE SPECIFIED FØR A VARIABLE'
SV-1   'AN ARRAY ØR SUBPRØGRAM NAME IS USED INCØRRECTLY WITHØUT A LIST'
SV-2   'MØRE THAN 7 DIMENSIØNS ARE NØT ALLØWED'
SV-3   'DIMENSIØN ØR SUBSCRIPT TØØ LARGE (MAXIMUM 10**8-1)'
SV-4   'A VARIABLE USED WITH VARIABLE DIMENSIØNS IS NØT A SUBPRØGRAM
            PARAMETER'
SV-5   'A VARIABLE DIMENSIØN IS NØT ØNE ØF SIMPLE INTEGER VARIABLE, SUB-
            PRØGRAM PARAMETER, IN CØMMØN'

'SYNTAX ERRØRS'
SX-0   'MISSING ØPERATØR'
SX-1   'EXPECTING ØPERATØR'
SX-2   'EXPECTING SYMBØL'
SX-3   'EXPECTING SYMBØL ØR ØPERATØR'
SX-4   'EXPECTING CØNSTANT'
SX-5   'EXPECTING SYMBØL ØR CØNSTANT'
SX-6   'EXPECTING STATEMENT NUMBER'
SX-7   'EXPECTING SIMPLE INTEGER VARIABLE'
SX-8   'EXPECTING SIMPLE INTEGER VARIABLE ØR CØNSTANT'
SX-9   'ILLEGAL SEQUENCE ØF ØPERATØRS IN EXPRESSIØN'
SX-A   'EXPECTING END-ØF-STATEMENT'

'TYPE STATEMENTS'
TY-0   'THE VARIABLE HAS ALREADY BEEN EXPLICITLY TYPED'
TY-1   'THE LENGTH ØF THE EQUIVALENCED VARIABLE MAY NØT BE CHANGED.
            REMEDY: INTERCHANGE TYPE AND EQUIVALENCE STATEMENTS'

WATFIV

'I/Ø ØPERATIØNS'
UN-0   'CØNTRØL CARD ENCØUNTERED ØN UNIT 5 AT EXECUTIØN. PRØBABLE CAUSE:
            MISSING DATA ØR INCØRRECT FØRMAT'
UN-1   'END ØF FILE ENCØUNTERED (IBM CØDE IHC217)'
UN-2   'I/Ø ERRØR (IBM CØDE IHC218)'
UN-3   'NØ DD STATEMENT WAS SUPPLIED (IBM CØDE IHC219)'
UN-4   'REWIND, ENDFILE, BACKSPACE REFERENCES UNIT 5, 6, ØR 7'
UN-5   'ATTEMPT TØ READ ØN UNIT 5 AFTER IT HAS HAD END-ØF-FILE'
UN-6   'AN INVALID VARIABLE UNIT NUMBER WAS DETECTED (IBM CØDE IHC220)'
UN-7   'PAGE-LIMIT EXCEEDED'
UN-8   'ATTEMPT TØ DØ DIRECT ACCESS I/Ø ØN A SEQUENTIAL FILE ØR VICE
            VERSA. PØSSIBLE MISSING DEFINE FILE STATEMENT (IBM CØDE IHC231)'
UN-9   'WRITE REFERENCES 5 ØR READ REFERENCES 6 ØR 7'
UN-A   'DEFINE FILE REFERENCES A UNIT PREVIØUSLY USED FØR SEQUENTIAL I/Ø
            (IBM CØDE IHC235)'
UN-B   'RECØRD SIZE FØR UNIT EXCEEDS 32767, ØR DIFFERS FRØM DD STATEMENT
            SPECIFICATIØN (IBM CØDES IHC233, IHC237)'
UN-C   'FØR DIRECT ACCESS I/Ø THE RELATIVE RECØRD PØSITIØN IS NEGATIVE,
            ZERØ, ØR TØØ LARGE (IBM CØDE IHC232)'
UN-D   'AN ATTEMPT WAS MADE TØ READ MØRE INFØRMATIØN THAN LØGICAL RECØRD
            CØNTAINS (IBM CØDE IHC236)'
UN-E   'FØRMATTED LINE EXCEEDS BUFFER LENGTH (IBM CØDE IHC212)'
UN-F   'I/Ø ERRØR - SEARCHING LIBRARY DIRECTØRY'
UN-G   'I/Ø ERRØR - READING LIBRARY'

WATFIV

UN-H   'ATTEMPT TØ DEFINE THE ØBJECT ERRØR FILE AS A DIRECT ACCESS FILE
          (IBM CØDE IHC234)'
UN-I   'RECFM ØTHER THAN V(B) IS SPECIFIED FØR I/Ø WITHØUT FØRMAT CØNTRØL
          (IBM CØDE IHC214)'
UN-J   'MISSING DD CARD FØR WATLIB. NØ LIBRARY ASSUMED'
UN-K   'ATTEMPT TØ READ ØR WRITE PAST THE END ØF CHARACTER VARIABLE BUFFER'
UN-L   'ATTEMPT TØ READ ØN AN UNCREATED DIRECT ACCESS FILE (IHC236)'

'UNDEFINED VARIABLES'
UV-0   'VARIABLE IS UNDEFINED'
UV-3   'SUBSCRIPT IS UNDEFINED'
UV-4   'SUBPRØGRAM IS UNDEFINED'
UV-5   'ARGUMENT IS UNDEFINED'
UV-6   'UNDECØDABLE CHARACTERS IN VARIABLE FØRMAT'

'VARIABLE NAMES'
VA-0   'A NAME IS TØØ LØNG. IT HAS BEEN TRUNCATED TØ SIX CHARACTERS'
VA-1   'ATTEMPT TØ USE AN ASSIGNED ØR INITIALIZED VARIABLE ØR DØ-PARAMETER
          IN A SPECIFICATIØN STATEMENT'
VA-2   'ILLEGAL USE ØF A SUBRØUTINE NAME'
VA-3   'ILLEGAL USE ØF A VARIABLE NAME'
VA-4   'ATTEMPT TØ USE A PREVIØUSLY DEFINED NAME AS A FUNCTIØN ØR AN ARRAY
VA-5   'ATTEMPT TØ USE A PREVIØUSLY DEFINED NAME AS A SUBRØUTINE'
VA-6   'ATTEMPT TØ USE A PREVIØUSLY DEFINED NAME AS A SUBPRØGRAM'
VA-7   'ATTEMPT TØ USE A PREVIØUSLY DEFINED NAME AS A CØMMØN BLØCK'
VA-8   'ATTEMPT TØ USE A FUNCTIØN NAME AS A VARIABLE'
VA-9   'ATTEMPT TØ USE A PREVIØUSLY DEFINED NAME AS A VARIABLE'
VA-A   'ILLEGAL USE ØF A PREVIØUSLY DEFINED NAME'

'EXTERNAL STATEMENT'
XT-0   'A VARIABLE HAS ALREADY APPEARED IN AN EXTERNAL STATEMENT'

WATFIV

WATFIV

FLOATING-POINT AND INTEGER NUMBERS WITH A DECIMAL EXPONENT

This appendix is a discussion of floating-point and integer numbers with a decimal exponent and the E and D exponent format codes.

FLOATING-POINT AND INTEGER NUMBERS WITH A DECIMAL EXPONENT

Single Precision Floating-Point Numbers with a Decimal Exponent   The range of a single precision floating-point number is either plus or minus .0000000 through 9999999. There are instances, however, when it is desirable to exceed this range without incurring the two disadvantages of double precision floating-point numbers. This can be accomplished through the addition of a decimal exponent to a single precision floating-point number.

A decimal exponent attached to a single precision floating-point number is composed of the character E followed by either a signed or unsigned 1- or 2-character integer number. If the 1- or 2-character integer number is unsigned, it is assumed to be positive by the computer. The decimal exponent causes the computer to multiply the single precision floating-point number by 10 raised to the power signified by either the signed or unsigned 1- or 2-character integer number. This increases the range of a single precision floating-point number to approximately 10^{75} or exactly 16^{63} through approximately 10^{-78} or exactly 16^{-65}.

The following are examples of *valid* single precision floating-point numbers with a decimal exponent:

5.0E0	(equivalent: $5.0*10^0$)	= 5.0
250.34E05	(equivalent: $250.34*10^5$)	= 25034000.
250.34E+05	(equivalent: $250.34*10^5$)	= 25034000.
250.34E5	(equivalent: $250.34*10^5$)	= 25034000.
−2195.634E15	(equivalent: $-2195.634*10^{15}$)	= −2195634000000000000.
7.1E−3	(equivalent: $7.1*10^{-3}$)	= .0071
890.75E−08	(equivalent: $890.75*10^{-8}$)	= .0000089075
890.75E−8	(equivalent: $890.75*10^{-8}$)	= .0000089075
−64375.19E−12	(equivalent: $-64375.19*10^{-12}$)	= −.00000006437519

The following are examples of *invalid* single precision floating-point numbers with a decimal exponent.

7534.52E	(a signed or unsigned 1- or 2-character integer number after the character E is missing)
315.2E1.4	(the 1- or 2-character number following the character E must be integer mode)
435.27E85	(the value of the 2-character integer number following the character E exceeds the maximum magnitude)

Double Precision Floating-Point Numbers with a Decimal Exponent   The maximum magnitude of a double precision floating-point number is either plus or minus .0000000000000000 through 9999999999999999. There are instances, however, when it is desirable to exceed this range. This can be accomplished through the addition of a decimal exponent to the double precision floating-point number.

A decimal exponent attached to a double precision floating-point number is composed of the character D followed by either a signed or unsigned 1- or 2-character integer number. If the 1- or 2-character integer number is unsigned, it is assumed to be positive by the computer. The decimal exponent causes the computer to multiply the double precision floating-point number by 10 raised to the power signified by either the signed or unsigned 1- or 2-character integer number. This increases the range of a double precision floating-point number to approximately 10^{75} or exactly 16^{63} through approximately 10^{-75} or exactly 16^{-65}.

A number composed of 1 through 7 characters is automatically considered by the computer as a double precision floating-point number *provided* it has a decimal exponent containing the character D. Even though there are only 1 through 7 characters, this number is subject to the same two disadvantages of a double precision floating-point number.

The following are examples of *valid* double precision floating-point numbers with a decimal ɔonent:

45.12D0	(equivalent: $45.12 * 10^0$)	$= 45.12$
1750.2D02	(equivalent: $1750.2 * 10^2$)	$= 175020.$
1750.2D+02	(equivalent: $1750.2 * 10^2$)	$= 175020.$
1750.2D2	(equivalent: $1750.2 * 10^2$)	$= 175020.$
−99831.573D8	(equivalent: $-99831.573 * 10^8$)	$= -9983157300000.$
73452198.152D+10	(equivalent: $73452198.152 * 10^{10}$)	$= 734521981520000000.$
15.23D-05	(equivalent: $15.34 * 10^{-5}$)	$= .0001534$
15.34D-5	(equivalent: $15.34 * 10^{-5}$)	$= .0001534$
−8345764.27D-11	(equivalent: $-8345764.27 * 10^{-11}$)	$= -.0000834576427$

The following are examples of *invalid* double precision floating-point numbers with a decimal exponent:

834.17D	(a signed or unsigned 1- or 2-character integer number after the character D is missing)
8951507.61D27.5	(the 1- or 2-character number following the character D must be integer mode)
7456398.134-90	(the value of the 2-character integer number following the character D exceeds the maximum magnitude)

Integer Numbers with a Decimal Exponent   When a decimal exponent is attached to an integer number, the number is classified as one of two types of floating-point numbers:

1. If the decimal exponent begins with the character E, the integer number can contain 1 through 7 characters.

2. If the decimal exponent begins with the character D, the integer number can contain 1 through 16 characters.

In both types, a decimal point *cannot* be used by the programmer. However, it is placed in its proper location in the number by the computer.

The following are examples of *valid* integer numbers with a decimal exponent:

4E6	(equivalent: $4 * 10^6$)	=	4000000.
9374658E08	(equivalent: $9374658 * 10^8$)	=	937465800000000.
9374658E+08	(equivalent: $9374658 * 10^8$)	=	937465800000000.
−837425E15	(equivalent: $−837425 * 10^{15}$)	=	−837425000000000000000.
25D-3	(equivalent: $25 * 10^{-3}$)	=	.00025
65125498D-05	(equivalent: $65125498 * 10^{-5}$)	=	.0000065125498
65125498D-5	(equivalent: $65125498 * 10^{-5}$)	=	.0000065125498
−77341298425D-13	(equivalent: $−77341298425 * 10^{-13}$)	=	−.0000000000000077341298425

The following are examples of *invalid* integer numbers with a decimal exponent:

719E	(a signed or unsigned 1- or 2-character integer number after the character E is missing)
5541721375D	(a signed or unsigned 1- or 2-character integer number after the character D is missing)
37264E80	(the value of the 2-character integer number following the character E exceeds the maximum magnitude)

THE E AND D EXPONENT FORMAT CODES

The E and D exponent format codes are used when it is desirable to read either an integer or a floating-point number with an exponent from a record or write a floating-point number with an exponent into a record of a data set. The general form of either the E or D exponent format codes are illustrated in Figure D-1.

```
cc 123456789...

   ccccc FØRMAT (aEw.d)
```

and

```
cc 123456789...

         FØRMAT (aDw.d)
```

where

a represents an optional unsigned integer number that specifies the number of times that particular format code is used each time the computer scans from the left to the right parenthesis of the FØRMAT statement. It may be omitted if the format code is to be used only once each time the computer scans from the left to the right parenthesis.

E   specifies that the datum is either an integer or a single precision floating-point number with an exponent.

or D   specifies that the datum is either an integer or a double precision floating-point number with an exponent.

w represents an unsigned integer number that specifies the number of record characters that are to be either read from or written into a record of a data set.

. is a necessary delimiter between w and d.

d represents an unsigned integer number that specifies the location of the decimal point within the number.

Figure D-1. The General Form of the E and D Format Codes.

Input Considerations   The characters that may read from a record are the numerical characters, the optional plus or required minus sign (if the number is negative) preceding the numerical characters, a decimal point, and an exponent (the character E or D and/or a plus or minus sign preceding either a 1- or 2-character integer number). Any leading, embedded, or trailing blanks are replaced by zeros when read. If the exponent of an integer or floating-point number contains the character E, the number may be composed of 1 through 7 characters. However, if the exponent contains the character D, the number may be composed of 1 through 16 characters. The number represented by w must be large enough to read the numerical characters on either side of the decimal point, the sign, if present, preceding the most significant numerical character, the decimal point, if present, and the exponent (the character E or D and/or a plus or minus sign, and a 1- or 2-character integer number). Figure D-2 illustrates the use of the E and D exponent codes in reading a datum from a record and storing it in the computer's memory.

Data Card	Format Code	Number Stored
cc `123456789...` `25034E05`	cc `123456789...` `1` `FØRMAT (E8.2)`	`250.34E05`
cc `123456789...` `5034E+05`	cc `123456789...` `1` `FØRMAT (E9.2)`	`050.34E+05`
cc `123456789...` `-25034E5`	cc `123456789...` `1` `FØRMAT (E8.2)`	`-250.34E5`
cc `123456789...` `17502D02`	cc `123456789...` `1` `FØRMAT (D8.1)`	`1750.2D02`
cc `123456789...` `7502D+02`	cc `123456789...` `1` `FØRMAT (D9.1)`	`0750.2D+02`
cc `123456789...` `-17502D2`	cc `123456789...` `1` `FØRMAT (D8.1)`	`-1750.2D2`

Figure D-2. The Effect of the Exponent Format Codes when Reading Data.

If a decimal point is not located in the number being read from the record, the computer will place a decimal point to the left of d positions beginning with the least significant character in the number (excluding the exponent). The decimal point must not be considered in this situation when computing w. However, if a decimal point is located in the number being read but d does not indicate the correct location of the decimal point in the number, the computer will ignore d's indication of the location of the decimal point and consider the location of the decimal point in the number as being correct.

Output Considerations   A floating-point number that uses an exponent format code is written as a decimal fraction followed by an exponent. A zero will always be written immediately preceding the decimal point. If the number is negative, a minus sign will be written immediately preceding this zero. The most significant nonzero character of the number will be written immediately to the right of the decimal point. The number represented by w must be large enough to write a leading minus sign if the number is negative, a decimal point, the number of numerical characters to the right of the decimal point specified by d, and a 4-character exponent (the alphabetic character, the positive or negative sign following the alphabetic character, and the 2-character integer number). If w provides an additional position, a zero will be written immediately preceding the decimal point.

If the number of numerical characters specified by d is greater than the actual number of characters, beginning with the most significant nonzero character, composing the number in storage being written, the number of trailing zeros required to make up the difference between this number of characters and d will be added by the computer. However, if the number of numerical characters specified by d is less than the actual number of characters, beginning with the most significant nonzero character, composing the number in storage being written, only the most significant d specified number of characters of the number will be written.

Figure D-3 illustrates the use of the E and D exponent codes in writing a datum into a record of a data set. To determine how to interpret the number written, move the decimal point to the right the number of positions indicated by the two integer characters of the exponent from its location in storage.

Number Stored	Format Code	Number Written	Interpretation of Number Written
	cc 123456789...		
250.34E05	1 FØRMAT ('1',E11.5)	0.25034E+05	25034000
	cc 123456789...		
050.34E+05	1 FØRMAT ('0',E11.5)	0.50340E+05	5034000
	cc 123456789...		
−250.34E5	1 FØRMAT ('0',E12.5)	−0.25034E+05	−25034000
	cc 123456789...		
1750.2D02	1 FØRMAT ('0',D11.5)	0.17502D+02	175020
	cc 123456789...		
0750.2D+02	1 FØRMAT ('0',D11.5)	0.75020D+02	175020

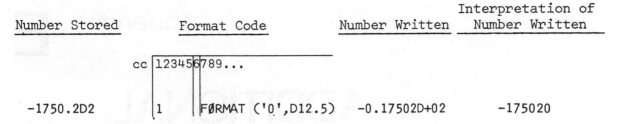

Figure D-3. The Effect of the Exponent Format Codes when Writing Data.

ADDITIONAL FORMAT OPTIONS

THE MATCHING OF SYMBOLIC NAMES AND FORMAT CODES

If there are two or more sets of parentheses in a FØRMAT statement referred to by either a READ and/or WRITE statement, the computer will match from left to right a symbolic name with a format code until it reaches the rightmost right parenthesis. If one or more of the symbolic names have not yet been matched with a format code when it encounters this parenthesis, the computer will terminate writing into this record if it is referred to by a WRITE statement, transfer back to the first left parenthesis it encounters, and begin writing data into another record of the data set, if it is referred to by a READ statement it will transfer back to the first left parenthesis it encounters, progress to the next record, and begin reading data from this record of the data set. The computer will continue repeating this process until each symbolic name in the *list* either has had a datum stored under it or until the datum stored under each symbolic name has had a duplicate of it written into a record of a data set. Conversely, if the number of symbolic names is less than the number of format codes within the parentheses of the referred to FØRMAT statement, the computer writes each datum stored under the symbolic names into a record of a data set, matching from left to right a symbolic name with a format code; any remaining codes are ignored by the computer.

Considering first the READ statement in the following illustration,

```
cc | 123456789...


   | READ (5,1,END=99) I,J,K,L,M,N
 1 | FØRMAT ((I2,I1),(I5, I3))
   | WRITE (6,2) I,J,K,L,M,N
 2 | FØRMAT (' ',I2,(I1),I5,I3)
```

the variable names I, J, K, and L will be matched respectively with the format codes I2, I1, I5, and I3. Upon encountering the rightmost parenthesis, the computer will return to the first left parenthesis it encounters, progress to the next record, and begin reading and storing in its memory a number from the new record under the variable names M and N again using the format codes I5 and I3 respectively. Considering now the WRITE statement, the computer will write a duplicate of each number stored under the variable names I, J, K, and L into a record of data set using the format codes I2, I1, I5, and I3 respectively. Upon encountering the rightmost parenthesis, it will terminate writing into that record and transfer back to the first left parenthesis it encounters. It will then write a duplicate of each number stored under the variable names M and N into a new record of the data set again using the format codes I1 and I5 respectively.

Certain format codes can have an optional unsigned integer number that specifies the number of times the particular format code is used each time the computer scans from the left to the right parenthesis of the FØRMAT statement (refer to the topic "The Format Codes" in Chapter 3). This unsigned integer number can also be used with several format codes by placing the referred to format codes within a set of parentheses and placing the unsigned integer number immediately prior to the left parenthesis. For example, in the following illustration,

```
cc │123456│789...
   │      ││
   │      ││
   │      ││
   │      │READ (5,1,END=99) I,J,K,L,M,N
   │1     │FØRMAT (I3,I2,2(I5,I7))
```

the variable names I, J, K, L, M, and N will be matched respectively with the format codes I3, I2, I5, I7, I5, and I7. The number 2 immediately preceding the set of parentheses enclosing the format codes I5 and I7 causes the computer to read these two codes as if they had been written I5, I7, I5, I7.

THE PUNCHING AND SKIPPING OF MORE THAN ONE RECORD

In certain situations, it is desirable to either punch and/or skip more than one record of a data set located on a card punch during the execution of a WRITE statement. This is accomplished through the use of one or more slashes within the FØRMAT statement. For example, in the following illustration,

```
cc │123456│789...
   │      ││
   │      ││
   │      ││
   │      │WRITE (7,1) I,J,K,L
   │1     │FØRMAT (I5,I2,//,I6,I4)
```

the computer will punch a duplicate of each number stored under the variable names I and J into a record of a data set located on a card punch. The computer will then, upon encountering a slash, terminate punching data into that record and advance to the next record. Upon encountering the second slash, the computer will immediately advance to the next record without punching any data. The computer will then punch a duplicate of the number stored under the variable names J and K into this record.

LOGICAL OPERATIONS

In addition to the six regional operators, there are three logical operators which cause the evaluation of the truth or falsity of two *logical expressions*. Two of these three logical operators are the connectives .AND. and .ØR. and the third logical operator is the inverter .NØT.. A basic requirement of the two logical expressions connected by the two connectives .AND. or .ØR. and the logical expression immediately following the inverter .NØT. is that each either be or be reducible to either a true or false condition. Like the relational operators, each of the logical operators must be immediately preceded and followed by a period for the same previously discussed reason. Two logical operators may appear in sequence only if the sequence is either .AND. .NØT. or .ØR. .NØT.; the sequence .NØT. .NØT. is invalid.

The connective .AND. requires that the logical expression both preceding and following it be true for the resultant condition to be true. If either are false or both are false, then the resultant condition will be false.

The connective .ØR. requires that the logical expression either preceding and/or following it be true for the resultant condition to be true. If both are false, then the resultant condition is false.

The inverter .NØT. causes the resultant condition to be true if the immediately following logical expression is false. However, if the immediately following logical expression is true, the resultant condition is false.

To illustrate the use of the logical operators, assume the following:

Variable	Type
I,J	Integer
A,B	Single precision floating-point
C,D,K,L	Logical

Considering the preceding information, the first logical expression in the following illustration

```
cc 123456789...

     C = K .AND. L
     C = (A+2.5 .LT. B) .AND. L
     D = .NØT. K .AND. .NØT. L
     D = K .AND. .NØT. L .ØR. I .EQ. J
```

will result in the logical constant .TRUE. being stored under the logical variable name C if both the logical variable names K and L have the logical constant .TRUE. stored under each of them. However, if either of the logical variable names K or L or both of them have the logical constant .FALSE. stored under them, the logical constant .FALSE. will be stored under the logical variable name C. In the second logical expression, if the number stored under the variable name A plus 2.5 is less than the number stored under the variable name B and the logical constant .TRUE. is stored under the logical variable name L, the logical constant .TRUE. will be stored under the logical variable name C. However, if the number stored under the variable name A plus 2.5 is not less than the number stored under the variable name B and/or the logical constant .FALSE. is stored under the logical variable name L, the logical constant .FALSE. will be stored under the logical variable name C. In the third logical expression, if the logical constant .TRUE. is stored under both the logical variable names K and L, the logical constant .FALSE. will be stored under the logical variable name D. However, if the logical constant .FALSE. is stored under either the logical variable names K and/or L, the logical constant .FALSE. will be stored under the logical variable name D. In the last logical expression, if the logical constant .TRUE. is stored under the logical variable name K and if the logical constant .FALSE. is stored under the logical variable name L or if the number stored under the variable name I is equal to the number stored under the variable name J, the logical constant .TRUE. will be stored under the logical variable name D. However, if the logical constant .FALSE. is stored under the logical variable name K and/or the logical constant .TRUE. is stored under the logical variable name L and/or if the number stored under the variable name I is not equal to the number stored under the variable name J, the logical constant .FALSE. will be stored under the logical variable name D.

The use of a set of parentheses is particularly important in certain instances with respect to what resultant condition is obtained when the logical operator .NØT. evaluates two arithmetic expressions whose relationship is being evaluated by a relational operator. For example, assume that the logical constants .FALSE. and .TRUE. are stored under the logical variable names I and J respectively. In the following illustration,

```
cc │123456789...
   │
   │
   │L = .NØT. (I .ØR. J)
   │MAP = .NØT. I .ØR. J
```

the resultant condition stored under the logical variable name L will be the logical constant .FALSE. whereas the resultant condition stored under the logical variable name MAP will be the logical constant .TRUE.. The reason for the different resultant conditions is due to the fact that in the first logical expression I .ØR. J was evaluated first. The resultant condition is .TRUE.; however, .NØT. (.TRUE.) is evaluated as .FALSE. (the logical operator .NØT. inverts the resultant condition). In the second logical expression .NØT. I is evaluated first. The resultant condition is .TRUE. (the logical operator .NØT. inverts the false condition stored under the logical variable name I) and .TRUE. .ØR. J is evaluated as .TRUE.. While the resultant conditions were different under the given circumstances, if the conditions stored under the logical variable names I and J had been reversed, the resultant conditions would have been identical. Also, this is one of those instances when it is not necessary for the computer to evaluate all the operands composing a logical expression prior to its obtaining a valid resultant condition (the condition stored under the second expression (J) is irrelevant to the resultant condition).

THE READING OF TWO OR MORE DATA DECKS

Occasionally, it is desirable to sequentially read two or more data decks. The problem arises as to how the computer can determine when all of the data cards comprising a particular data deck have been read. The use of the END= option is not appropriate in this situation as it only detects the absence of a data card. Thus, it is necessary to use another technique. The following are illustrations of four of these techniques:

THE USE OF A COUNTER

In the following illustration, a counter is used to determine when the number of data cards composing a data deck have been read. When the variable name KØUNT has a number stored under it that is greater than the number stored under the variable name NUMBER, execution of the program is terminated.

```
cc  123456789...

C       THE USE ØF A CØUNTER
        .
        .
        .
2       READ (5,1,END=99) NUMBER
1       FØRMAT (I3)
        KØUNT = 0
4       KØUNT = KØUNT+1
        IF (KØUNT .GT. NUMBER) GØ TØ 2
        READ (5,3,END=99) QUANT,PRICE,TØCØST
3       FØRMAT (F3.0,T10,F5.2,T20,F7.2)
        .
        .
        .
        GØ TØ 4
99      STØP
        END
```

THE USE OF THE FIRST CARD OF A
DATA DECK AS A CONTROL CARD

In the following illustration, the number of data cards comprising a data deck is punched in an otherwise blank punch card located in front of the data deck. This number is read and stored under the variable name NUMBER. Then the variable name NUMBER is placed in the DØ statement to control the number of loops and, in turn, the number of data cards read by the second READ statement.

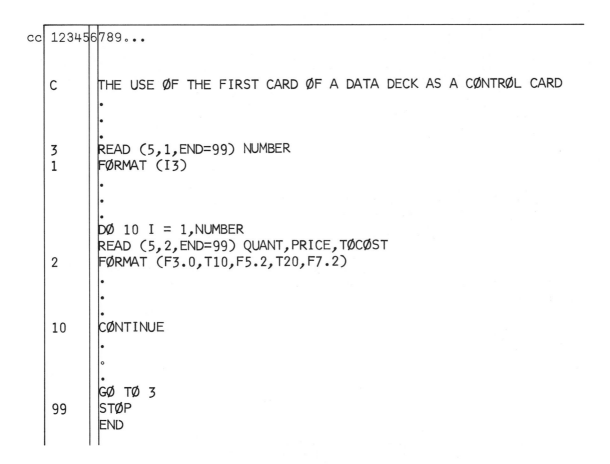

```
cc  123456789...


C        THE USE ØF THE FIRST CARD ØF A DATA DECK AS A CØNTRØL CARD
         .
         .
         .
3        READ (5,1,END=99) NUMBER
1        FØRMAT (I3)
         .
         .
         .
         DØ 10 I = 1,NUMBER
         READ (5,2,END=99) QUANT,PRICE,TØCØST
2        FØRMAT (F3.0,T10,F5.2,T20,F7.2)
         .
         .
         .
10       CØNTINUE
         .
         °
         .
         GØ TØ 3
99       STØP
         END
```

THE CHECKING OF A USED FIELD OF DATA
IN A BLANK PUNCH CARD, WHICH IS
THE LAST CARD OF A DATA DECK

In the following illustration, a check is made of a *used* field of data to determine whether or not a number is punched in the field. The absence of a number indicates that the blank punch card has been read.

```
cc 123456789...

   C     THE CHECKING ØF A USED FIELD ØF DATA IN A BLANK PUNCH CARD
         .
         .
         .
   3     READ (5,1,END=99) QUANT,PRICE,TØCØST
   1     FØRMAT (F3.0,T10,F5.2,T20,F7.2)
         IF (QUANT .EQ. 0) GØ TØ 2
         .
         .
         .
         GØ TØ 3
   2     WRITE ...
         .
         .
         .
         GØ TØ 3
   99    STØP
         END
```

THE CHECKING OF A UNUSED FIELD OF DATA
IN A PUNCH CARD, WHICH IS THE
LAST CARD OF A DATA DECK

In the following illustration, a check is made of an *unused* field of data to determine whether or not a number is punched in the field. The presence of a number indicated that the otherwise blank punch card has been read.

```
cc 123456789...

   C     THE CHECKING ØF AN UNUSED FIELD ØF DATA IN A PUNCH CARD
         .
         .
         .
   3     READ (5,1,END=99) QUANT,PRICE,TØCØST,ICØDE
   1     FØRMAT (F3.0,T10,F5.2,T20,F7.2,T78,I3
         IF (ICØDE .EQ. 999) GØ TØ 2
         .
         .
         .
         GØ TØ 3
   2     WRITE...
         .
         .
         .
         GØ TØ 3
   99    STØP
         END
```

Appendix H

SYSTEM AND PROGRAM FLOWCHARTING

Regardless of the degree of complication of a program, flowcharting is an important step in the process of preparing it for execution by a computer. A flowchart is a graphical representation of the definition, analysis, or solution of a problem in which symbols are used to represent operations, data, flow, equipment, etc.* There are two basic types of flowcharts.

1. SYSTEM FLOWCHART

A system is composed of the procedures and devices required to produce some end result. While this definition is valid for either manual or automated data processing systems, the following discussion is oriented toward automated and, specifically, electronic data processing systems.

A system flowchart describes the flow of data through the interrelated hardware elements of an electronic data processing system. It depicts the over-all plan of procedure of data processing operations. As such, emphasis is placed on the media involved in converting the source data into information. This is reflected in the type of symbols composing a system flowchart. The specific operations to be performed on the data are described briefly, if at all, in a system flowchart.

2. PROGRAM FLOWCHART

A program flowchart is a detailed depiction of the operations and decisions required to solve a problem. Specifically, it shows how the data is to be processed, i.e., the sequential performance of the operations and decisions. Three uses of a program flowcharts in computer applications are:**

    1. An aid to computer program development

    2. A guide for the coding of instructions that make up a computer program

---

*American National Standard Flowchart Symbols and Their Usage in Information Processing. Business Equipment Manufacturers Association, Sponsor. New York, New York: American National Standards Institute, Inc., 1971, p. 7.

**Introduction to IBM Data Processing Systems. White Plains, New York: International Business Machines Corporation, Third Edition, March 1969, p. 69.

3. Part of the documentation of a computer program.

The following are some of the conventions and techniques that should be considered when preparing a system and program flowchart:

1. In the program development stage, a system flowchart may serve as a means of experimenting with various approaches to processing the data. When actual programming begins, a system flowchart depicts the various data processing runs. A program flowchart is then prepared for each run to serve as a basis for actual program writing.

2. One of the most important uses of a program flowchart is its provision of a pictorial sequence of logic and arithmetic operations. As such, the relationship of one portion of a program to another should be recognizable both during development of the program and after its completion.

3. The program processing steps should start at the top of a page and move down and to the right to the lower right-hand corner. If the flow goes in a reverse direction, arrowheads are used on the flowlines. The arrowheads can also be used with normal flow to increase clarity and readability.

4. A program flowchart should be referenced to its corresponding written program. This greatly aids in program testing and debugging, maintenance, and modification. One way to cross-reference is to place a notation either above the flowchart symbol to either the right or left of the vertical flowline or inside the symbol separated by a stripe.

5. Titles should be short but not confusing. For better understanding, the language in the flowchart should be English rather than a machine-oriented or program system language. Whenever the text pertaining to a symbol cannot be placed within a symbol, it should be
   a. placed alongside
   b. referenced to a narrative located elsewhere on the flowchart
   c. placed within the annotation, comment symbol.

The following is an illustration and accompanying description of the more commonly used system and program flowchart symbols. The shape of each of these symbols and its accompanying description is recommended by the American National Standards Institute, Inc. (ANSI X3.5-1970):

INPUT/OUTPUT   represents the function of either making information available (input) or recording processed information (output)

PROCESS   represents any kind of processing function

FLOWLINE   represents the function of linking symbols. It indicates the sequence of available information and executable operations

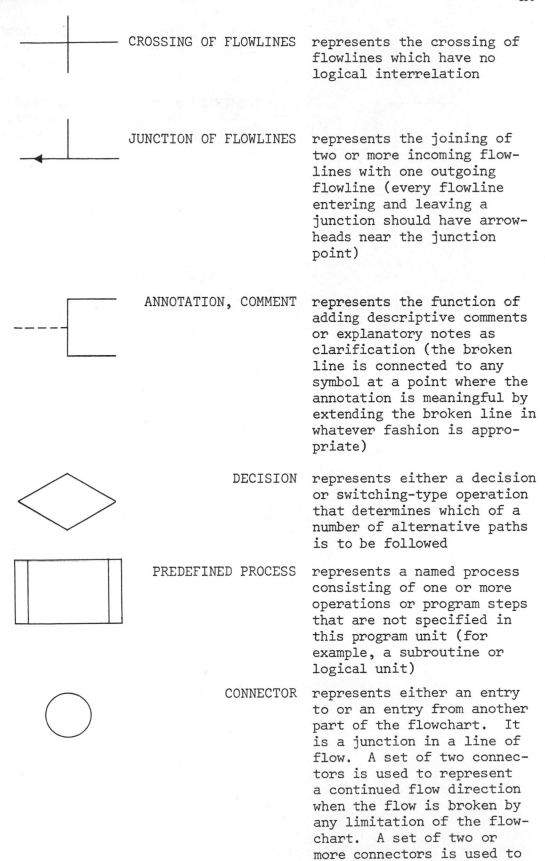

CROSSING OF FLOWLINES   represents the crossing of
                        flowlines which have no
                        logical interrelation

JUNCTION OF FLOWLINES   represents the joining of
                        two or more incoming flow-
                        lines with one outgoing
                        flowline (every flowline
                        entering and leaving a
                        junction should have arrow-
                        heads near the junction
                        point)

ANNOTATION, COMMENT   represents the function of
                      adding descriptive comments
                      or explanatory notes as
                      clarification (the broken
                      line is connected to any
                      symbol at a point where the
                      annotation is meaningful by
                      extending the broken line in
                      whatever fashion is appro-
                      priate)

DECISION   represents either a decision
           or switching-type operation
           that determines which of a
           number of alternative paths
           is to be followed

PREDEFINED PROCESS   represents a named process
                     consisting of one or more
                     operations or program steps
                     that are not specified in
                     this program unit (for
                     example, a subroutine or
                     logical unit)

CONNECTOR   represents either an entry
            to or an entry from another
            part of the flowchart. It
            is a junction in a line of
            flow. A set of two connec-
            tors is used to represent
            a continued flow direction
            when the flow is broken by
            any limitation of the flow-
            chart. A set of two or
            more connectors is used to
            represent the junction of
            several flowlines with one

flowline, or the junction
of one flowline with one
of several alternative
flowlines.

TERMINAL   represents a terminal point
in a flowchart (start, stop,
halt, delay, or interrupt)

FORTRAN-SUPPLIED SUBPROGRAMS

There are two types of FORTRAN-supplied subprograms: mathematical functions and service subroutines. The following discussion of each of these types of subprograms is centered around a table depicting the main characteristics of each of them.

Table I-1 contains the FORTRAN-supplied mathematical function subprograms. It is divided into two segments: in-line and out-of-line subprograms. *In-line* subprograms are part of the FORTRAN compiler and thus available at all computer installations. An in-line subprogram is inserted by the FORTRAN compiler at each point in the program where it is called. *Out-of-line* subprograms are not part of the FORTRAN compiler, but for programming purposes are treated as if they were part of it. Since they are not part of the FORTRAN compiler, they are available at most, but not necessarily all, computer installations. An out-of-line subprogram is located in a library and whenever it is called in a program the FORTRAN compiler transfers control to it.

The FORTRAN name of a subprogram is used by the computer to identify three things: (1) the particular mathematical function subprogram being called, (2) the type of the argument(s) accompanying the subprogram name, and (3) the type of the value returned by the subprogram to the calling program.

IN-LINE MATHEMATICAL FUNCTION SUBPROGRAMS

General Function	FORTRAN Name	Definition	Number of Arguments	Type of Argument	Type of Function Number Returned by the Subprogram
Absolute value	IABS	$\lvert Arg \rvert$	1	Integer *4	Integer *4
	ABS		1	Real *4	Real *4
	DABS		1	Real *8	Real *8
Modular arithmetic†	MØD	$Arg_1 \ (mod \ Arg_2) =$ $Arg_1 - (x) \cdot Arg_2$ Where: (x) is the largest integer whose magnitude does not exceed the magnitude of Arg_1/Arg_2. The sign of the integer is the same as the sign of Arg_1/Arg_2.	2	Integer *4	Integer *4
	AMØD		2	Real *4	Real *4
	DMØD		2	Real *8	Real *8
Truncation	INT	Sign of Arg times largest integer $\leq \lvert Arg \rvert$	1	Real *4	Integer *4
	AINT		1	Real *4	Real *4
	IDINT		1	Real *8	Real *8
Convert from integer to real	FLØAT	Convert from integer to real	1	Integer *4	Real *4
	DFLØAT		1	Integer *4	Real *8

†MØD and AMØD are not defined when the value of the second argument is zero.

Description	Function	Definition	Args	Argument type	Result type
Convert from real to integer	IFIX	Convert from real to integer	1	Real *4	Integer *4
	HFIX		1	Real *4	Integer *2
Transfer of sign††	SIGN	Sign of Arg_2 times $|Arg_1|$	2	Real *4	Real *4
	ISIGN		2	Integer *4	Integer *4
	DSIGN		2	Real *8	Real *8
Positive difference	DIM	$Arg_1 - \mathrm{MIN}(Arg_1, Arg_2)$	2	Real *4	Real *4
	IDIM		2	Integer *4	Integer *4
Obtain most significant part of a REAL number	SNGL		1	Real *8	Real *4
Obtain real part of a complex number	REAL		1	Complex *8	Real *4
Obtain imaginary part of a complex number	AIMAG		1	Complex *8	Real *4
Precision increase	DBLE		1	Real *4	Real *8
Express two REAL arguments in complex form	CMPLX	$C = Arg_1 + iArg_2$	2	Real *4	Complex *8
	DCMPLX		2	Real *8	Complex *16
Obtain conjugate of a complex number	CØNJG	$C = X - iY$ For $Arg = X + iY$	1	Complex *8	Complex *8
	DCØNJG		1	Complex *16	Complex *16

††SIGN, ISIGN, and DSIGN are not defined when the value of the second argument is zero.

OUT-OF-LINE MATHEMATICAL FUNCTION SUBPROGRAMS

Description	Function	Definition	Args	Argument type	Result type
Natural logarithm	ALØG	ln (Arg)	1	Real *4	Real *4

Function	FORTRAN name	Definition	No. args	Argument type	Result type
Natural logarithm	DLØG	ln (Arg)	1	Real *8	Real *8
	CLØG	ln (Arg)	1	Complex *8	Complex *8
	CDLØG	ln (Arg)	1	Complex *16	Complex *16
Common logarithm	ALØG10	$\log_{10}$ (Arg)	1	Real *4	Real *4
	DLØG10	$\log_{10}$ (Arg)	1	Real *8	Real *8
Exponential	EXP	e^{arg}	1	Real *4	Real *4
	DEXP	e^{arg}	1	Real *8	Real *8
	CEXP	e^{arg}	1	Complex *8	Complex *8
	CDEXP	e^{arg}	1	Complex *16	Complex *16
Square root	SQRT	$(Arg)^{1/2}$	1	Real *4	Real *4
	DSQRT	$(Arg)^{1/2}$	1	Real *8	Real *8
	CSQRT	$(Arg)^{1/2}$	1	Complex *8	Complex *8
	CDSQRT	$(Arg)^{1/2}$	1	Complex *16	Complex *16
Arcsine	ARSIN	arcsin (Arg)	1	Real *4	Real *4
	DARSIN	arcsin (Arg)	1	Real *8	Real *8
Arccosine	ARCØS	arccos (Arg)	1	Real *4	Real *4
	DARCØS	arccos (Arg)	1	Real *8	Real *8
Arctangent	ATAN	arctan (Arg)	1	Real *4	Real *4
	ATAN2	arctan (Arg_1/Arg_2)	2	Real *4	Real *4
	DATAN	arctan (Arg)	1	Real *8	Real *8
	DATAN2	arctan (Arg_1/Arg_2)	2	Real *8	Real *8
Trigonometric sine	SIN	sin (Arg)	1	Real *4	Real *4
	DSIN	sin (Arg)	1	Real *8	Real *8
	CSIN	sin (Arg)	1	Complex *8	Complex *8
	CDSIN	sin (Arg)	1	Complex *16	Complex *16
Trigonometric cosine	CØS	cos (Arg)	1	Real *4	Real *4
	DCØS	cos (Arg)	1	Real *8	Real *8
	CCØS	cos (Arg)	1	Complex *8	Complex *8

Description	Name	Definition		Argument Type	Function Type
Trigonometric cosine	CDCØS	$\cos(Arg)$	1	Complex *16	Complex *16
Trigonometric tangent	TAN DTAN	$\tan(Arg)$ $\tan(Arg)$	1 1	Real *4 Real *8	Real *4 Real *8
Trigonometric contangent	CØTAN DCØTAN	$\cotan(Arg)$ $\cotan(Arg)$	1 1	Real *4 Real *8	Real *4 Real *8
Hyperbolic sine	SINH DSINH	$\sinh(Arg)$ $\sinh(Arg)$	1 1	Real *4 Real *8	Real *4 Real *8
Hyperbolic cosine	CØSH DCØSH	$\cosh(Arg)$ $\cosh(Arg)$	1 1	Real *4 Real *8	Real *4 Real *8
Hyperbolic tangent	TANH DTANH	$\tanh(Arg)$ $\tanh(Arg)$	1 1	Real *4 Real *8	Real *4 Real *8
Absolute value	CABS CDABS	$\sqrt{(a^2 + b^2)}$ for $a + bi$	1 1	Complex *8 Complex *16	Complex *8 Complex *16
Error function	ERF DERF	$\dfrac{2}{\sqrt{\pi}} \displaystyle\int_0^x e^{-u^2}\, du$	1 1	Real *4 Real *8	Real *4 Real *8
Complemented error function	ERFC DERFC	$1 - \mathrm{erf}(x)$	1 1	Real *4 Real *8	Real *4 Real *8
Gamma function	GAMMA DGAMMA	$\displaystyle\int_0^\infty u^{x-1} e^{-u}\, du$	1 1	Real *4 Real *8	Real *4 Real *8
Natural log of the gamma function	ALGAMA DLGAMA	$\log_e(x)$	1 1	Real *4 Real *8	Real *4 Real *8

Description	Name	Definition	No. of Args	Argument Type	Result Type
Largest value among the arguments†††	AMAX0	$Max(Arg_1, Arg_2, \ldots,)$	≥2	Integer *4	Real *4
	AMAX1		≥2	Real *4	Real *4
	MAX0		≥2	Integer *4	Integer *4
	MAX1		≥2	Real *4	Integer *4
	DMAX1		≥2	Real *8	Real *8
Smallest value among the arguments††††	AMIN0		≥2	Integer *4	Real *4
	AMIN1		≥2	Real *4	Real *4
	MIN0		≥2	Integer *4	Integer *4
	MIN1		≥2	Real *4	Integer *4
	DMIN1		≥2	Real *8	Real *8

†††For the FORTRAN IV (H) Compiler, these functions are in-line.
††††For the FORTRAN IV (H) Compiler, these functions are in-line.

TABLE I-1. FORTRAN-Supplied Mathematical Function Subprograms.

The second type of FORTRAN-supplied subprograms are called service subprograms. Table I-2 contains these subprograms.

TABLE I-2.   FORTRAN-Supplied Service Subroutines.*

Purpose	CALL Statement	Argument Information
Alter status of sense lights	CALL SLITE (i)	i is an integer expression. If i = 0, the four sense lights are turned off. If i = 1, 2, 3, 4, the corresponding sense light is turned on.
Test and record status of sense lights (After the test, the sense light that was tested is turned off.)	CALL SLITET (i,j)	i is an integer expression that has a value of 1, 2, 3, or 4 and indicates which sense light to test. i is an integer variable that is set to 1 if the sense light was on, or to 2 if the sense light was off.
Dump storage on the output data set and terminate execution	CALL DUMP $(a_1,b_1,f_1, \dots,a_n,b_n,f_n)$	a and b are variables that indicate the limits of storage to be dumped. (Either a or b may be the upper or lower limits of storage, but both must be in the same program or subprogram or in common.) f indicates the dump format and may be one of the following: 0 – hexadecimal 1 – LØGICAL*1 2 – LØGICAL*4 3 – INTEGER*2 4 – INTEGER*4 5 – REAL*4 6 – REAL*8 7 – CØMPLEX*8 8 – CØMPLEX*16 9 – literal 10 – REAL*16 11 – CØMPLEX*32
Dump storage on the output data set and continue execution	CALL PDUMP $(a_1,b_1,f_1, \dots,a_n,b_n,f_n)$	a, b, and f are as defined above for DUMP.

IBM System/360 and System/370 FORTRAN IV Language (Order No. GC28-6515-8, January 1971) p. 118.

Test for divide check exception	CALL DVCHK(j)	j is an integer variable that is set to 1 if the divide-check indicator was on, or to 2 if the indicator was off. After testing, the divide-check indicator is turned off.
Test for exponent overflow or underflow	CALL ØVERFL(j)	j is an integer variable that is set to 1 if an exponent overflow condition was the last to occur, to 2 if no overflow condition exists, or to 3 if an exponent underflow condition was the last to occur. After testing, the overflow indicator is turned off.
Terminate execution	CALL EXIT	None

Answers to Questions and Exercises

ANSWERS TO CHAPTER 1 QUESTIONS AND EXERCISE

Questions

1. A) *Electronic*   Achieves its results through the movement of electronic impulses rather than the physical movement of internal parts.
    B) *Internal storage*   The ability to simultaneously store program statements and data in its memory. This ability enables the computer to consecutively execute several program statements without human intervention and thus takes advantage of its ability to accurately execute these statements at a high rate of speed.
    C) *Stored program*   A series of statements stored in the computer's memory which instruct the computer in detail as to both the specific operations it is to perform and the order in which it is to perform these operations.
    D) *Program execution modification*   The ability to change the course of the execution of program statements because of a decision based on data stored in its memory and/or the result of one or more arithmetic operations.

2. A) *Analog computers*   The analog computer, in contrast to the digital computer, measures either continuous electrical or physical magnitudes rather than counting digits; decimal digits are obtained indirectly. Thus, such magnitudes as speed, current, length, pressure, temperature, shaft rotations, and voltage are directly measured and then converted to analogous decimal digits.
    B) *Digital computers*   The digital computer, in contrast to the analog computer, operates directly on decimal digits that represent either discrete data or symbols in the process of obtaining desired objectives. Digital computers are the type of computers most commonly thought of and referred to when the term "computer" is used either by itself or in context.

3. The acronym FORTRAN is derived from the term FORmula TRANslator. This computer language is especially appropriate for writing computer programs for applications that involve mathematical computations and other manipulation of numerical data.

4. A) *TRUE*
    B) *FALSE*   The computer normally executes program statements in the order in which they are located in the program rather than by their statement number.
    C) *FALSE*   In addition to FØRMAT statements, all program statements to which a transfer is made during execution of the program must have a statement number.

D) *FALSE*   Only 1 through 5 numeric characters are usable as statement numbers.

E) *TRUE*

F) *TRUE*

G) *FALSE*   Each program statement number must be a unique numeric character so that the computer is able to determine what specific program statement is being referred to by another program statement.

H) *TRUE*

I) *FALSE*   Any alphabetic, numeric, or special character other than either a blank (this character cannot be punched) or a zero may be placed in it.

J) *FALSE*   FORTRAN statements can begin and end at any punch card column 7 through 72.

K) *TRUE*

L) *TRUE*

5. The alphabetic character C in punch card column 1.

6. Punch card columns 2 through 80.

7. A)   Alphabetic characters

   B)   Numeric characters

   C)   Special characters

8. FORTRAN statements instruct the computer when, how, and where to read, process, and store the data being processed. Data cards contain the original source of data that is processed by the computer.

9. A source program is a set of FORTRAN statements in FORTRAN language form.

10. An object program is a set of FORTRAN statements in Machine Language form.

11. During compilation, FORTRAN statements are converted (compiled) into Machine Language statements.

Exercise

Line

1. Alphabetic character C must be punched in card column 1. Otherwise, the computer will not recognize this program statement as a comment statement.

2. This program statement is correct.

3. Only numeric characters can compose a statement number.

4. This program statement has the same statement number as another program statement. Thus, the computer will not know which of the two program statements the programmer is referring to.

5. There is no statement number, and all FØRMAT statements must be assigned a statement number.

6. A program statement cannot begin in a punch card column prior to column 7.

7. This program statement is correct. The computer will interpret the statement number as the number 99.

ANSWERS TO CHAPTER 2 QUESTIONS AND EXERCISES

Questions

1. A)   *FORTRAN key words*   FORTRAN key words are the means by which the computer distinguishes among the FORTRAN statements.

   B)   *Numbers*   An integer number is one or more numerical characters. A floating-point number is one or more numerical characters and a decimal point that may be followed by one or more of the numerical characters to form what is called the fraction part of the number.

   C)   *Symbolic names*   A symbolic name is a symbolic representation of a number, an alphabetic character, an array of numbers, or a subprogram.

   D)   *Expressions*   An arithmetic expression involves an arithmetical computation. A logical expression expresses either a true or false condition.

2. A) *Alphabetic characters*   The alphabetic characters are used to form FORTRAN key words and symbolic names and may be used to partially form numbers and expressions.

   B) *Numeric characters*   The numeric characters are used to form numbers and may be used to partially form symbolic names and expressions.

   C) *Special characters*   The special characters may be used to partially form numbers and expressions.

3.

Alphabetic Character	Numeric Character
Ø	0
I	1
Z	2
S	5

4. Either establishment or replacement of the datum stored under the symbolic name on the left side with either the datum or data on the right side.

5. A FORTRAN key word is the means by which the computer determines the specific type of execution it is to perform when executing that program statement.

6. An integer number can never include a decimal point whereas a floating-point number must always include a decimal point.

7. A single precision floating-point number can have 1 through 7 numerical characters whereas a double precision floating-point number can have from 1 through 16 numerical characters.

8. A symbolic name can only contain alphabetic and numeric characters; the first character must be alphabetic.

9. The alphabetic characters I, J, K, L, M, or N.

10. The alphabetic characters A through H, Ø through Z, and $.

11. The symbolic name appears in either a DØUBLE PRECISIØN or a LØGICAL specification statement prior to the first program statement in which the symbolic name is used.

12. A double precision floating-point or logical symbolic name can have as its first character any alphabetic character.

13. .TRUE. and .FALSE.

14. A logical variable name is a symbolic name that can have either the logical constant .TRUE. or the logical constant .FALSE. stored under it.

Exercises

1. (1) contains a decimal point
    (2) correct
    (3) correct
    (4) correct
    (5) correct
    (6) exceeds the maximum numerical character length
    (7) correct
    (8) contains a decimal point
    (9) correct
    (10) exceeds the maximum magnitude
    (11) correct
    (12) contains an embedded comma

2. (1) correct
    (2) exceeds the maximum numerical length
    (3) correct
    (4) no decimal point
    (5) correct
    (6) correct

(7) correct
(8) correct
(9) minus sign incorrectly located
(10) correct
(11) contains an embedded comma
(12) correct
3. (1) correct
(2) correct
(3) exceeds the maximum numerical character length
(4) correct
(5) no decimal point
(6) correct
(7) correct
(8) minus sign incorrectly located
(9) correct
(10) contains embedded commas
(11) correct
(12) correct
4. (1) correct
(2) a signed or unsigned 1- or 2-character integer number after the alphabetic character is missing
(3) correct
(4) correct
(5) correct
(6) the 1- or 2-character number following the alphabetic character D must be integer mode
(7) correct
(8) the value of the 2-character integer number following the alphabetic character E exceeds the maximum magnitude
(9) correct
5. (1) correct
(2) a signed or unsigned 1- or 2-character integer number after the alphabetic character E is missing
(3) correct
(4) a decimal point is not allowed to be placed by the programmer
(5) correct
(6) the value of the 2-character integer number following the alphabetic character E exceeds the maximum magnitude
(7) correct
(8) a signed or unsigned 1- or 2-character integer number after the alphabetic character D is missing
(9) correct

ANSWERS TO CHAPTER 3 QUESTIONS

Questions

1. A record is composed of one or more fields of data that have a logical relationship.
2. A data set is composed of one or more records.
3. The READ statement causes data to be read from one or more records located on a specific input device and the storing of this data in the computer's memory.
4. The END= option provides the means for the computer to transfer to the program statement indicated by the statement number following the equal sign when the computer attempts to read data from a record located on a specific input device and encounters the end of the data set. The ERR= option provides the means for the computer to transfer to the program statement indicated by the statement number following the equal sign when the computer encounters an error condition during its attempt to read data from a record located on a specific input device.

5. The WRITE statement causes data to be transferred from the computer's memory and written into one or more records located on a specific output device.

6. Because in most instances either the structure of each record or the form of data within a record is quite different.

7. The matching process is based on a left to right sequence. That is, the first symbolic name is matched with the first format code, the second symbolic name is matched with the second format code, etc.

8. More than one record can be either read or written through the use of the slash. Each slash causes termination of either reading or writing of a record and the progression to the next record.

9. A carriage control character is the means of determining the desired number of print lines to vertically advance on a page of printer paper before printing.

10. A format code indicates the location, type, field size, and location of the decimal point (if applicable) of a datum that is either read from or written into a record.

11. When it is necessary to either read an integer number from a record or write an integer number into a record.

12. When it is necessary to either read a floating-point number from a record or write a floating-point number into a record.

13. When it is necessary to read either an integer or a floating-point number with an exponent from a record or write a floating-point number with an exponent into a record.

14. When it is necessary to either read from or write into a record heading, labels, and general information.

15. When it is necessary to either read from or write into a record either one or more of the FORTRAN Character Set characters and/or the 15 additional characters in their literal form.

16. When it is necessary to begin either reading from or writing into a specific record position by means of the format code (or literal data if writing) following it.

17. When it is necessary to either skip one or more positions within a record being read or insert blanks in one or more positions within a record being written into.

ANSWERS TO CHAPTER 4 QUESTIONS AND EXERCISES

Questions

1. A) The arithmetic statement is the means through which arithmetical computations are performed. It also provides the means through which both a number may be stored under either a variable name or array element and a number that is stored under a symbolic name may be utilized in a program.

   B) The logical statement is the means through which a true or false condition is stored under a logical variable name.

2. A) A single variable name or array element must be located on the left side of the equal sign.

   B) The variable name or array element on the left side of the equal sign is "defined" by the result of the evaluation of the expression on the right side of the equal sign.

   C) The variable name of array element on the left side of the equal sign need not be the same type as the operand(s) composing the arithmetic expression on the right side of the equal sign.

   D) The result of an arithmetic expression on the right side of the equal sign is stored under the type of the variable name or array element on the left side of the equal sign.

3. The three possible components of an arithmetic expression are:

   A) Operands

   B) Arithmetic operators

   C) Parentheses

4. A) An arithmetic expression may be composed of either a single number or symbolic name.

   B) An arithmetic expression may be composed of two or more numbers and/or symbolic names.

   C) A symbolic name cannot be used in an arithmetic expression until it has been "defined" in the program.

   D) Two or more arithmetic operators cannot appear in sequence in an arithmetic expression.

   E) One or more sets of parentheses may be used in an arithmetic expression.

F)   The evaluation of the various operands comprising an arithmetic expression is based upon a hierarchy of arithmetic operations.

G)   The operands comprising an arithmetic expression should be of the same type.

5.   True or false

6.   A relational operator is a symbol by which either a true or false relationship is established between two arithmetic expressions. The six relational operators and their corresponding arithmetic meaning and flowchart notation are:

Relational Operator Symbol	Arithmetic Meaning	Flowchart Notation
.GT.	Greater than	$>$
.GE.	Greater than or equal to	$\geq$
.LT.	Less than	$<$
.LE.	Less than or equal to	$\leq$
.EQ.	Equal to	$=$
.NE.	Not equal to	$\neq$

7.   A)   Numerical numbers whose type may be either integer, single precision floating-point, or double precision floating-point.

B)   A logical constant or variable name.

8.   A logical operator causes the evaluation of the truth or falsity of two logical expressions.

9.   That the two logical expressions connected by the two connectives .AND. or .ØR. and the logical expression immediately following the inverter .NØT. either be or be reducible to either a true or false condition.

10. A)   The connective .AND. requires that the logical expression both preceding and following it to be true for the resultant condition to be true. If either are false or both are false, then the resultant condition will be false.

B)   The connective .ØR. requires that the logical expression either preceding and/or following it be true for the resultant condition to be true. If both are false, then the resultant condition is false.

C)   The inverter .NØT. causes the resultant condition to be true if the immediately following logical expression is false; if it is true, then the resultant condition is false.

11. It interrupts the normal left to right evaluation both within and outside a set of parentheses.

12. It instructs the computer to terminate execution of an object program.

13. A STØP statement may be located anywhere in a program.

14. It instructs the computer to terminate compilation of a source program.

15. An END statement must be the last physical statement in the program.

Exercises

1.   A)   A single variable or array name must be located on the left side of the equal sign.
     B)   Correct
     C)   Correct
     D)   Correct
     E)   Correct

2.   A)   Correct
     B)   The type of the variable name on the left side of the equal sign must be logical.
     C)   Correct
     D)   A relational operator cannot compare a character whose type is logical.
     E)   A required period immediately preceding the relational operator is missing.
     F)   A relational operator compares two arithmetic expressions.
     G)   Correct

3.   A)   Correct
     B)   The variable name J is not a logical expression.
     C)   The logical operator .ØR. is not preceded by a logical expression.

D) Correct

E) The logical operators .AND. and .ØR. cannot appear in sequence.

F) Correct

G) A required period immediately preceding the relational operator .ØR. is missing.

ANSWERS TO CHAPTER 5 QUESTIONS AND EXERCISES

Questions

1. One group, composed of the STØP and END statements, is concerned with the *termination* of a program. Another group, composed of the arithmetic and logical IF, unconditional GØ TØ, computed GØ TØ, and ASSIGN and assigned GØ TØ statements, is concerned with *branching* to a specific program statement. Another group, composed of DØ statements, is concerned with *looping* one or more program statements a specific number of times.

2. Because it provides the computer with the capability of executing specific sequences of program statements based upon a decision it arrives at without human intervention.

3. To evaluate an arithmetic expression and, depending upon the results of the evaluation, transfer to one of three possible program statements.

4. To evaluate a logical expression and, depending upon the result of the evaluation, transfer to either the true or false branch.

5. To transfer to an executable statement on the basis of the current value of a number stored under an integer variable name.

6. To transfer to an executable statement on the basis of the current value of a number stored under an integer variable name.

7. To loop the same set of program statements a desired number of times.

8. The range of a DØ statement extends from the DØ statement through the program statement assigned statement number *sn*.

9. An integer variable name.

10. An executable program statement.

11. The last program statement within the range of a DØ statement must be an executable statement. It cannot be a GØ TØ statement of any form, PAUSE, STØP, RETURN, arithmetic or logical IF, or another DØ statement.

12. Yes, the DØ variable may be used in appropriate program statements within the range of the DØ statement.

13. The next executable program statement following the program statement assigned *sn*.

14. A) The values of in, in_1, and in_3 must not have been changed by a program statement outside the range of the DØ statement.

    B) If a DØ statement is nested within the range of one or more other DØ statements, both the transfer and return must be made from and to the innermost DØ statement.

15. To serve as a convenient last statement within the range of a DØ statement. It is especially appropriate when the last statement might otherwise be one of the forbidden statements. It is also a convenient statement to use when an arithmetic and/or logical IF statement is used with the range of a DØ statement.

Exercises

1. A) Correct

   B) While this statement is correct with respect to construction, it is not logically sound as the positive branch causes a DØ loop to be initiated that would continue until interrupted by the computer operator.

   C) The right parenthesis is omitted.

   D) The positive branch is missing.

   E) Correct

F)   While this statement is correct with respect to construction, it is not logically sound as all three branches transfer to the same program statement. An unconditional GØ TØ statement would be more appropriate in this situation.

G)   There is an implied arithmetic operator (multiplication sign) in the arithmetic expression.

H)   The computer will always transfer to the same program statement, in this case the program statement assigned statement number 51.

I)   Correct

2.   A)   Correct

B)   The logical expression is not enclosed in a set of parentheses.

C)   The decimal point following the logical operator is omitted.

D)   An arithmetic expression is included in a logical arithmetic statement.

E)   .GL. is not a valid relational operator.

F)   Correct

3.   A)   The comma that must follow the right parenthesis is omitted.

B)   The variable name following the comma must be integer.

C)   The integer variable name I cannot exceed the number of statement numbers located within the set of parentheses.

D)   Correct

4.   A)   The variable name following the key word TØ must be integer.

B)   The statement number 50 is not located within the set of parentheses in the assigned GØ TØ statement.

C)   The comma following the integer variable name in the assigned GØ TØ statement is omitted.

D)   Correct

ANSWERS TO CHAPTER 6 QUESTIONS AND EXERCISES

Questions

1.   An ordered set of computer memory storage spaces identified by an array name.

2.   When it is desirable to both reflect in a program the fact that these data are related and retain each datum's identity for processing reasons.

3.   To assign an array name to one or more arrays and specify the number of computer memory storage spaces that are allocated to each array.

4.   The ability to specify the type of an array name.

5.   It must precede any other program statement that refers to an array name located in the specification statement.

6.   The first number specifies the number of allocated rows of storage spaces, the second number specifies the number of allocated columns of storage spaces, and the third number specifies the number of allocated ranks of storage spaces composing the array.

7.   A subscript is composed of either 1 through 7 unsigned integer numbers, variable names with an unsigned integer number stored under each of them, and/or array elements, each of which is separated by a comma, enclosed in a set of parentheses.

8.   If it is located in a specification statement, the computer is provided information concerning the type of data that will be stored in an array and the number of storage spaces allocated to an array. However, if it is located in another type of program statement, reference is being made to a specific array element within that array.

9.   The normal order is rows first, then columns (if present), and finally ranks (if present).

10.   It is the means through which a number is transferred into and from a specific storage space within an array.

11.   An indexed subscript is the means by which more data may be transferred either into or from certain array elements of an array that is economically feasible by means of listing all of the individual array elements.

12.   In either a READ or WRITE statement.

Exercises

1.
```
cc  123456789...

        DIMENSIØN NØB(5)
        READ (5,1) NØB(1),NØB(3),NØB(5)
    1   FØRMAT (3I2)
```

2.
```
cc  123456789...

        DIMENSIØN M(50)
        READ (5,1) (M(I), I = 1,25)
    1   FØRMAT (25I5)
```

3.
```
cc  123456789...

        DIMENSIØN M(50)
        READ (5,1) (M(I), I = 2,50,2)
    1   FØRMAT (25I5)
```

4.
```
cc  123456789...

        DIMENSIØN IN(100)
        READ (5,1) IN
    1   FØRMAT (80I1,20I1)
```

5.
```
cc  123456789...

        DIMENSIØN IN(100)
        WRITE (6,1) (IN(I), I = 1,100,2)
    1   FØRMAT (50I1)
```

ANSWERS TO CHAPTER 7 QUESTIONS AND EXERCISES

Questions

1. A) A subprogram is a group of statements that solve part of an overall problem and as such should not be used by itself, but rather as part of a larger program.

   B) In those programs that require, at various points within the program, identical computation to be performed on different data.

2. A) A calling program may be either the main program itself or another subprogram that is either directly or indirectly connected to the main program.

B)   It is the means by which a subprogram is either directly or indirectly connected to a main program.

3.   A FORTRAN-supplied subprogram, unlike a FUNCTIØN or SUBRØUTINE subprogram, is a group of statements that is part of the FORTRAN compiler. As such, the statements need not be written but rather only called by writing the subprogram name, immediately followed by one or more arguments, in the arithmetic expression portion of an arithmetic statement located in the calling program.

4.   It must be the first statement in the subprogram.

5.   A)   Any kind of statement, except another FUNCTIØN, SUBRØUTINE, or BLØCK DATA statement, may be located in a FUNCTIØN subprogram. If an IMPLICIT statement is located in the subprogram, it must immediately follow the FUNCTIØN, SUBRØUTINE statement.

     B)   Any kind of statement, except a FUNCTIØN, another SUBRØUTINE, or BLØCK DATA statement, may be located in a SUBRØUTINE subprogram. If an IMPLICIT statement is located in the subprogram, it must immediately follow the FUNCTIØN statement.

6.   The datum stored under at least one argument must be transferred from a calling program to a called FUNCTIØN subprogram and at least the datum stored under the subprogram name must be returned from the called FUNCTIØN subprogram to the calling program.

7.   Each argument and its corresponding dummy argument must agree in order, number, and type.

8.   The symbolic name of an argument in a calling program can be either identical to or different than the symbolic name of its corresponding dummy argument in the called subprogram.

9.   Because the statement numbers and symbolic names in the called FUNCTIØN or SUBRØUTINE subprogram are completely independent of those used in the calling program.

10.   The array name must be specified as an array in either a DIMENSIØN or explicit specification statement in the subprogram prior to any other statement that references it.

11.   In either the *list* portion of a READ statement, as the symbolic name on the left side of the equal sign of either an arithmetic or logical statement, or as an argument in a CALL statement.

12.   Execution of the statements in the subprogram is terminated and the computed datum and control are returned to the calling program.

13.   Whereas a FUNCTIØN subprogram is called by citing its name accompanied by one or more arguments in an arithmetic expression of an arithmetic statement in the calling program, SUBRØUTINE subprogram is called by a CALL statement in the calling program; whereas a FUNCTIØN subprogram is limited to always returning at least one datum to the calling program, a SUBRØUTINE subprogram may return none, one, or more datum to the calling program; whereas in a FUNCTIØN subprogram a datum may be returned to the calling program via the FUNCTIØN subprogram name and one or more of its dummy arguments, in a SUBRØUTINE subprogram if one or more datum are to be returned, it must be via one or more of the dummy arguments located in the SUBRØUTINE statement.

14.   The standard (normal) entry into a called subprogram is the first executable program statement following the FUNCTIØN or SUBRØUTINE statement. If a reference is made in the calling program to an ENTRY statement in the called subprogram, entry is made at the first executable program statement following the ENTRY statement.

15.   The subprogram is executed and the resultant datum transferred to the called subprogram; it can be transferred to the called subprogram and the subprogram is executed during the execution of the called subprogram.

16.   Because it is located in the same program unit that it references whereas a called subprogram is not in the same program unit as the program unit calling it.

17.   To specify that a subprogram named used as an argument, without its argument(s), by another subprogram is to be considered a subprogram name rather than a variable name.

18.   The CØMMØN statement makes one or more single storage spaces and/or arrays of storage spaces in the computer's memory simultaneously available to both a calling program and its one or more called subprograms.

19.   The EQUIVALENCE statement, similar to the CØMMØN statement, permits the same storage space in the computer's memory to be shared by two or more symbolic names.

20. The CØMMØN statement makes the same storage spaces simultaneously available to symbolic names located in a calling program and its one or more called subprograms whereas the EQUIVALENCE statement makes the same storage spaces simulatenously available to symbolic names located in the same program unit.

Exercises

```
cc  123456789...


C       EXERCISE 1
3       READ (5,1,END=99) VAR
1       FØRMAT (F5.2)
        VNEW = TEST(VAR)
        VNEW = SQRT(VNEW)
        WRITE (6,2) VAR,VNEW
2       FØRMAT (' ',F5.2,10X,F5.2)
        GØ TØ 3
99      STØP
        END
        FUNCTIØN TEST(VAR)
        TEST = ABS(VAR)
        RETURN
        END
```

```
cc  123456789...


C       EXERCISE 2
        DIMENSIØN INDR(25),GRØSS(25)
        REAL NETPAY(25)
        DEDUCT(Z) = Z*.10
        I = 1
2       READ (5,1,END=99) IDNR(I),PAY
1       FORMAT (I9,T15,F5.2)
        NET = PAY-DEDUCT(PAY)
        GROSS(I) = PAY
        NETPAY(I) = NET
        IF (I .EQ. 25) GØ TØ 3
        I = I+1
        GØ TØ 2
3       WRITE (6,4) (IDNR(I),GRØSS(I),NETPAY(I), I = 1,25)
4       FØRMAT ('','EMPLØYEE ID IS', 1X,I9,10X,'GRØSS PAY = $',F6.2,
       110X, 'NET PAY = $',F6.2)
99      STØP
        END
```

```
cc  123456789...

    C       EXERCISE 3
            DIMENSIØN X(4)
            CØMMØN /A/A,B,C,D
            EQUIVALENCE (X(1),A)
            READ (5,1) (X(I), I = 1,4)
    1       FØRMAT (4F5.1)
            CALL TEST
            WRITE (6,2) A,B,C,D
    2       FØRMAT (' ',F6.2,10X,F6.2,10X,F6.2,10X,F6.2)
            STØP
            END
            SUBRØUTINE TEST
            CØMMØN /A/X(4)
            DØ 1 I = 1,4
    1       X(I) = SQRT(X(I))
            RETURN
            END
```

```
cc  123456789...

    C       EXERCISE 4
            CØMMØN /A/ITEM(4)
            REAL ITEM
            PW = 0
            S = 0
            READ (5,1) (ITEM(I), I = 1,4)
    1       FØRMAT (4F5.0)
            I = 1
    6       IF (ITEM(I) .LE. 10) CALL TESTA(I,PW)
            IF (ITEM(I) .GT. 10) CALL TEST(I,PW,SQ)
    3       WRITE (6,4) ITEM(I),SQ,PW
    4       FØRMAT (' ',F5.2,10X,F5.2,10X,F5.2)
            IF (I .GE. 4) GØ TØ 99
            I = I+1
            SQ = 0
            GØ TØ 6
    99      STØP
            END
            SUBRØUTINE TEST(I,PW,SQ)
            CØMMØN /A/ITEM(4)
            REAL ITEM
            SQ = SQRT(ITEM(I))
            ENTRY TESTA(I,PW)
            PW = ITEM(I)**2
            RETURN
            END
```

```
cc│1234567789...

  C       │EXERCISE 5
          │CØMMØN /A/ITEM(4)
          │REAL ITEM
          │PW = 0
          │READ (5,1) (ITEM(I), I = 1,4)
  1       │FØRMAT (4F5.2)
          │I = 1
          │CALL TEST(I,PW,&2)
          │SQ = 0
          │SQ = SQRT(ITEM(I))
  2       │WRITE (6,3) I,ITEM(I),SQ,PW
  3       │FØRMAT (' ',I5,10X,F7.2,10X,F7.2,10X,F7.2)
          │IF (I .GT. 4) GØ TØ 99
          │I = I+1
          │GØ TØ 5
  99      │STØP
          │END
          │SUBRØUTINE TEST(I,X,*)
          │CØMMØN /A/ITEM(4)
          │REAL ITEM
          │X = ITEM(I)**2
          │IF (ITEM(I) .LE. 10.) RETURN 1
          │RETURN
          │END
```

ANSWERS TO CHAPTER 8 QUESTIONS AND EXERCISES

Questions

1. When the particular program in which it is located is written with the intention of it being executed in one or more computer installations that have possibly assigned different data set reference numbers to either the card reader and/or the printer.

2. It provides the means to either read from or write into one or more records of a data set via the READ (i,n) or the WRITE (i,n) statements without using either the "list" portion of the statement or having the statement refer to a FØRMAT statement.

3. To cause the computer to stop its execution of the program.

4. The PAUSE statement, unlike the STØP statement, permits execution of the program to be restarted again at that point in the program.

5. It provides the means by which a datum may be stored under one or more variables, array elements, and/or array names.

6. By placing an optional integer number followed by an asterisk (*) immediately preceding the number or condition.

7. It permits the assigning of an initial datum to either one or more variable names and/or array elements assigned to a labeled common storage area.

8. To explicitly indicate the type of specific variable names appearing in the program.

9. To permit the storage of a complex number under either a variable or array name, FUNCTIØN subprogram name, or statement function name.

10. The standard length of an INTEGER symbolic name is 4 bytes and the optional length is 2 bytes; the standard length of a REAL symbolic name is 4 bytes and the optional length is 8 bytes; the standard length of a LØGICAL symbolic name is 4 bytes and the optional length is 1 byte; and the standard length of a CØMPLEX symbolic name is 8 bytes and the optional length is 16 bytes.

Exercises

```
cc | 123456789...

   C       EXERCISE 1
           IMPLICIT REAL(A-Z)
           INTEGER I,X,J
           DIMENSIØN GRØSS(10),FEDTAX(10),NET(10),RATE(2),ID(10,3)
           DATA RATE/.10,.15/
           READ 1, ((ID(I,J),J = 1,3), GRØSS(I), I = 1,10)
   1       FØRMAT (2A4,A3,4X,F6.2)
           DØ 2 I = 1,10
           X = 1
           IF (GRØSS(I) .GT. 200.) X = 2
           FEDTAX(I) = RATE(X)*GRØSS(I)
   2       NET(I) = GRØSS(I)-FEDTAX(I)
           PRINT 3
   3       FØRMAT ('1',2X,'S.S.NR',10X,'GRØSS',20X,'FED TAX',10X,
          1'NET PAY'//)
           PRINT 4 ((ID(I,J), J = 1,3), GRØSS(I),FEDTAX(I),NET(I), I = 1,10)
   4       FØRMAT (' ',2A4,A3,1X,' ',F7.2,9X,' ',F7.2,9X,' ',F7.2)
           STØP
           END
```

```
cc | 123456789...

   C       EXERCISE 2
           NAMELIST/TED/A,B,C,D/TEX/E,F,G,H
           DØ 1 I = 1,5
           READ (5,TED)
           E = SQRT(A)
           F = SQRT(B)
           G = ABS(C)
           H = ABS(D)
           WRITE (6,TED)
           WRITE (6,TEX)
   1       CØNTINUE
           STØP
           END
```

```
cc | 123456789...

   C       EXERCISE 3
   C       IF X IS GREATER THAN 500, PAUSE '10001'
   C       IF X IS NEGATIVE, PAUSE 'NEG'
   3       READ (6,1,END=99) X
   2       FØRMAT (F5.2)
           IF (X .LT. 0) PAUSE 'NEG'
           IF (X .GT. 500.) PAUSE '10001'
           GØ TØ 2
   99      STØP
           END
```

```
cc  123456789...

C       EXERCISE 4
        CØMMØN /A/GRØSS(25),FEDTAX(25),NET(25),RATE(2)
        REAL NET, MATCH
3       READ 1, ID,PAY
1       FØRMAT (I2,3X,F6.2)
        IF (ID .EQ. 0) GØ TØ 2
        GRØSS(ID) = PAY
        NET(ID) = MATCH(ID)
        GØ TØ 3
2       DØ 4 I = 1,25
        IF (GRØSS(I) .LE. 0) GØ TØ 4
        PRINT 5, I,GRØSS(I),FEDTAX(I),NET(I)
5       FØRMAT (' ','EMPLØYEE NUMBER',3X,I2,5X,'GRØSS PAY=',1X,F6.2,
       15X,'DEDUCTIØNS=',1X,F5.2,5X,'NET PAY',1X,F6.2)
4       CØNTINUE
        STØP
        END
        BLØCK DATA
        CØMMØN /A/GRØSS(25),FEDTAX(25),NET(25),RATE(2)
        REAL NET
        DATA GRØSS/25*0/.FEDTAX/25*0/RATE/.10,.15/
        END
        REAL FUNCTIØN MATCH(ID)
        CØMMØN /A/GRØSS(25),FEDTAX(25),NET(25),RATE(2)
        I = 1
        IF (GRØSS(ID) .GT. 200) I=2
        FEDTAX(ID) = (GRØSS(ID)*RATE(I))
        MATCH = GRØSS(ID)-FEDTAX(ID)
        RETURN
        END
```

ANSWERS TO CHAPTER 9 QUESTIONS AND EXERCISES

Questions

1. Because a record may only be sequentially written on and read from a magnetic tape.
2. Eighteen record columns (bytes).
3. A formatted WRITE or READ statement is used when the one or more records on a magnetic tape are to be written on an output device such as a printer. An unformatted WRITE or READ statement is used when the one or more records on a magnetic tape are to be used by the computer and not written on an output device such as a printer.
4. To cause the computer to backspace one record on a magnetic tape each time it is executed.
5. To cause the computer to rewind the magnetic tape to the first record on the tape.
6. To cause the computer to write an end-of-file mark on a magnetic tape.
7. To indicate to the computer that the last record of the file has either been written on or read from the magnetic tape.
8. Because the process involves random accessibility by the computer (the ability to proceed directly to any point on a disk with equal accessibility) and either the sequential writing or the sequential reading of one or more records.
9. The sequential-access method does not provide the means of designating specific records on a tape whereas the direct-access method does provide the means of designating specific records on disk.

10. One record column (byte).
11. To describe the characteristics of one or more data sets associated with a data set reference number located in the statement.
12. To reduce the time it takes the computer to read a record of a data set located on a magnetic disk by seeking the specific record of a data set while the computer is simultaneously executing one or more of the following statements in the program.

Exercises

1.

```
cc 123456789...

C        EXERCISE 1
         DIMENSIØN NN(5),NNN(5)
4        READ (5,1,END=5) (NN(I), I = 1,5)
1        FØRMAT (5I2)
         DØ 2 I = 1,5
2        NNN(I) = NN(I)**2
         WRITE (8,3) (NN(I),NNN(I), I = 1,5)
3        FØRMAT (5I2,5I10)
         GØ TØ 4
5        END FILE 8
         REWIND 8
8        READ (8,3,END=99) (NN(I),NNN(I), I = 1,5)
         DØ 6 I = 1,5
6        PRINT 7, NN(I),NNN(I)
7        FØRMAT (' ',5X,I2,5X,I10)
         GØ TØ 8
99       STØP
         END
```

2.

```
cc 123456789...

C        EXERCISE 2
         DIMENSIØN ACCT(10,3)
         IMPLICIT INTEGER(A-Z)
         DATA ACCT,TGRØSS,TMILES,TCØST/33*0/
3        READ (5,1,END=2) NR,GRØSS,MILES
1        FØRMAT (3I5)
         CØST = 1*GRØSS*MILES
         WRITE (8) NR,GRØSS,MILES,CØST
         GØ TØ 3
2        END FILE 8
         REWIND 8
5        READ (8,END=4) NR,GRØSS,MILES,CØST
         ACCT(NR,1) = ACCT(NR,1)+GRØSS
         ACCT(NR,2) = ACCT(NR,2)+MILES
         ACCT(NR,3) = ACCT(NR,3)+CØST
         TGRØSS = TGRØSS+GRØSS
         TMILES = TMILES+MILES
         TCØST = TCØST+CØST
         GØ TØ 5
```

```
4        BACKSPACE 8
         BACKSPACE 8
         BACKSPACE 8
         DØ 6 I = 1,3
         READ (8) NR,GRØSS,MILES,CØST
6        PRINT 7, NR,GRØSS,MILES,CØST
7        FØRMAT (' ', 5X, 4(I5,2X))
         DØ 8 I = 1,10
         IF (ACCT(I,1) .EQ. 0) GØ TØ 8
         PRINT 9, (I,ACCT(I,J), J = 1,3)
9        FØRMAT (' ', 5X, 4(I5,2X))
8        CØNTINUE
         STØP
         END
```

3.   cc 123456789...

```
C        EXERCISE 3
         DEFINE FILE 92(100,50,L,N)
         IMPLICIT INTEGER(A-Z)
3        READ (5,1,END=2) NN,A
1        FØRMAT (I3,2X,I5)
         FIND (92'NN)
         AA = A**2
         WRITE (92'NN) A,AA
         GØ TØ 3
2        N = 1
6        READ (92'N) A,AA
         N = N-1
         PUNCH 4, N,A,AA
4        FØRMAT (I3,2X,I5,5X,I8)
         IF (N .EQ. 100) GØ TØ 99
         N = N+1
         GØ TØ 6
99       STØP
         END
```

4.   cc 123456789...

```
C        EXERCISE 4
         DIMENSIØN NUMB(10)
         IMPLICIT INTEGER(A-Z)
         DATA NUMB,THØURS,TCØST/12*0/
         DEFINE FILE 8(200,80,E,NR)
         DEFINE FILE 9(20,22,U,NRR)
         NR = 1
         NRR = 1
         DØ 1 I = 1,4
         DØ 1 J = 1,5
         DØ 2 K = 1,10
         READ (5,3,END=99) ACCT,HØURS
3        FØRMAT (2I10)
         CØST = HØURS*4
         NUMB(ACCT) = NUMB(ACCT)+CØST
         WRITE (8'NR,4) ACCT,HØURS,CØST
4        FØRMAT (3I10)
         THØURS = THØURS+HØURS
         TCØST = TCØST+CØST
2        CØNTINUE
         WRITE (9'NRR) THØURS,TCØST,(I,NUMB(I), I = 1,10)
         THØURS = 0
         TCØST = 0
1        CØNTINUE
         FIND (8'1)
         FIND (9'1)
         NR = 1
         NRR = 1
         DØ 5 I = 1,4
         PRINT 6, I
6        FØRMAT (' ',10X,'SUMMARY FØR WEEK',1X,I3)
         DØ 5 J = 1,5
         PRINT 7, J
7        FØRMAT (' ',15X,'DAY',1X,I2)
         DØ 8 K = 1,10
         READ (8'NR,4) A,B,C
8        PRINT 9, A,B,C
9        FØRMAT (' ',5X,'ACCT NUMBER',1X,I2,1X,'HØURS =',1X,
        1I3,1X,'CØST=',1X,I4
         READ (9'NRR) A,B,(L,NUMB(L), L = 1,10)
         DØ 10 1 = 1,10
10       PRINT 11, I,NUMB(I)
11       FØRMAT (' ',5X,'CHARGES TØ DATE FØR ACCØUNT',1X,I2,
        11X,'=',1X,I6)
5        PRINT 12, A,B
12       FØRMAT (' ',5X,'TØTAL HØURS FØR THIS WEEK ARE',1X,
        1I5,1X,'AND TØTAL CØSTS ARE $',1X,I5,'.00')
         STØP
         END
```

INDEX

ABS, 98, 202
Addition, 12, 50
A format code, 39-41
ALOGIO, 98, 204
Alphabetic characters, 11
Alphanumeric FORMAT specification, 39-41
Analog computer, 1-2
.AND. 55, 192
Apostrophe, 36-37
Arithmetic expression, 50-53 (Also see Expression)
Arithmetic IF (See IF statements)
Arithmetic, integer, 14
Arithmetic operations, hierarchy of, 52
Arithmetic operators, 50
Arithmetic statements, 48-53
Argument, 98, 100, 103, 104, 107
Array names, 16
Arrays, 81-96
ASSIGN statement, 69-71
Assignment statements, 48-62
Associated variable name, 145-146, 151-152
AT, 163

BACKSPACE statement, 142-143
Blank, 12, 13
Blank fields (See X FORMAT code)
BLOCK DATA, 129-130
Branching, 63-71
Byte, 133

C, 6
CALL statement, 104-105
Card, 5-8
    control, 8
    data, 7
Carriage control characters, 30
Characters, 11

(Characters cont.)
    FORTRAN, 11
    numeric, 11
    special, 11
Coding form, 2-4
Comment, 6
COMMON statement
    blank, 114
    labeled, 114-117
Compilation
    object, 8-9
    source, 8-9
Compiler programs, 160
    Fortran IV, G and H level, 161
    WATFOR and WATFIV, 167
Complex statement, 131-132
Computed GO TO, 68-69
CONTINUE statement, 76-77
Control statements, 63-80
    CONTINUE statement, 76-77
    DO statement, 71-76
    END statement, 57
    GO TO statement, 56, 58
    IF statement, 63-68
    STOP statement, 56-57
COS, 98, 204

D exponent, 184-189
D format code, 186-188
DATA, 127-129
Data set, 22
Data set reference number, 23
DEBUG, 161-166
Debugging, 160-166
    At debug statement, 163
    DEBUG statement, 161-163
    DISPLAY statement, 164-166
    error messages, 167-183
    TRACE OFF statement, 164

(Debugging cont.)
    TRACE ON statement, 163-164
DEFINE FILE statement, 145-146
Delimiters, 12-13
Digital computer, 1-2
DIMENSION statement, 83-84
Direct-access I/O Statements, 144-153
    DEFINE FILE statement, 145-146
    FIND statement, 152-153
    READ statements, 148-152
    WRITE statements, 146-147
    DISPLAY, 164-166
Division, 12, 50
DO statement, 71-76
Double precision numbers, 15
DOUBLE PRECISION statement, 18-19, 84-85
DSQRT, 98, 204

E exponent, 184-189
E format code, 186-188
END FILE statement, 144
END statement, 144
END= option, 24
.EQ., 54
EQUIVALENCE statement, 117-119
ERR= option, 24
Error messages, 167-183
Errors, types, 160
EXP, 98, 204
Explicit specification
    statements, 17-19, 84-85
    DOUBLE PRECISION statement, 18-19, 84
    INTEGER statement, 17, 84-85
    REAL statement, 18, 84-85
Exponentiation, 184-189
Expression, 20, 50-53
EXTERNAL statement, 112

F format code, 32-34
.FALSE., 19
File format letters, 145-146
    E, 145-146
    L, 145-146
    U, 145-146
FIND (i'r) statement, 152-153
FLOAT, 98, 202
Floating-point numbers, 14-16
Flowcharting, 63, 194-196
    program, 197-200
    system, 197
FORMAT code, 26-43, 125-126
    A (alphanumeric) code, 39-41
    Apostrophe (literal) code, 36-37

D and E (exponent) code, 184-189
F (floating-point) code, 32-34
G (general) code, 125-126
H (Hollerith) code, 38-39
I (integer) code, 30-32
L (logical) code, 34-35
Literal data, 36-39
    Apostrophe (literal) code, 36-37
    H (Hollerith) code, 38-39
T (tab) code, 41-42
X (blank) code, 42-43
Z (hexidecimal) code, 126-127
FORMAT statement, 26
    matching with read and/or write, 26-28
FORTRAN supplied subprograms, 97-99
    character set, 11
    categories of statements, 20
    coding form, 2-5
FUNCTION statement, 99-101, 136-137

.GE., 54
GO TO statement
    computed, 68-69
    unconditional, 56
    assigned, 69-70
.GT., 54

H format code, 38-39
Hierarchy of arithmetic operations, 52
    of logical and relational operators, 55

I format code, 30-32
IABS, 98, 202
IFIX, 98, 203
IF statement, 63-65
    arithmetic, 63-65
    logical, 65-68
IMPLICIT statement, 130-131, 133
Implied DO loops, 90-94
INIT, 162-163
Input/Output statements, 22-47
INTEGER statements, 17-18

Key words, 13, 159

L format code, 34-35
Labeled COMMON 114-117
.LE., 54
Literal data, 36-39

LOGICAL statement, 19, 53-54
   logical operators, 55, 192-193
   relational operators, 54-55
   hierarchy of execution, 55
Logical constant, 19
Logical IF statement, 65-68
Looping, 71-76
.LT., 54

Magnetic disk, 144-153
Magnetic tape, 177-184, 139-144
Magnetic tape control, 141-144
Matrix, (See Arrays)
Multiplication, 12, 50

NAMELIST, 123-125
.NE., 54
Nested DO statements, 74-76
.NOT., 55
Numbers, 13
   double precision, 15
   floating-point, 14-15
   integer, 14
   real, 14-15
   single precision, 14-15
   statement, 5-6
Numeric characters, 11

Object program, 8-9
Operators
   arithmetic, 50
   logical, 54
.OR., 55

PAUSE, 121-123, 127
PUNCH, 121-123

READ (i) List statement, 140-141
READ (i,n) List statement, 22-23, 139-140
READ (i'r,n) List statement, 148-149
READ statement, 18
Reference number, data set, 23, 25
Relational operators, 54-55
RETURN statement, 101-103, 105-106
REWIND statement, 143

Sequential input/output statements, 139-144
   BACKSPACE statements, 142-143
   END FILE statement, 144

(Sequential input/output statements cont.)
   READ statements, 139-142
   REWIND statement, 143
   WRITE statement, 139-142
SIN, 98, 204
Slash, 28-29, 191
   used in reading, 28-29
   used in writing, 28-29, 191
Source program, 8-9
Special characters, 11-12
Specification statements, 17-19
   COMMON statement, 112-117
   COMPLEX statement, 131-132
   EQUIVALENCE statement, 117-119
   Explicit specification statements, 84-85, 111-112
   DOUBLE PRECISION statement, 18-19
   INTEGER statement, 17-18
   LOGICAL statement, 19
   REAL statement, 18
SQRT, 98, 204
Statement numbers, 5-6
Statement function, 110-111
Statements, 5-6
   categories of, 20
STOP statement, 56-57
SUBCHK, 162
Subprograms,
   FORTRAN supplied, 97-98
   FUNCTION, 99-101
   SUBROUTINE, 103-105
SUBROUTINE statement, 103-105
Subscripts, 86
   indexed, 91
SUBTRACE, 163
Subtraction, 12, 50
Symbolic names, 16-17, 132-133

T format code, 41-42
TRACE, 162
TRACE OFF, 164
TRACE ON, 163-164
.TRUE., 19

Unconditional GO TO statement, 56

Variable names (See Symbolic names)

WATFOR, 167
   compiler, 167
   error messages, 175-183

WATFIV, 167
   compiler, 167
   error messages, 175-183
WRITE (i) List statement, 140-141

WRITE (i,n) List statement, 139-140
WRITE (i'r,n) List Statement, 146-147

X format code, 42-43